long time no see

diaries of an unlikely messenger

Carrie Triffet

A Wealth of Wisdom LLC
Keauhou Hawaii

Published in the United States by A Wealth of Wisdom, LLC
PO Box 390038
Keauhou, Hawaii 96739
www.aWealthOfWisdom.com

ISBN: 978-0-9843125-9-7

Library of CongressControl Number: 2009911842
Printed in the United States of America

Book Design: Carrie Triffet
Author photos: Isabel Lawrence Photographers www.isabellawrence.com

THANK YOU

Does anybody really read the acknowledgements? Or is it like that guy at the Oscars® who wins for Best Teeny Tiny Documentary, and insists on thanking his accountant, his 5th grade English teacher and each of his children by name on national television?

Well, I'm doing it anyway.

Many thanks to Natalie, Dawn, Deb, Kate, Adam (whose name is not really Adam), Steve and Claudia for reading, suggesting and commenting on these many, many revisions. Many thanks also to Kathy, for laughing in all the right places. I couldn't have done it without you guys.

Belated thanks to the members and leaders of SGI-USA for doing your best, against all odds, to teach me Buddhist practice. Thanks to Fran at InnerVision12—so much of this story could never have happened without you. Thanks to Renée at A Wealth of Wisdom for being quite fabulous to work with.

And thanks to too many friends to name here, for all your support and love and eagerness to toast my authorial accomplishments with rounds of champagne. I'm truly blessed. Either that, or you all just really, really like champagne.

Oh, and thanks to my children.

Nah, just kidding.

CONTENTS

IN THE BEGINNING

BUDDHISM

BEYOND RELIGION

(DON'T SKIP THE) PROLOGUE

Messenger—that's some job description, you may be thinking right about now. *How did she land a gig like that?*

Funny you should ask.

My qualifications are simple. I hear a Voice.

I didn't always. The first time I heard that Voice I was twenty-seven years old. My best friend Johnny and I were inseparable; two very cool peas in an ultramod pod, we prowled the local thrift stores for vintage clothing by day, and by night we hit the dance clubs, decked out in our finest hipster couture. Life was good—that is, until one day out of the blue he confessed suddenly that he had become a Buddhist over the weekend.

Just like that. A *Buddhist*, for Christ's sake.

He set up a stylish little altar, the sleek black box remaining carefully closed whenever I was around. That was fine with me; I wanted no part of this irritating turn of events. Then one afternoon many weeks later, out of boredom or curiosity I finally asked whether I could see it, this mysterious Gohonzon I'd been hearing so much about.

Johnny opened the altar doors and that's when it happened. Visible waves of sparkly, effervescent joy tumbled out to greet me, followed by a crystal clear Voice that spoke out loud inside my head.

And the Voice said:

Long time no see.

It's not as strange as it might seem, y'know. I'm pretty sure a lot of people have experienced clairaudience* at one time or another—yet the common tendency is to dismiss that "little voice" along with the guidance it gives.

I didn't dismiss it. And maybe that's the only thing that sets me apart from so many others. I learned how to listen.

Well, ok, maybe listening is not the *only* thing that sets me apart. My life was pretty uncommon long before the Voice showed up. Yet when that Voice spoke, I listened and it led me on a strange and wonderful journey of faith that continues to this day.

But I'm getting ahead of myself. Before I tell you about the spiritual journey itself, we'd better go back to those seemingly unspiritual early days when the story first began, so you'll better understand everything that came after.

---

* The power to hear things outside the range of normal perception. Like clairvoyance, in other words, except with hearing instead of sight.

IN THE BEGINNING

.

CHAPTER ONE

TOXIC AVENGER

My soon-to-be mother had a bad case of the flu. Just before Christmas of 1957 a snowstorm began to pummel the Midwest, bringing record low temperatures with it. As he prepared to leave town for the holidays, her obstetrician made the decision to admit her to the hospital for the final days of her pregnancy, just to be safe.

That big, drafty maternity ward was the last place anybody would choose to spend the holidays, even in the best of weather. Dreary and institutional, it was also the worst possible place to be pregnant in a snowstorm; cracked panes in its upper windows sent the snow swirling in on gusting winds, where it settled in delicate drifts by my mother's bedside. Over the next several days her flu bug ripened rapidly into pneumonia, abetted by a well-meaning skeleton staff of clueless candy stripers.

"Save the mother or save the baby?" barked the on-call emergency doctor, striding down the hall as he addressed my shell-shocked dad. "It's too late to save both."

My father hesitated. "Save my wife," he whispered at last. "We can always have another child."

And so my mother was hustled into emergency surgery. Under anesthesia her heart began to fail; a rabbi was hastily brought in to witness the end, yet somehow, against all odds, she rallied. We both did.

Many years later I remembered this birth-and-death experience and its aftermath firsthand:

July 6, 1986

I knew I was killing my mother. I didn't mean to. I wanted to tell them—the doctor, the rabbi—that I wasn't doing it on purpose. I couldn't help myself. Something about me was poisonous, and it was her fault for getting too close to me. She should've known better than to trust me with her life and body.

I was whisked away from the scene of the crime and shot full of drugs that made me woozy and sick. Then it was off to solitary confinement. I went willingly, gladly. I knew I was guilty and wanted to pay for the monstrous thing I had done.

Alone in the dark, I had plenty of time to think. These were my conclusions:

1. *Babies kill their mothers, so I'd be damned if I would ever give birth to one of the treacherous little bastards.*
2. *Since I couldn't control the toxic effect I had on others, I would never again risk letting anyone love me. One murder on my conscience was all I could stand.*

Home at last from the hospital, a cold and wary little ex-con, I was surprised to find my mother alive and waiting for me with open arms. Though not nearly surprised enough to ever forgive her for abandoning me. ❖

Out of the frying pan, as they say, and into the brimstone and hellfire. By some celestial mistake, I'd been allowed to live. And that clerical error didn't seem to sit well with the universe at large.

SUPERNATURAL

In some ways my childhood was as normal as any. I rode a trike, and then later a bike adorned with long handlebar streamers that fluttered in the breeze; I played hopscotch, went through a horse phase, owned a stuffed animal or two. To the casual observer it might have seemed like the typical suburban experience of the 1960s. But it wasn't, not by a long shot.

I knew I was different, that I didn't belong here. The universe knew it too, and loved to torment me with glow-in-the-dark ghosts that no one but me seemed able to see. Least of all my parents and sister, three solid citizens who were as normal and down to Earth as they could possibly be. Think of the Munsters, except in reverse: They were all Marilyn, and I was that spooky little werewolf kid, the one who never fit in at school.

I coped with this supernatural state of affairs as best I could. Life was always most terrifying after the sun went down (since that was when the glowing ghosts came out to play), yet daytime wasn't much better. The physical world of houses and trees and blue-sky sunshine seemed pale and unconvincing, a cheap B movie set. Bleeding through its veneer of bright normalcy was the ever-present dread; big, juicy Technicolor horror that whispered my name from every dark corner, its cold, sticky tendrils lying in wait beneath the floorboards for that foolish, unguarded footstep.

I mostly kept this ongoing phantasmagoria to myself. Sure, my parents were aware that something was up; they knew I was afraid to go upstairs by myself, the lingering byproduct of an unfortunate afternoon spent watching Chiller Theater at the neighbor kids' house. The Crawling Eye had taken up permanent residence in our second story after that terrible day. Having watched it murder dozens of

European mountain climbers, I felt sure this awful eye would do the same to any careless Midwestern five-year-old if given the chance. So I made my parents watch me from the foot of the stairs every time I went up there to use the house's only bathroom.

And I'm sure Mom and Dad were aware of the terror I felt each time the Magic Hand appeared on our after-school TV screen. Silent sidekick to the host of *Cap'n Jim's Popeye Club*, the Magic Hand was just a white hand that interacted with Cap'n Jim between Popeye cartoons. Yet that eerie, dismembered hand crawled deeply into my waking nightmares.

At the time, I made no distinction between my daytime shadow world of bloodthirsty hand and eyeball—which was, of course, imaginary—and my nighttime ghost infestation, which was unfortunately quite real. They frightened me equally. Yet even if I'd recognized and prioritized the difference between them, I still would have been unable to communicate to anyone the true nature of the nocturnal problem: The semi-permeable wall of perception that oozed endless other-worldly images; the shifting netherworld of competing realities that threatened at all times to swallow me whole.

No, I couldn't tell them about any of that. The Marilyns, bless their hearts, would never have understood. ❖

LOST IN SPACE

Here's another thing I never told anybody: Time and space used to play tricks on me. Nowadays it's a fairly rare occurrence but when I was a kid, spatial and temporal hiccups happened a lot. Time stood still or skipped a step without warning. Buildings or whole city blocks appeared or disappeared at will from the neighborhoods where they belonged; sometimes I found them elsewhere, sometimes not at all. After awhile I lost all faith in my ability to get around in the world.

This sort of thing happened only when I was alone. If I wanted a house or a bus stop to show up in the same spot twice, I knew I'd better take another person along for insurance. It was always ok if I had someone with me—time and space didn't seem to want any witnesses when they did their crazy dance.

Although seemingly not directly connected to the supernatural issue, I nevertheless interpreted each of these random pranks as yet more proof that the universe hated me and wanted me dead. Or if not dead, exactly, then at least lost in a strange part of town or hopelessly late for supper. ❖

It wasn't just the perversely scary antics of the unseen universe that made my early childhood so hard to navigate. There was also that other aspect of the unseen universe, the one everybody else seemed to take for granted like it was the most natural thing in the world.

NEVER BUY A VOLKSWAGEN

My hometown held a large, close-knit Jewish community, and within its population an unusual number of concentration camp survivors. As a young kid I had regular contact with two of these: The mother of my best childhood friend, a lovely lady who'd managed to avoid the gas chamber by random chance; the other, my Hebrew school teacher, who'd seized his moment to escape from camp into the relative safety of the frozen forest beyond.

These stories and others like them hadn't yet taken on the safe sepia-toned patina of history. In those days the narratives felt real, and dangerously current. I was born a mere thirteen years after the war's end, and in my formative years the Jewish community still grieved as one, unmoored by the staggering enormity of its loss.

I had nothing to compare it to. This all-consuming sadness, crushing isolation and paralyzing fear of outsiders was just business as usual. The Jews clung to each other for support and sustenance, seeming to take urgent comfort and lifeblood nourishment from religious observance and their shared Jewish identity.

I didn't get it. The religion of my forefathers fit me like scratchy wool underpants two sizes too small, and I chafed bitterly against its restrictions. Nothing about Judaism—or God or religion in general, for that matter—inspired or comforted me, and I saw little point in pretending. I knew the universe was a malicious prankster, and this nonsensical insistence on worshiping it cramped my style.

All those hundreds of commandments. *Why can't we just have ten like everybody else?* I wanted to know. *Or better yet none at all?* ❖

HE WHO MUST NOT BE NAMED

And then there was that whole Jesus situation, which was… complicated. On the one hand He looked like a nice enough guy—His blond, blue-eyed portrait smiling down on my sleepovers at the neighbor kids' house. And of course it was widely known that if you believed in Him, Santa brought you all kinds of magical swag on Christmas.

Yet He was also the reason I wasn't allowed into some of the other kids' houses. I was a dirty Jew, or so their mothers informed me, and Jesus wouldn't like it if I spread those cooties around.

Meanwhile, school brought a whole different kind of challenge. I learned nothing at all about Christ or Christianity at home or in my Hebrew school studies, except that He was somehow associated with unspeakable evil, and so the name of Jesus was never to be uttered aloud.

"Why? What happens if you say it?" I figured it must be bad because nobody would ever tell me. Maybe saying Jesus' name was what killed those six million Jews?

This was back in the day when public school kids were routinely made to sing religious songs, so for these occasions I was forced to adopt a weird sort of ventriloquist's dummy approach:

Wag-wag (soundlessly my jaw moved up and down)
Loves me, yes I know
For the Bible tells me so. ❧

CHAPTER TWO

I had survived early childhood, learning gradually to ignore the daytime yammerings of TV monsters and other assorted beasts. Nighttime yammerings were not as easily dismissed, though I was working on it.

As for the oppressive religious atmosphere of my earliest years, some progress had been made on that front as well. I had graduated from Hebrew school, thus freeing up my weeknight evenings, and was looking forward to Sunday school graduation, which meant I might finally taste the joy of sleeping in one morning a week like regular people.

Well, a girl could dream, anyway. Just when things seemed most hopeful, fate tossed our family a game-changing curveball that permanently redefined the subject of Judaism.

IT'S TEN O'CLOCK—DO YOU KNOW WHERE YOUR CHILDREN ARE?

For most of my early life, our family's brand of Judaism could have been described as solid Suburban-Orthodox. Meaning we kept a strict Kosher home, observed the Sabbath and all requisite holidays, yet we dressed and, for the most part, behaved like ordinary citizens of twentieth century America.

Then, in her eleventh year of life, my sister won free tuition to a Lubavitch summer camp for girls and nothing was ever the same after that. Lubavitch Judaism, for those unfamiliar with the term, is a branch of Hasidism named for the town in Russia where it first became fruitful and multiplied. Perhaps you've seen Lubavitch Jews on the street, walking to or from the synagogue on Saturday mornings. Bearded men dressed in black wool suits and hats regardless of the weather; modest ladies wearing blouses with necklines rising above the collarbone, sleeves falling below the elbow and skirts—*always* skirts, pants are strictly forbidden—demurely covering the knee. And if the lady in question is married, a wig covers her hair, for only her husband is allowed to see that hair, and only behind closed doors.

Something about this Ultra-Orthodox lifestyle called my sister's name, and she fell for it body and soul. Eventually convincing my cash-strapped parents to pull her out of the public junior high school half a mile from our house and enroll her instead at the Yeshiva for girls two cities away, she embraced Lubavitch Judaism on its own terms and never looked back.

Although my sister seemed happy, she no longer wanted to sleep under our roof or eat off our plates since we weren't Kosher enough for Lubavitch liking. And the folks who ran that Yeshiva for girls had begun to set their sights on my enrollment too, with the tacit approval of my parents, who were becoming uneasy with my budding black sheep tendencies. Clinging to the unlikely hope that a strictly gender-segregated lifestyle would keep me off the streets and out of trouble, they allowed the Lubavitchers to pursue me with abandon.

One incident comes to mind.

I was thirteen years old. The doorbell rang one sunny summer morning; an ancient rabbi and his small entourage had come calling. My parents welcomed the group into our home, then my whole family vanished mysteriously along with the entourage, leaving me alone with the antique Bearded One.

He smelled like dentures. Backing me into a corner of the dining room, he began haranguing me in heavily accented Eastern Bloc English-as-a-second-language on the joys of Yeshiva enrollment. I was angry and scared so I harangued right back, loudly defending all the reasons I didn't want to go. At each of my increasingly impassioned arguments he would shake his head, perplexed, before launching back into his prepared speech. (At the time I thought he was only pretending not to understand my protests; I realize now he was unable to keep up with my rapid-fire American kid slang.)

The others reappeared and the school's principal, a native English speaker, took over. Her eyes traveled down to my illicit bell-bottom jeans and back up to my flushed and angry face as she prepared her arguments.

"I want to go to a regular junior high," I informed her sullenly before she could open her mouth. "I don't want to go to the Yeshiva."

"Why not? We're a very good school."

"Because I want to play in the marching band!" I bellowed. I'd practiced like crazy for my band audition and had recently learned I'd been accepted into the super-cool "A" band, the Tigers, instead of the loser "B" band, the Cubs, which meant I'd be marching at all the football games in the fall.

"We could have a marching band," she volunteered brightly.

I eyed her caustically. Seven preteen girls in dresses dragging cellos up the road were not what I had in mind.

"I want. To march. At football games."

"We could have football games…" she began, then her voice trailed off. Even she could see the absurdity in it.

Not long after this incident the Yeshiva and my parents jointly admitted defeat, and I was left to enjoy the public school system in peace. Still my sister's religious influence plagued me. The primary function of an older sibling, as I saw it, was to pave the way, to wear down parental resistance to dating and curfews and other acts of teenage autonomy. Yet my sister never dated. Never kissed a boy, as far as I knew. When the time came for her to be married, matchmakers arranged it all; my sister and her prospective husband, a rabbi, met once and sealed the deal at the New York Public Library.

All of which left my parents wholly unprepared for the next little hell-raiser in line.

It's not that I was a bad kid. I just ached to get the hell out of that place, dreaming of the day I could blow town for good. Although my folks kept me on the tightest leash they dared, my mother's long, heartbreaking battle with colon cancer, which was raging at this same time, offered an occasional power vacuum to be exploited while everyone's focus was elsewhere.

Sleepovers were a prime opportunity. Slipping out of the house after the family went to bed, my friends and I would get high and spend the night roaming the city. Ending up typically at the town's only twenty-four-hour doughnut shop, we'd enjoy the gray pre-dawn quiet with our powdered sugared breakfast before sneaking home to bed, nobody the wiser for our nocturnal wanderings.

I also hung out with, yet did not belong to, two separate schoolyard gangs. They weren't gangs in today's sense of the word, of course. These kids were peaceable stoners, high school dropouts, mostly, with no job prospects and thousands of empty hours to kill. I considered it a privilege to help them kill as many of those late-night hours as I could.

Surprisingly, given my taste in recreational activities, I was never arrested. That includes the time I got busted with one of those gangs, illuminated plainly in the police cruiser's headlight beam while passing a joint to the boy next to me. And the time a couple of years later in California that a bicycle cop glided quietly alongside my boyfriend's parked car (good God, since when did cops ride bicycles?), demanding I roll down my window to let the swirling clouds of pot smoke billow out into the evening air.

Although the others were invariably taken downtown and booked, somehow I always got sent away with a sincere lecture instead. Authority figures have always liked me. ❖

As if the supernatural situation wasn't abnormal enough, a whole new kind of unwanted uniqueness was beginning to take shape—or not—as I moved into my teen years.

THE MIRROR HAS TWO FACES

I'm built like Olive Oyl, except without all the curves.

This one fact has single-handedly distorted my perception of the world more than any other. Or, maybe not single-handedly. Truth be told, I was feeling pretty unpretty long before anybody realized what my body would turn out to be. Long before it became clear that I wasn't just a "late bloomer," in the euphemistic parlance of my aunts; that in fact there would be no blooms at all issuing from this unnatural weed.

For the first five or six years of life I was a cute kid like any other. Then I entered, oh I don't know, let's call it an awkward phase. Walking home from elementary school, all gangly eyeglasses and knobbly knees, I'd encounter roving packs of older boys headed home in the opposite direction.

"Uggleh," they'd mutter darkly as they approached, howling with laughter as I ran past them in tears, "You look like you been hit with an uggleh stick."

By age thirteen or fourteen the uggleh incidents were thankfully a thing of the past (although I did carry the nickname "Woof" in certain circles until high school graduation); by then the vicious catcalls had mostly been replaced by equally vicious wolf whistles. The mystifying change brought no comfort. Approval or disapproval made little difference; it all sounded the same to my ears.

Try as I might in all the years since then, I never became more comfortable inside my own skin. I had no idea what I looked like as an adult, any more than I did as a kid. The world acted as one big funhouse mirror, shape-shifting minute by minute to keep me frightened and off balance. Sometimes I seemed to be attractive, other times a freak of nature. There was apparently no middle ground; love me or hate me, everybody had an unwanted opinion about my strangely unfeminine body, and I could never predict what that response was going to be.

Some found me beautiful, often going to embarrassing lengths to tell me so. Yet I never dared believe it, because for every one of those guys, two or three others would gawk openly at me with icy, incredulous disgust. God, I knew that hateful expression well. I came to think of it as the Death Stare, since it would have burned the scrawny flesh right off my bones if it could. It was a stare that said, *You're a blight on the landscape, an appalling genetic mistake. And now, having accidentally gazed upon you, I'll have to wash my eyeballs out with soap.*

I used to do whatever was necessary to avoid that Death Stare. Or any stare, if I could help it. All attention was bad attention, and I couldn't figure out how to stop being an attention-getter. Outside world: Bad. Staying home: Good. For years I dreaded walking out the front door even to retrieve the mail, and avoided eye contact at all costs.

I became much braver as I got older, of course. I went out into the world and fraternized like a normal person. Yet on bad days, letting strangers look at me still felt like acid on my skin.

I don't usually talk about this stuff. Partly because it's always been steeped in shame, but also because it dredges up other peoples' issues, too. What they think they hear me say is, *Oh poor me, I'm so tall and thin and I can't seem to put on any weight.*

To which the only logical response would be, *Oh for Christ's sake, eat a cookie!*

I get it. I do. It's hard to step outside your own pain long enough to understand someone else's. Especially when the source of their anguish would be the answer to your own prayers. More than one oversized woman has insisted she could be happy if only she were in my shoes. But I'll tell you right now, I wouldn't wish these crazy flip-flops on anybody.

It used to frustrate the hell out of me when someone would suggest that my "look" was a lifestyle choice I could easily remedy with three squares a day.

Jesus, I would want to shout, *If I could release myself from this torment just by eating extra helpings of mac 'n cheese, don't you think I would?*

In fact, I do. I eat like a hungry, hungry hippo and it's never made a damned bit of difference. Oh yes, I do gain weight—I get a splendid spare tire right around the middle, and pretty much nowhere else.

Picture a corn dog wearing an onion ring. Mmmm, sexy. ❖

High school social dynamics can be brutal. Did any of us *not* have a really bad week now and then?

THE GAUNTLET

Our high school campus consisted of a large, modern building that housed all the traditional classrooms and amenities, and a much older structure that used to be a separate vocational-technical school and now mainly held the high school's shop classes.

Kitty-corner across the highway from the repurposed vocational school sat an outpost of Boy's Town, a series of drab brownstone high-rises that warehoused hundreds of disadvantaged or "troubled" teenage boys from all over the country, many of whom took most of their classes in the vocational-technical building. I attended commercial art classes in a room at the very back of that building and down a long hall, past all the other classrooms.

It was a Monday afternoon in the spring of my junior year. I was headed to class down the long, long hallway, where a captain-of-the-football-team-type named Chad was lounging outside his classroom door with a couple of friends. One of them said something stupid and typical like, *"Hey, Chad, here comes your girlfriend."*

I guess I must have smart-mouthed a retort that made Chad look foolish in front of his boys, because he was out for blood after that. The next day, half a dozen guys were waiting in the hall to watch the fireworks; on the following day it was more like twenty. By Thursday every boy from every classroom crowded the hallway to participate in the awful spectacle as I tried to make my way past them to commercial art class.

Days, weeks—I'm not sure how long it went on. Long enough to consider dropping out of school. Finally when I couldn't take it anymore I did what no bully-ee ever does gladly: I told my teacher, a crusty old guy with a good heart and some seriously outdated commercial art skills. I never found out what he did about it, but the next day (and every day after that) the hall was a ghost town as I walked alone to class, my heel clicks echoing hollowly on the terrazzo floors.

Funny, how the past can stick with you. For decades, every time I saw two or more men congregating on the sidewalk up ahead I had to force myself not to automatically cross the street to avoid them.

For a brief period in my twenties those tables were turned.

Although desperately shy in real life, I knew how to make myself look scary as hell to the casual observer. Multicolored hair, bits of metal sticking out here and there.

Occasionally I'd find myself walking the streets alone at night— on my way home from a concert at the seedy old Florentine Gardens in Hollywood, let's say—when I'd encounter a gaggle of unsuspecting guys heading toward me on the same side of the street. So I'd play a little game to amuse myself: Beef up my swagger, put on a vicious sneer and start radiating a big dark cloud of evil, ugly energy.

Then I'd count the seconds until they crossed the street to avoid me, their uneasy sideways glances darting my way as they scurried past. One…two…three…

Extra points for big and muscular, double score for gang members. ❖

CHAPTER THREE

WAR STORIES

Having been raised on a steady diet of Holocaust trauma, it was perhaps not surprising that by the age of fifteen I was thoroughly obsessed with Nazis. Well, not just Nazis—if it had anything at all to do with World War II, you could count me in. I collected an impressive library of books on the subject, but soon realized reading about it wasn't enough. This stuff didn't feel like yesterday's news; it was real and heart-stoppingly immediate, and I knew that I needed to witness it firsthand.

Soon after graduating from high school, I started spending my summers roaming around Europe with a friend and a backpack. We hit the tourist landmarks and museums along with all the bars and discos, yet I was really there to visit the remnants of the war: Those gaping holes not yet fully rebuilt by the late 1970s, empty voids where homes and businesses had once stood in each exhausted city. In these forlorn open spaces I could feel the enormity of so many lives interrupted, their social networks destroyed along with all the structures.

Brussels, Cologne, Rotterdam. Evidence of the war revealed itself everywhere I looked, yet I always felt the connection most strongly in London. I especially loved to get old British people reminiscing about the war at home. Rationing. Air raids. One especially enthusiastic church docent pulled out archival photos of volunteers on the rooftop of St. Paul's—average civilians pitching in to pass buckets of water down the line, helping to quell the fires after bombs had fallen nearby. Those images felt hauntingly real. I could almost taste the smoke.

Here's the funny thing about all of this: I could swear I was carrying other peoples' simultaneous first-hand memories of the war. And no, it wasn't just an overactive imagination brought on by reading too many books. I knew how it felt, how it *smelled* to momentarily inhabit the thoughts and experiences of different people from that era.

I recalled, for instance, the experience of being an unremarkable Nazi government functionary, casually racist and mild as milk. I remember sitting at a desk, twirling a pair of wire-rimmed glasses between my fingers as I glanced through my meticulous bookkeeping ledgers.

That was it. Just a flash, a sensory moment without context of any kind, yet I remembered exactly how it felt: The weight of the glasses, the texture of the paper, the satisfaction of seeing page after page of neat ledger entries.

Yet I seemed to remember the experience of someone else too, a short-tempered young Londoner lying cheek by jowl with family and neighbors in the close confines of the underground station, cocooned in rough wool blankets while nighttime bombs destroyed my beloved city overhead.

And then there was the day a few years later, while walking up a sunny street in Los Angeles, that I suddenly remembered how it felt to dig a mass grave and be machine-gunned into it, the bullets tearing across my back as I fell face forward to join the other crumpled bodies below.

These were not my own memories, obviously. How could they be? Yet if they weren't mine, whose recollections were they?

I didn't really want to know the answer to that question, fearing the exploration might bring uninvited interaction with ghosts. This "no ghosts" policy was all that really mattered to me; by the time I turned fourteen or so I had figured out how to keep a nice tight lid on all those supernatural terrors. War victims or not, I wasn't about to let any random dead people start oozing out into my awareness if I could help it. ❖

It wasn't all weirdness and pain. That era was accompanied by a really good soundtrack.

THE LONG AND WINDING ROAD

George Harrison was coming to the Nassau Coliseum in Long Island! To my ecstatic sixteen-year-old ears, the news seemed too good to be true. In those days, a Beatle just didn't tour. Even more incredible: My friend Patty and I had inexplicably been granted permission to travel by Greyhound bus all the way to New York—*alone!*—to see the concert.

I was six years old when the Beatles played *The Ed Sullivan Show*. After a relatively brief *Paul is so cute!* phase, I moved on to the Monkees along with most of the other kids I knew. Because, let's face it, Davy Jones was even cuter.

Rediscovering the Beatles a year or two after they'd already broken up and fallen off the pop cultural radar altogether, I belatedly became a single-minded devotee. They hadn't toured live since I was small, and over the intervening years I'd come to think of the Beatles as something akin to papal figures—elevated beings who could be heard and witnessed on film or radio, yet never experienced in live audience. This miraculous George Harrison show would be my first opportunity to see a living, breathing Beatle in the flesh.

I had a month to prepare myself for this landmark concert event. What to wear? Nothing ordinary would do; my clothing had to express the very essence of sincere devotion. I bought a child's size Fruit of the Loom tee, dyed it black in a pot on the stove. There were no such things as concert tees yet (at least not where I lived), yet I was making one.

And I knew exactly what to put on it. There was this odd squiggle that appeared somewhere on every George Harrison album cover. I had no idea what the squiggle meant—*This side up* in Hindustani, for all I knew—yet I used to gaze at that symbol lovingly for hours, tracing its shape over and over with my finger as I listened to his records. I just really liked the way it looked.

So I bought a mess of tiny glass bugle beads in a pretty shade of iridescent dusty pink, and spent the month painstakingly hand beading that mysterious squiggle onto the front of my shirt. Night after night as I worked to create those undulating swirls, my mind would empty itself of conscious thought and become filled instead with the blissfully transcendent sitar strains of all my favorite Harrison songs, played over and over again on the stereo.

I've looked back and wondered about that shirt many times since, yet it was only a couple of years ago that the squiggle's meaning finally dawned on me. One day while flipping idly through an illustrated book on Eastern spirituality I suddenly saw the image represented there.

It was Om, of course.

Like many small-town teenagers I was supremely oblivious in those days, exposed only to mainstream American influences and not yet open to any form of alternative spiritual philosophy. Yet something about that squiggle shirt hinted at a rich, mysterious undercurrent at work even way back then, a hidden ocean of spirituality surging deep beneath the unknowing surface of my life. And although I did my best to remain ignorant of its presence, the power and majesty of that vast ocean would not be denied for much longer. ❖

Despite what I considered my overwhelming physical deformity, I did date a bit in high school. Had a few nice boyfriends, went to the prom. I even turned down a perfectly lovely proposal of marriage because it interfered with my longstanding plan to split for California the moment the ink was dry on my high school diploma.

By the time I hit the West Coast I thought of myself as a somewhat jaded expert on the subject of romance. Ah, youth.

FIRST LOVE

You know the kind. Ooey-gooey, all-consuming love. The kind where you think you invented it; a shimmering, magical, transcendent state of being never before experienced in all of human history, and blah blah blah. I fell without caution, without wisdom, without a lick of self-awareness or common sense. The falling was glorious; the landing, not so much.

I met him at a place called the FUBAR* which should give you some indication right there, a dive whose chief virtue was that it allowed entry to eighteen-year-olds like myself with a stamp on the opposite hand and a stern warning to stay away from the alcohol. Wink, wink.

He was thirty-two. Newly separated from his wife, with two kids closer in age to me than I was to him. None of this sounded good to me, yet it sounded good to him and I found it impossible to resist the mesmerizing force of his will. We became a couple at his insistence, and although my instinct at first was to get the hell away from this guy and all his adult commitments, I stayed instead. Over time I fell for him, mind, body and soul, blissfully letting him reshape everything about me to suit his liking. I lost myself altogether in the process.

And then the bliss wore off. Still, we remained together for four turbulent and mutually unsatisfying years. In year three he declared we should see other people and I reluctantly complied, heartbroken

* Fucked Up Beyond All Recognition

yet obedient as ever. But when I met someone I liked better than him, the ultimatum was swiftly delivered: Ditch the new guy and agree to move in together, or it was over between us for good.

So we moved in together, just my love and me. Oh, and his two kids plus a handful of industrial engineers who worked eight-to-five every day with him in the main hall of the converted church where we lived. I had to pass through their office space every morning to get from the bedroom to the bathroom or into the shared kitchen.

In this very public love nest our already unstable relationship continued its slow rot from the inside out. And then one day just before I left for one of my European world-war-witnessing backpacking trips, he confessed he'd met someone else.

She was living with her guy, my guy was living with me, yet they knew they were destined to be together someday in the unspecified future. But I was not to worry—this was my home, and I would be welcome here for as long as I wanted to stay.

A wiser or more perceptive person than I would surely have realized what lay in store. Yet when I returned from Europe a month later, I was gob-smacked to find my few possessions piled in the basement and another woman living my life, entertaining my friends, hanging with my kids.

Having burned through my savings on the trip, it hadn't occurred to me to make a backup plan. And now suddenly, to my complete surprise, I found I was homeless. No job, no money, no household items (he'd thrown away all my starving-student junk when I moved in, because his grownup stuff was nicer). No friends. And no clue.

Looking back on that terrible period it's clear to me my wounds were largely self-inflicted, yet at the time I staggered around in dumbfounded agony, undone by the unexpected cruelty of the betrayal. I continued to live at the scene of the crime for six desperate days while trying to devise a plan for starting over somewhere else. One day as I lay crying bitterly in the bedroom, I heard him come in, pause and then scribble something before walking out. It was a check for five hundred dollars.

I took the money. And when I did, something inside me shattered.

For years afterward I fixated on that check, fantasizing that I would save up five hundred dollars and send it back because I didn't need his goddamned charity. Or, no. I'd save it up, write a check, tear it into a million little pieces, and mail it back to him. Or, no. I'd do it in person; I'd throw those confetti bits of blood money right in his face. Or, no. Why should I give him five hundred dollars? He owed me that and more.

I took the money and left the same day with one change of clothes and a hairbrush.

I couldn't eat, couldn't sleep, losing twenty-two pounds while living on the sofas of strangers. The weeks oozed by in an agonized blur. A skeletal, hollow-eyed wraith, I managed to behave calmly around people who knew me, yet displayed the awkward tendency to burst into tears in the company of strangers.

Time passed. I got a job, a place to live, some new friends and lovers. Gradually I built a new life, one household utensil at a time. But I was never the same after that.

A new kind of rage overtook me. Anger had always been my primary fuel of choice, hot and bothered, yet this was different and a lot more dangerous. This anger was made of ice, and it numbed me.

A few months after moving out, I described the changes this way:

December 8, 1979
...It's like I walked through fire and the white-hot heat changed my molecular structure. I feel crystalline, glittery on the inside, with all the impurities—or maybe all the purities?—burned away. Like a phoenix risen from my own ashes, except with an empty hole where my heart used to be.

A second internal transformation began to reveal itself as the months rolled by. Over time I became so identified with the abusive lover I'd left behind that I gradually took on his attributes, preying on men weaker than myself, men who wanted to lose themselves in me. Calculatedly undoing my lovers as I felt I had been undone.

The pattern was always the same. First, a blissful month or so. Then a transitional period where I started to notice his flaws. Like: His shirt gets untucked sometimes. Or: He's not witty enough to keep up with my hip-sophisticate friends. Or: He likes me too much. Or he doesn't like me enough.

Any guy who dated me during that period was guaranteed to fail the perfection test, and the punishment for failure wasn't pretty. As his transgressions mounted, my destroyer instinct took over and I would begin to torture him, coolly, dispassionately and with ruthless precision. The worst part (for me, anyway) was that I knew I was doing it, yet was helpless to stop the horrifying process once the auto-destruct button had been pressed.

That final sorry phase of the affair would last another month or so before I grew bored with the carnage, dumping the bloody, dismembered body parts (metaphorically speaking) and heading out in search of a newer, shinier, future ex-boyfriend.

The serial mayhem went on unchecked for years. Despite periodic attempts at counseling and therapy, I remained unable to hold any form of relationship—or job, come to think of it—for more than a few vicious months at a time.

But hey, I had a to-die-for apartment and fabulous friends. And we all went out dancing almost every night, magnificent in our rooster tail haircuts and cutting-edge, modern vintage clothes.

Had anyone asked, I'd have insisted I was completely happy. ❖

BUDDHISM

CHAPTER FOUR

SAY WHAT?

Long time no see. What the hell did that mean? And how had Johnny's Gohonzon—it was a scroll of paper, after all, not even a statue—been able to talk to me?

I thought I'd better check out this Buddhism thing more closely. Johnny attended weekly Buddhist meetings at the home of a beloved TV actress from my 1970s childhood, so on the appointed Friday evening the two of us drove there together.

I'd like to report that I began my Buddhist practice out of a desire to help others, or even a desire to help myself. The truth is this: I began my Buddhist practice because Bob Newhart's secretary asked me to. It so unnerved me that a famous person cared one way or the other about my spiritual wellbeing that I agreed to give it a try just to make her stop looking at me.

She signed me up to go receive a Gohonzon the very next day.

"You don't have to wait until then to start chanting," she advised. "Do it on your way home tonight and see what happens!"

And so I did. After leaving Johnny at his place, I gave chanting a try on the ten-block trip home. It was late at night; there wasn't a soul on the road, my windows were rolled up tightly, yet I still felt like an asshole, and kept looking around to make sure there were no witnesses.

"Nam...Myo...Ho," *is anybody watching, can they see my lips move?* "Ren...Ge Kyo...Nam Myo Ho...Ren Ge...Kyo...Nam...," *whoops, here comes a car* "...Myo Ho Ren...Ge Kyo..."

I parked the car and went in to bed, but found there was no sleep to be had. In those days I expected and got eight solid hours every night, yet to my surprise I couldn't sleep a wink. *Because I was wildly euphoric.* Wait, no, not just euphoric—I was also profoundly at peace. This was strange. I knew how it felt to be energized and elated, the endorphins rushing through my system; I also knew how it felt to be calm and serene. But to be both deeply calm and joyfully ecstatic at the same time? This was new. This was weird. Too weird for sleeping, and it was pissing me off.

January 11, 1986
I didn't get to sleep until probably four o'clock in the damned morning after last night's bizarre Buddhafest, and now it's far too early to be out of bed on a Saturday morning. And that totally sucks. Johnny and those other people are coming by any minute to take me out to the temple to get my Gohonzon and I don't want to go. I called them up a little while ago and tried to back out. They're persistent little buggers.

Ugh. What have I gotten myself into? ❖

WHAT GOES AROUND

I had entered a brave new Buddhist world, a whirlwind of mostly unwelcome activity. Meetings in the evenings, meetings on the weekends. The unflagging care and attention I received from total strangers at these events was flattering and mystifying by turns. I didn't get it. What could possibly have been in it for them? Given the option, I'd have preferred to skip those meetings altogether, to take my Gohonzon and run—which was probably why I was never given the option. Instead other people were always insisting on picking me up and taking me to meetings, or coming to my house to teach me how to chant. Oddly enough, their efforts were beginning to pay off. Sort of.

January 28, 1986
Seventeen days since I got my Gohonzon. I don't know which is more amazing: That I'm still chanting, or that I ever started in the first place. Just getting past the incense and peppermint, the karma and the candles…I never thought I'd go in for all that smiley faced hippie crap.

And then at the study meetings there's all this stuff about reincarnation—please. Spare me. I kind of like the way the chanting feels, but I really don't need to hear about any of that wacko past-life bullshit. ❖

GOOD MORNING, STARSHINE

Forty-two Nam-Myoho days and counting. For that first month or so it seemed like all I ever did was: Wake up/chant/go to work/come home/chant/go to sleep/wake up and chant all over again, day after day after tedious day. It was a drag, frankly, learning all that Sanskrit mumbo jumbo. But once I more or less had it down and it no longer took me an hour to stumble through the prayers every morning, something funny was starting to happen. And I could find no words to describe it.

February 22, 1986
It's kind of like the sunrise is happening on the inside of my life for the very first time. It's such a good feeling, I want to tell everybody I know. And that's where the "no words to describe it" part gets to be a problem. I cringe as I hear myself saying perky-ass Valley Girl things, like: "Chanting is so totally awesome!"

And my friends just look at me with that expression that says: Are you fucking kidding me?

I think I heard one of them call me the Stepford Buddhist behind my back. Ouch. ❖

PARTY LIKE IT'S 1998

I don't know where the idea came from, yet all my life I knew I'd be dead by the age of forty. It wasn't worry or opinion; I considered it immutable fact, and this premature expiration date was never far from my thoughts.

In the decade following high school I coped by not coping, plunging headlong into the last days of disco before moving on to enthusiastically embrace the "live fast/die pretty" club scene of the early 80s.

Then in 1986 as I settled into my Buddhist practice, something unexpected happened as a side benefit of all the chanting. The "dead by forty" fixation just melted away all by itself.

This was a startling development, and as time went on it became clear the phenomenon wasn't just confined to the issue of early mortality. My ongoing Nazi preoccupation disappeared in much the same way at about the same time. Yet here's the most astonishing part: I don't know how or when, but in those lovely rays of gentle Buddhist sunshine, I forgot my fear of the supernatural. It just sort of slipped my mind.

How could total terror simply fade away as if it had never existed? That howling horror, the unspeakable dread that clamored constantly for my attention? Although I'd managed to firmly lock away all supernatural occurrences years earlier, I lived in constant fear they'd resurface. Throughout my teens and twenties, I scrupulously avoided all scary images, all paranormal books, movies and TV commercials—anything that might accidentally activate that ever-present shadow world. I took no chances. Even the possibility of a benign visit from a deceased loved one was too risky, too terrible to contemplate; to ensure my safety I repeated these words aloud like a prayer every night, just after settling myself beneath the magic covers and before turning out the light: *"I know you're out there, so please don't come visit me until after I'm dead."*

All these constant obsessions had somehow evaporated like the morning dew and I never even noticed their passing. Only months or years later did it occur to me I hadn't thought even once about early mortality, or blitzkrieg, or things that go bump, in a very long time. ❧

WOO WOO

My practice of Buddhism was four months old when my friend Laurie introduced us. She said she just had a feeling her chiropractor, Stephen, and I were supposed to meet.

Tall, charming, handsome; I couldn't say whether or not we were "supposed" to meet, but was very glad Laurie thought so. Stephen seemed to feel the same way, or at least he focused all his attention on me from the moment we were introduced. It wasn't long before I found out why.

He was a follower of the teachings of Alice Bailey, he told me, and had been mentored for several years in the esoteric healing arts by those affiliated with her philosophies and writings. I had never heard of Alice Bailey or her teachings, and didn't know what he meant by esoteric healing arts. But he was cute, so I kept listening.

Alice Bailey channeled the teachings of an ascended master *(I'm sorry, she did what?)* and Stephen belonged to a meditation group that put these teachings into practice. And he'd been studying occult techniques—I recoiled at the word—for use in his healing work.

"Relax," he said, as he smiled reassuringly. "The dictionary definition of 'occult' just means 'that which isn't readily seen.' There's no black magic involved, I promise." He leaned in closer.

"You're an open window between worlds, you know," he continued. "I'd like you to join our meditation group if you're interested."

Holy Christ on a crutch—I'm an open window between worlds?

I have no idea what that means, but excuse me for just one sec while I slam down the sash, draw the blinds and hammer those shutters closed...

I did not join Stephen's meditation group.

Coincidentally, however, I'd thrown my back out quite severely a few weeks earlier. Partway through fashion school at the time, I typically spent all day, everyday, on my feet in patternmaking or draping classes; when I wasn't busy doing that I was hunched over a sewing machine or hauling around a thirty-pound canvas bag of tools and textbooks. And my back just wasn't getting any better on its own.

Stephen the chiropractor to the rescue. I'd never tried chiropractic treatment before, let alone the "esoteric" kind that healed by manipulating invisible energy. Yet my back was killing me and it meant this hot guy would come to my apartment, so I agreed to give it a go.

The healing was quick and near-miraculous. I felt my spine rearrange itself into the picture of perfect health, seemingly without having been physically touched at all during the treatment. Jubilant and one hundred percent sold on those occult techniques of his, I wanted to celebrate. The house call rapidly evolved into something else altogether, and that evening marked the beginning of an eight-month romantic relationship.

About that affair I will say this: If you are an intensely insecure individual with trust and privacy issues, and you're thinking of dating an all-too-human guy who, by the way, can read your mind and see your invisible energy patterns…

I don't recommend it. ❖

CHAPTER FIVE

EARTHLY DESIRES = ENLIGHTENMENT

It's funny; Nam-Myoho-Renge-Kyo gets a bad rap here in the U.S. for not being "spiritual" enough.

"Everybody chants for parking spaces," is the typical sniffy comment.

All I know is, a spiritual practice was the very last thing I was in the market for at the time, so all the serene and lofty ones floating above the fray would never have grabbed me. I didn't want to bliss out, didn't care about saving the whales, and, trust me, I was not the slightest bit interested in becoming a better person.

Yet this Buddhist practice could—did—help me get right down in the muck and start to fix the things that were so achingly wrong with my world. So I grabbed it tight and held on for dear life. And if a little compassion or wisdom crept in as a silent side benefit of all that chanting...well, no harm in that, I guess. Which turns out to be an actual tenet of Nichiren Buddhist practice: Earthly desires are enlightenment.

Meaning (or so I understood it at the time), you can chant for whatever you want. The object of desire doesn't matter. As long as something causes one to chant with sincerity, the very action of chanting to a Gohonzon automatically begins the awakening process, polishing one's life condition so the nature of the desires themselves imperceptibly begin to elevate. Start out chanting for drugs or boyfriends, in other words, and gradually end up chanting for somebody else's happiness.

Well, that and boyfriends. ❖

GOD'S LITTLE SOCIOPATH

Late 1987. I'd been chanting for almost two years, and found it strange to be practicing Buddhism a whole lot harder than I'd ever intended when I first signed up. Although I adored the Gohonzon itself, I still wasn't sure I even liked this Buddhist organization. Yet there I was, attending meetings day and night, participating regularly in unbelievably unhip events with people I had no desire to know better.

I probably should have felt bad for my Buddhist leaders. It was their job to "raise" me within the Buddhist family, to teach me how to become a leader myself, to help me stretch and grow and learn to practice Buddhism to the fullest. They were a perpetually cheery pain in my ass, in other words. I made no secret of my feelings; I suspected most of the younger leaders were afraid of me, and that was just the way I liked it.

Yet I had to admit, their annoying shtick really did seem to work: The more I tried taking the actions they so enthusiastically recommended, the more my life opened up and changed for the better. Career breakthroughs, better boyfriends, healthier family relationships.

Some karmic sludge stayed persistently the same, of course. I was still ice-cold numb, still dead on the inside and exquisitely immune to the sufferings of others. Things were only changing in the sense that I had previously been absolutely ok with that, yet now it was starting to dawn on me this might not be such a good thing. It was becoming genuinely uncomfortable to be so unfeeling, so monstrously lacking in basic humanity.

Maybe this wasn't right. ❧

ANIMAL GUILT

And then even the karmic sludge gradually started to shift a little bit, too. It wasn't a comfortable sensation.

March 27, 1988

Things are changing, I can feel it. Over the past few months I've started to join the human race, I've actually begun to care—but about animals, not about people. I still don't give a shit about humans yet I'm really beginning to empathize with animals, noticing whether they're happy or sad, taking their side if somebody isn't treating them right. This is brand new, and at first I welcomed it as proof I'm not a monster after all—that I can feel something for somebody. Anybody.

That's the good part. The weird part, the troubling part is that once it shoved its tiny, hairy paw in the door, this newfound animal empathy somehow metastasized into a giant, unrecognizable obsession. Somehow I've gone from not caring at all about animal mistreatment to becoming completely devastated by it. But it's not just the abuse of animals out in the world that brings me to my knees. Now all my own unthinking interactions with childhood pets come flooding back to haunt me, too; every careless betrayal I've perpetrated against them is suddenly seen in a terrible new light. Now it's like I'm the unforgivable abuser. In truth, I probably wasn't any more oblivious or unfeeling toward animals than the next little kid, yet that's no consolation. The memories sicken me. This thing seems to be taking over my life and it brings with it a bottomless pit of guilt and darkness that immobilizes me each time it appears.

And the issue keeps getting worse. It's no longer just about humans mistreating animals. I can't even watch a lion take down a zebra on a nature show anymore without being haunted for a week. A stray cat saves its kittens from a burning building and I'm paralyzed with grief and guilt at the sight of her tiny, bandaged body on the evening news. And now even fictional animal stories—cartoons, for God's sake—are doing it, too.

This can't be progress. I wish I knew what the hell is happening. ❖

ANGER

Two-and-a-half years as a Buddhist, and I'd been chanting long enough to begin to understand the nature of the sludgy obstacles I was up against, yet not nearly long enough to be able to do much about any of them. These were the "terrible twos" of spiritual practice.

October 19, 1988

Argh. Sometimes I just can't stand it. The good thing about waking up and smelling the spiritual coffee is that it's helping me make sense of the jumbled mess that is my life. The bad thing is: Change comes painfully slowly, and in the meantime the acute awareness of all that needs to be changed makes me want to scream.

Take anger, for instance. Blinding rage has always been such a big part of me—my protector, my fuel, my best friend. Yet I hate the uncontrollable destruction it brings and would love to leave the fireworks behind forever, if I only could.

Sometimes after I've made a terrible mess of a situation, I sit and chant about my anger for hours at a time. I'd give anything to be released from it. I get so desperate for relief that the only thing I can think to do is use my anger to fight my anger. So as I chant, I picture my rage as a really repulsive, many-headed beast and my prayers as a big-ass sword. And I spend those hours furiously slicing and dicing each slavering head that appears, until I'm too exhausted to go on.

I have no idea if it works to chant that way. Luckily I'm pretty sure any form of chanting is good chanting, and no harm can come of it. So I guess for now I'll keep on slaying the beast like my life depends on it, and wait to see what happens after that. ❖

It took awhile, a good three years or more, but eventually I began to see that all those annoyingly chipper people in the Buddhist organization weren't really so annoying after all. In fact, lots of them were kind of wonderful. Why hadn't I noticed it before?

KURT

December 11, 1989

We had a very nice turnout for tonight's year-end meeting at John and Natalie's place. After the chanting was over, they surprised us by unveiling a "tree of dreams," a branch that John had affixed to a base so it stood upright like a small tree. Then they handed out pretty little cards and asked us all to write down one personal goal or desire we'd like to see happen in the coming year, and tie it to the tree; this time next year we'd all get together again to read the cards aloud and celebrate the successes.

I drew a blank on what to write, then something funny happened…it almost felt like somebody else took over the pen and started to write without me. I watched my hand from a hazy distance as it wrote: In 1990 I'm going to meet and marry the right man for me.

All the while I was thinking: What? No! Don't write that— what if it doesn't happen? They'll read it out loud next year and I'll look like an ass!

Yet I wrote it anyway and handed it in.

I don't know where that came from. A date with the right guy would be nice, but marriage isn't even on my list right now.

As it turned out, I'd already met him two weeks earlier. I'd been volunteering at a Buddhist art facility for the past couple of years, spending most evenings and weekends designing or painting whatever banners, scenic backdrops, parade floats or miscellaneous signage the membership needed for its many meetings and public events. I was proud of the work I did there, happy to give something back to the organization that had done so much for me.

After my most recent love relationship had ended the year before (extremely nice guy, just not especially right for me), I decided it would be a good idea to take a break from dating. For once, instead of plunging unthinkingly right back into the pool, maybe it would be helpful to spend a little time reflecting, chanting, cleaning up my still-a-piece-of-work-in-progress relationship karma. The long hours required at the art facility were perfect for this; just the thing to keep me out of trouble and off the dating scene.

And then Kurt showed up to volunteer at the art facility. Not only that—he'd shown up in response to *my* prayers. I was a member of the staff in charge of getting these art projects completed. Usually I insisted on doing most of the work myself to guarantee it would be done properly, rather than taking the time to train a volunteer to help me. Not terribly Buddhist in spirit, maybe, but at least the art always looked good and got done on time.

Now we had a whole series of projects that required architectural renderings, and I suck at perspective drawing. That meant I had to find a new volunteer with major art skills, pronto. I didn't know of any. So I put the call out into the universe instead, chanting with crystal clear determination and focus: *I need the right artist to show up right now, so my crew can successfully deliver the drawings that help support this beautiful Buddhist organization in its goals.*

Kurt arrived the next day. He was perfect. By early January I started to notice he was perfect in lots of other ways too, and he was clearly noticing the same thing about me. Over the next several weeks as we worked together on a hectic succession of art projects, we fell deeply in love.

One Monday shortly before Valentine's Day, he handed me a small watercolor sketch. He had an odd look on his face.

"What is it?" I asked, not sure whether to be alarmed.

"I just ran across this watercolor yesterday when I was cleaning my apartment. I completely forgot I'd painted it."

I glanced at the painting. It was a nice peaceful scene, a girl sitting by a riverbank. I looked back at Kurt questioningly.

"Look at the face," he said.

I did as he instructed. It was unmistakably a picture of me.

"Oh! How nice." I was pleased—it was a terrific likeness. Very flattering.

"Now look at the date," he said. "I painted this almost a month *before* we met."

It really did feel like mysterious forces were at work between us, like the cosmos itself had preordained our meeting. Being with Kurt was the easiest, most natural thing in the world, like no other relationship I'd ever known. We moved in together right away; I loved him so much that three months after that, in October of 1990, I agreed to let eighty-five pairs of eyes watch me walk down the aisle to marry the right man for me. ❖

BOB

Kurt and I had been married only a few months when our pet-loving sister-in-law brought us the news: A fantastic litter of kittens had been discovered under a friend's wheelbarrow on Easter Sunday.

That wheelbarrow happened to be located all the way down in South Orange County, a good fifty miles away, yet she assured us it would be well worth the trip. Whip-smart, adorable and filled with personality, these rambunctious kittens were clearly something special. If we wanted one, we'd better act fast. Kurt drove to Orange County the next day, where a feisty little gray and white kitten adopted him on sight. We named it Bob.

Bob was a holy terror. Incorrigible, stubbornly opinionated and unable to stay out of trouble, he left a trail of chaos and destruction wherever he went. We kept the spritz bottle handy in a futile attempt to train the unwanted behavior out of him, yet it only spurred him on to greater acts of badness.

It was like the damned kitten wanted to be punished. Always on the lookout for creative ways to taunt me, he'd do things like climb the curtains all the way up to the ceiling, wait until I'd gotten a good look at him up there, then crash to the floor and go thundering past me into the bedroom. Or he'd wait until I wasn't looking, sneak *under* the closed door to my art studio, jump onto my table and tromp through the wet blobs of paint he found there. I'd take off after him up the hallway as he left vivid green paw prints on the hardwood ahead of me, squirting the water bottle at him furiously until long after his fur was soaked through. The game was over when the soggy little beast found somewhere safe to hide, out-waiting me there until I eventually stopped looking for him.

One afternoon after yet another such skirmish, we found ourselves at that old, familiar impasse: Bob soaked to the skin, glaring at me defiantly from the bedroom where I'd finally cornered him; me panting angrily, half-empty squirt bottle in hand. Nothing seemed to get through to this little monster. And the bad behavior was only getting worse; the harder I tried to teach him to be good, the more of a marauding outlaw he became. I was at my wit's end, so frustrated with him I could have put my fist through a wall.

Now I understand what makes a person a child beater, I thought suddenly, and the idea staggered me. I guess I'd never realized just how thin the veneer of loving non-violence could be when one felt pushed to extremes. Uh-oh. I felt a nauseating wave of animal guilt coming on.

Then that familiar guilt cycle was unexpectedly disrupted by what seemed to be a sudden electrical flash of direct insight, a momentary window into Bob's little mind. All at once I understood that he didn't enjoy being bad at all; he wanted my attention desperately, and didn't know how to get it except by engaging me in these war games.

He just wants to be loved.

It was that Voice talking. More than five years had passed since I'd first heard it speak. My anger vanished instantly. I sat down on the bed in wonderment, held out my arms to the bedraggled kitten. Bob's expression changed to one of utter joy as he leapt into my embrace. For the first time (yet by no means the last) we'd understood each other perfectly.

We were inseparable after that, my extremely good little kitty and me. He worked hard to learn and follow the house rules, always doing his best to please. We grew to adore one another, our mutual bond of love and trust more perfect than any I had previously known.

Needless to say, the squirt bottle was happily retired—until several years later, at least, when little Morgan Furchild arrived on the scene and we began that old kitten training tug-of-war all over again. ❖

CHAPTER SIX

TURNING 40: TIME TO DIE?

December 22, 1997

*O*ne day last week during morning prayers it hit me suddenly—
good God, I'm almost forty. I hadn't given that silly fixation a
single thought in the past dozen years. Now that I think about
it, I realize there are a bunch of worrisome things wrong with
me physically and I really should go have them checked out. So
I guess that'll be my resolution for the New Year: Go get medical
attention. Don't die by forty.

It took a month or so to work up the nerve to make that first visit
to the doctor, yet once made it was quickly followed by another
appointment. And another.

March 2, 1998

Well, I've been doing it. I've been having some tests done at the
clinic, each unfortunately showing inconclusive results. I seem to
have turned into a lemon somewhere along the way. Every time
I go into the shop the symptoms disappear or else their diagnostic
equipment just can't pinpoint the source of the problem. Now
I'm pretty sure they're grasping at straws. Tomorrow morning

Carrie Triffet **69**

(Saturday) I'm scheduled for an endometrial biopsy, for no specific reason that anybody can tell me.

On a sadder note, I got an emergency call from home this evening; poor Dad is failing fast, so I need to hop a flight tomorrow right after I get through at the clinic so I can be there to say goodbye.

As I waited at the airport for my flight back home to California on Monday morning, I reflected on the weekend's occurrences. It had been an eventful couple of days.

The biopsy had been a non-anesthetized drag, for starters.

"Ever given birth?" the nurse practitioner had chirped brightly in response to my outraged yowls. *"This is what labor feels like!"*

Afterward she handed me a couple of extra-strength Advil and sent me on my way with a small bag of feminine products, adding, "Oh, by the way, you may bleed a bit," as I headed out the door.

I guess the trauma of having a foot-long piece of innards torn out was too much for my body to accept without complaint; as I boarded the plane I felt the beginnings of an awful stomachache. And she wasn't kidding about the bleeding. By the time I made it to my dad's hospital in the early evening it was more like a rushing river, a torrential hemorrhagic downpour.

Yet I wasn't interested in my own physical distractions, which seemed petty by comparison. I had come there to offer whatever comfort I could to my shrunken sweet-pea of a dad. And to my stepmom, Audrey, and to my sister, both of whom were exhausted by their long hospital vigil, beaten down by stress and grief.

I'm not sure where I pulled it out from (nothing beats having a few zillion Nam-Myoho-Renge-Kyos in the bank, I guess), but I managed to transcend my own inconsequential stuff from the minute I got there, and instead floated Buddha-like above the whole situation. My stomach had become locked up, frozen, leaving me unable to eat for nearly forty-eight hours, and of course I was bleeding buckets the whole time, yet somehow none of that mattered. I just focused all my attention on bringing radiant peace and healing acceptance to all three family members in whatever ways I could, and felt absolutely great while doing it.

And I heard from my Voice again. Late Sunday afternoon a friend of my sister's came to visit Dad, which was really very sweet of her. Audrey and I were there when she arrived; my sister was not. As we were introduced, I saw the woman's eyes flick involuntarily down to my jeans and then back up—these people just can't help themselves—and it took me back to all those painful early skirmishes over my schooling, and the embarrassment I had represented to the Ultra-Orthodox community.

Despite our differences she turned out to be a very nice lady, staying around to visit with Audrey and me while my father slept. At around five o'clock Audrey began to get hungry and I thought I might finally be able to eat something too, so I offered to make a trip to the basement cafeteria.

As I walked around the sad little sandwich buffet to fix myself a meal, all I could think about was: *Protein!* Give me protein. I hadn't eaten since Friday night and was beginning to worry about the blood loss. Feeling only marginally hungry, I knew I needed as much fuel as I could manage. So I made a heaping sandwich of processed turkey and American cheese slices, and felt very grateful to have it.

On my way back up in the elevator, heavy purse slung over one shoulder and both hands balancing full, unwieldy cafeteria trays, I suddenly realized: *Oh my GOD! I just made myself an un-Kosher meat and cheese sandwich. What the hell was I thinking? I can't eat this in front of that woman. What am I going to do?*

The elevator opened at my floor. I looked around wildly for a place to stash either the meat or the cheese—*she mustn't find out what I did!*—yet no trashcan was to be found.

Ok then, I'll hide the cheese in my purse, there's only a little mayo on it—I can throw it away after she leaves. Yet I could find no bench to sit on, no place to set down one tray while I tore apart the sandwich on the other.

And while I stood panting at the elevators, drenched in shame and flop-sweat, my Voice calmly observed:

That's not who you are.

It stopped me in my tracks. In fact, everything in the world seemed to stop for a moment as scenes of my childhood flashed in front of me.

Oh. Yes, I forgot. That's not who I am.

Although it had only uttered that one statement, a complete set of unspoken concepts seemed to surround it. I knew the Voice was asking me to give up my lifelong dread of the Jewish community's disapproval; although I'd always obstinately acted the black sheep, fear of being caught breaking their rules had nevertheless remained a powerful source of bitterness and humiliation for me, even as an adult.

I realized I was also being asked to admit the plain truth about myself: I was not, nor had I ever been, a sincere practicing Jew. For better or worse, my spiritual path clearly pointed elsewhere and the time had come to find the courage to stop pretending. But did I really dare be myself in front of this woman, and openly flout religious law?

I turned around and floated, trance-like, into the hospital room with cafeteria trays intact, and watched myself from a serene distance as I polished off that turkey and cheese sandwich. It tasted mighty good.

And all the while, the very nice lady continued her pleasant and uneventful visit as my daddy slept peacefully on. ❖

CAKE

A month or two later, and a few more tests revealed the truth: I'd gone haywire on the inside, with a bad tendency to grow strange objects in inappropriate places.

"It's probably cancer; this sort of thing usually is," the various medical professionals agreed, "still, we can't know for sure until we do more tests."

And while we all waited for those new tests to roll around, I chanted my ass off.

I chanted with gratitude and appreciation for my body's efforts; as far as it knew, I'd spent my whole life asking to die by forty and now it was doing its best to comply. I apologized for the mix-up and gently explained the death sentence had been my mistake. Now it was our mutual job to survive.

And then I chanted hour upon hour with take-no-prisoners focus to obliterate those growths, to turn them into harmless nothings. And as the weeks of testing crawled by, the prognosis gradually changed from "probably" to "possibly" to "it's not looking cancerous at all." By the time I went in for my surgeries they were confident I was in the clear, and indeed that's the way it turned out.

I should really go out on a limb and live the second half of my life like it's a brand new ballgame, I thought to myself as I pictured the gift of all those extra years stretching out ahead of me. *I dodged that bullet and now the rest of the time I spend here on Earth is cake.* ❖

NO CAKE

The surgeries, as it turned out, were no help at all. Over the next seven or eight months, all original symptoms persisted, only now they were made much, much worse by my body's inability to bounce back from the physical trauma of the operations themselves. And a host of strange new effects had shown up as well. I thought of them as my "post-surgery symptoms," although they were later found to have no direct causal connection—terrible, acute stomach pains that came and went without warning, extreme debilitating fatigue and finally, beginning on Christmas Day and building steadily over the holidays to a swollen crescendo, a head-to-toe outbreak of hives so fierce and inflamed it sent me to the emergency room at five o'clock one morning, driven halfway mad by the puffy, allover itch.

And the doctors had no idea what to do for me. The hives never really went away despite double rounds of cortisone treatments, and the phantom pains and fatigue were seemingly un-diagnosable mystery ailments that refused to show up on any test. When I discovered a whole new series of growths in the same region from which the first set had been removed (and knowing another surgery was absolutely out of the question) I did the unthinkable: I called an "alternative" healer.

A few weeks earlier, I had dragged myself out to an evening chanting session during a particularly bad bout of post-surgery pain. Whenever these stomach spasms came on I had to drop what I was doing and go to bed, yet this time I crawled out after a few hours to get in the car and go chant seriously about my situation. Over the months since the surgeries, I'd slowly stopped making plans or taking on long-term projects because I knew I'd always be too tired or too sick, or both. I didn't want to live that way anymore.

I slunked into the room full of chanters, sitting down next to an acquaintance.

"What's wrong? You look awful," she observed helpfully, and when I told her about it she pressed a phone number into my hand.

"Call this woman," she instructed. "She can definitely help you. Her program is the pits, you'll have to give up all your favorite foods and the treatment costs a bundle. But she'll be able to figure out what's wrong with you."

I nodded, stuffing the phone number into my pocket. I had no intention of ever calling it. I lived for good food; I loved eating it, reading about it, cooking it, sharing it. I was one of those people who would sit at the dinner table with friends, planning future awesome meals we were going to have together while we were still in the middle of eating this one. No way was I going to follow some kind of ridiculous tofu-sprout diet, and spend a ton of money for the privilege.

Yet there I was, sick and tired, lumpy and itchy, and it was clear something drastic had to be done.

Elizabeth was a cellular biologist by training, and the cutting-edge nutrition program she developed with the help of that background and skill set is, as far as I know, unique. I credit her with saving my life. And yes, it cost a bloody fortune over a span of three-and-a-half years. Insurance didn't cover it, and, as promised, her program turned out to be a total pain in the butt. I drank only water during those years—ten glasses a day—water in and water out. That alone was something of a full-time job. I took no meds, not even an aspirin; ate no processed foods, no preservatives, no sugars, no wheat, no dairy, no vinegar, no caffeine, no alcohol…well, frankly, the list of what I *could* eat was far shorter than the list of what I couldn't.

The whole thing played hell with my social life. Restaurants were no fun anymore. *I* was no fun anymore. Out-of-town trips became a logistical nightmare, and bars and parties were always filled with other people having a raucously good time while I quietly nursed an Evian in the corner.

Yet I got undisputedly better as a result of that program. Then one day in the winter of 2004 I was unloading my fresh, whole-grain all-natural organic groceries from the car and reflecting wistfully on this extremely limiting dietary lifestyle and how very tired I was of the whole nutrition thing with its hundreds of supplements and herbs and tinctures and drops, and how awfully good a slice of pizza would taste right about now, when my Voice observed:

You're not that sick anymore.

And I was startled to realize it was the truth. This draconian emergency program was in fact a relic from a much sicker era, and I was given to understand that its time had passed and such measures were no longer necessary.

I gratefully quit the nutrition program the very same day.

The great thing about Elizabeth's program—I mean in addition to the fact that it worked—was that it took advantage of the skills of other very gifted healing arts professionals when needed, thereby introducing me to the crème de la crème of the local naturopathic scene. I certainly wouldn't have sought out any of these people on my own, yet being sent there by my primary caregiver for the treatment of specific ailments meant I learned to accept whatever mildly freaky spiritual component each of these treatments inevitably contained.

Highly instrumental in this adventure was an excellent chiropractor named Eileen. At certain points in the healing process I experienced quite a lot of structural disharmony—growing pains, if you will—so I saw her often. During one period in particular, my back was really giving me problems, yet each time I came in and got an adjustment, my spine slipped right back out of alignment even before I had written my check and gone home. After it happened three or four times in a row, I mentioned it to her.

She performed a few kinesiology tests and quickly determined the problem: I had developed an allergic reaction—*to myself.* There was a large mirror hanging behind the reception desk in the lobby, and apparently the very sight of me as I handed over my payment was enough to make my spine collapse into a self-hating heap.

That didn't sound plausible—or fixable—so I protested the diagnosis.

Eileen raised an eyebrow. "There are only three possible reasons for an inability to sustain a spinal adjustment: One–Nutritional or chemical imbalance, and that can't be it because you're under Elizabeth's care. Two–Bio-mechanical imbalance, and that can't be it because you're under *my* care. The only other possibility is emotional-spiritual imbalance. You, my dear, need therapy to get to the bottom of this issue."

Oh no, she did not just say that to me. Who the hell does she think she is, telling me I need to see a therapist? I fumed silently as Eileen handed me a pamphlet for something called trans-generational therapy: "Feeling hopelessly stuck and you don't know why? Maybe your pain is not your own!"

Oh puh-leeze. I took the pamphlet without a word and shoved it in my purse, my spine clattering into a disordered jumble as I stalked angrily out of the building.

Nobody was more surprised about it than me, but I did undergo the trans-generational therapy. My friend Michele called out of the blue a few days after I'd stormed out of Eileen's office and coincidentally asked me to attend *her* trans-generational therapy session as an observer. I readily agreed to be there for moral support, little realizing the so-called "observers" did most of the heavy lifting, while the "participants," like my friend, mainly stood by and watched the proceedings.

The theory behind trans-generational therapy seemed to be that emotional pain gets transmitted through families and continues to be carried, generation after generation, by unsuspecting individuals who hold an unconscious connection to the traumas of the deceased. Or something like that. And while there was no actual channeling involved (or so the therapist assured us), the observers were asked to open themselves to feel and describe the emotions and experiences of those deceased or absent loved ones, which enabled the participants to then make sense of this newly revealed information about their own family history.

Part group therapy, part detective work, this process was guided by the therapist who worked to uncover relationship after relationship from previous generations as she searched for the main nugget of trauma blocking the present-day participant's ability to thrive in the world. As each new ancestor was revealed, the therapist pulled another observer off the sidelines to stand in for that person, to feel what they were feeling.

I'd been sitting back and watching the whole thing quietly, then about three quarters of the way through the evening, someone's dead grandfather ushered in a new unknown presence; I was called in to observe for this new person. I lay down on the floor as instructed —yow, my back was killing me—while they tried to figure out who I might be. Could I have been a miscarriage? No, that didn't seem right. Well, then, was I an aborted baby?

Suddenly I felt this unknown person's experience as it flooded into me.

"No," I reported with absolute conviction. "I could not possibly have been aborted. I am loved and cherished and *wanted* more than anything in the world."

This certainty of my own worth was a completely foreign feeling, as I had never once felt that way in my own life. I liked it, it was nice.

I turned out to be Grandfather's first wife, his precious young darling who had died in the influenza pandemic of the early 1900s. Grandfather, a gifted doctor of great renown, had been powerless to save her and never got over his resulting guilt and grief. A devastated shell of a man, he immigrated to America and changed professions, erasing all evidence of his previous life, yet found he was unable to free himself from the past. Eventually he remarried yet discovered he had no love to give. This loveless marriage begat unloved children along with much sadness, loneliness and profound isolation for all concerned.

I was, in short, standing in for the "nugget" that had torn this present-day person's family apart.

"Will you release your hold on this woman's grandfather?" the therapist asked me/her.

"Oh, no," I answered. "It's wonderful to be so loved."

"Even now that you see the pain this love causes for so many others?"

I blinked and looked around me, startled. I/she meant no harm; it hadn't occurred to her that others were suffering on her account.

"Well, since I'm already gone I guess there's no harm in letting go, in allowing the living to have their time on Earth as I had mine," I said at last on her behalf. And I felt her peacefully release all attachment to her husband's remorse and sadness as everyone in the room breathed a collective sigh.

I couldn't say why or how that form of therapy was able to access the feelings of all those dead people; I just knew from my own experience that it did. And I surprised myself by not being overly freaked out by that. So, later the same evening I signed up to be a participant in my own therapy session the following week. ❖

NAZIS AND JEWS

Nearly everybody who showed up that evening seemed to be either German or Jewish or both. I guess we all end up right where we're meant to be, because, to my great surprise, my session turned out to be all about Nazis. I hadn't thought about Nazis in years. And never until that night had I stopped to wonder why I'd always disliked Judaism so much. We decided it was time to get some answers.

Back through the generations, to anonymous relatives in unmarked graves whose towns and villages had been forever wiped from the map. It was a gut-wrenching process, uncovering those people one by one to find out what made each of them tick. I cried and cried until my nose ran, until my tears met up in the hollow of my throat and streamed a salty river down the front of my shirt. Eventually we found my "nugget," coincidentally played by my friend Michele. A guy (at least I think it was a guy, it felt masculine to me) who refused to believe anybody would kill him just because he happened to be a Jew by random accident of birth.

He took no part of his self-identity from Jewishness. In his opinion, religion was old fashioned, superstitious nonsense, and he chose instead to live his very modern life without religious affiliation of any kind. He thrived on intellectual pursuits, leaving his provincial home and family to enjoy an artistically rich life in the big, glittery city—Vienna, maybe, or Berlin—making friends with other like-minded bohemian types from all walks of life. There was nothing remotely Jewish about him. He was absolutely sure the current tragedy befalling the Jews, while unfortunate, bore no relevance to his life at all.

Except that it did. Enraged at the stupidity of world events, he found it impossible to accept the bitter irony of his fate. And as much as he hated the Nazis, he was even more furious with Judaism, the unwanted religion that couldn't protect him, yet wouldn't leave him alone to live his life in peace.

This was the guy with whom I was so deeply bonded in trans-generational connection. It was seemingly his rage, his hatred and frustration that I had absorbed and carried all these years as my own.

The "dead" were lined up in a long row on the floor; the therapist now asked my guy to stand and face me. Beautiful little Michele rose and stood looking up at me, her eyes hard and angry at the memory of the injustice shown him/her. I just went on crying, feeling his pain and glad to do it, proud to honor his memory by keeping that trauma alive for him.

"This pain does not belong to you," the therapist addressed me in her soft German accent. "These experiences are not your own. This terrible atrocity did not happen to you. It happened to someone else. Will you give the burden of this hatred and anger back to the person to whom they belong?"

I shook my head as I stared helplessly into Michele's tortured eyes. I couldn't abandon her/him that way. If I didn't honor his sacrifice, who would?

The therapist paused a moment, then asked, "Are you physically strong?"

I nodded, even though that was a ridiculous lie at the moment. She disappeared into the next room and returned shortly with a medium-sized rock. I staggered a bit as she transferred it carefully to my arms; it was much heavier than it looked.

She let me hold it awhile as I continued to gaze into Michele's eyes, until my whole body shook with the effort.

"The burden of misplaced rage and pain that you carry is every bit as heavy as this rock. Are you ready to give it back now?"

I saw Michele's expression melt at last from unyielding fury to empathy and understanding as she/he realized the toll this bond was taking on me. She nodded his encouragement, urging me to release it. So I gave it back. And as she and I carefully lowered the rock to the ground, I sensed that both my unknown Jewish guy and I were now finally free.

The healing was profound. I cried for four days straight as I discovered a brand-new sense of peace, acceptance and connection with my Jewish heritage. After it was over I felt about forty pounds lighter, metaphysically speaking. And my spine, now able to hold an adjustment at last, breathed a grateful sigh of relief. ❖

CHAPTER SEVEN

REIKI

It was cold and damp, as February in California tends to be, and I had begun to notice a peculiar circulatory problem in my fingers and toes that became much more pronounced every time the weather took a turn for the worse. Nutrition couldn't help it and chiropractic treatment was having no effect.

"How about reiki?" Eileen suggested.

Immediately I agreed to try it. After the spectacular success of the trans-generational therapy a few months earlier, I'd finally stopped asking questions and had begun to trust every new treatment referral she came up with. I had never heard of reiki and had no idea what it was, but no matter.

Francesca, the reiki master in question, happened to live not far from our place in the Valley and she agreed to see me at her beautiful house instead of the office. She led me into a lovely little room on the first floor, told me to climb up on the table, gave me a blanket and an eye mask, and then she did I had no idea what for the remainder of the hour. It was quiet, the soft music played and she touched me only occasionally, a light brush on the shoulder, the forehead. The treatment was very relaxing, more like a middle-of-the-workday spa visit than a medical appointment.

When it was over, she had a strange look on her face.

"What form of meditation do you practice?" she asked.

"None," I replied. "I chant Nam Myo Ho Renge Kyo, which, as I understand it, is the opposite of meditation, since the mind stays focused and active. I have no experience at all with meditating. In fact, when you asked me to still my thoughts earlier, I was never able to get my mind to shut up for even a second. Why do you ask?"

"Oh, that was just surface chatter, I ignored it completely," she answered. "I ask because you went much, much deeper than a first-time reiki client ordinarily ever would."

"Oh. Huh," I replied absently, handing her a check and studying my calendar to schedule the next appointment. "Hey, by the way, what were you actually doing in there? I couldn't tell."

She hesitated. "I was balancing your chakras."

I froze. *Buddhists don't have chakras!* I spluttered inwardly, furious that I'd unwittingly been party to a "heretical" treatment based in some other religious practice than my own. I hastily gathered up my things, saying nothing to Francesca as she quietly watched me go.

I sat out front in my car for a long time, thinking. Her only motivation had been to help me; was I really so prejudiced, such a hard-line uptight fundamentalist that I couldn't accept healing if it didn't come from a pre-approved Buddhist source? (Yes.)

So what, exactly, was I afraid of? If my Buddhist practice was truly so powerful and correct, shouldn't it be strong enough to withstand the occasional health-related companionship of other belief systems? I chanted carefully about these questions in the weeks afterward, and was delighted to discover that my practice of Buddhism took a great stride forward in depth and faith as I learned to relax and trust it enough to allow other healing practices into my life.

March 16, 2000

Was back at Francesca's place again today. We're doing more guided meditations now and that's kind of fun, even though I never seem able to make my mind stop its jabbering.

One goofy thing: She was trying to get me to "visualize my spiritual guide" so that he or she and I could sit together in a garden and allow unconditional love to flow between us. Yeah, good luck with that. In the last session she tried to activate my heart and instead I got this crystal clear vision of jagged hundred-foot ice cliffs towering over a black lunar landscape… so something tells me there won't be much unconditional love in my near future.

Anyway, there I was, busy trying to visualize my guide, and the image that started forming was one of those blond, blue-eyed Jesuses from a bad 1960s painting—and I just cut it off completely because that was so ridiculously stupid. I mean really, is my imagination so weak that Jesus in a pale pink robe is all I can come up with for a guide? So Francesca suggested I visualize a column of radiant light instead of trying to make it a person. So that's what I did; just me and the column of light holding hands in the garden. And it actually felt kind of nice.

At the end of this same session she said, "I have a message for you." (I was afraid to ask from whom.) "You're perfect, exactly as you are."

I appreciated the sentiment, really I did, yet the idea was so ludicrously farfetched I didn't know what to do with it. Sure, I aspire to being perfect eventually after fixing all the poisonous wrongness about me. But was this some kind of unfunny joke, to tell me I'm perfect right now, exactly as I am? "…Thank you," I replied finally, not knowing what else to say.

Although they hadn't been doing much for my circulation problem, which by this time had been diagnosed as Raynaud's syndrome, I had really grown to love the reiki sessions. I couldn't quite identify how these guided meditations were helping me, yet I sensed they seemed to be gradually letting in the light on some dark and previously unknown part of my life I couldn't name. Mainly that was a good thing, and yet every so often it wasn't.

April 11, 2000

The other day while chanting, I was inspired suddenly to pray that I want to always be pure and focused in my faith; that I don't ever want to be at cross-purposes again on my spiritual path. And to please show me whatever might be standing in the way of my single-minded forward progression in faith.

Be careful what you ask for, I guess, because, WHAM! I immediately got hit full-force with that old supernatural terror. Worse than I've felt it since I was five years old and couldn't go upstairs by myself.

Like for instance, last night I was expecting an important client phone call and it came hours late, when I was already relaxing and flipping channels in the bedroom. Kurt's office adjoins the bedroom, and there's no light switch at that end of the room. And I could not make myself take the half-dozen steps into his darkened office to pick up the phone. I. Just. Couldn't. I stood there, paralyzed, and stared at the telephone from the safety of the bedroom until it stopped ringing.

Today I intended to chant about that whole supernatural mess, thinking if I finally face the fear instead of running away I might be able to make some headway. I'm pretty brave when it comes to tackling things head-on in front of the Gohonzon; nothing really scares me so much that I won't at least try to chant my way through it.

Except for this, as it turns out. When I sat down in front of the Gohonzon, I couldn't try. I was too terrified to even think about trying.

I mentioned it to Francesca in today's session, and she had the weirdest response: "In earlier times," she said, "healers used to be burned at the stake as witches. Maybe that's why you're so afraid of the supernatural."

I stared at her for a long minute, trying to make sense of the bizarre non-sequitur before giving up and pointing out the obvious instead: "Yuh… but I'm no healer."

She smiled a peculiar little smile. "Oh, I only attract healers," she said with such matter-of-factness that something in me was forced to believe her. ❖

A few months later, after a particularly blissful reiki session, Francesca informed me suddenly that she wouldn't be seeing me anymore.

"You've learned everything here that you were supposed to," she added as I handed her a check. "There's nothing more I can do for you now."

I nodded silently, my feelings a little bit hurt; I'd never been fired by a healing arts professional before. It felt surprisingly like being dumped, yet I accepted the verdict and moved on.

She was right, of course. It was time for me to make room for the next step. And before long that next step revealed itself in the form of yet another ailment, with its corresponding form of healing waiting patiently in the wings.

COLD SHOULDER

December 4, 2001

I was so pissed at Kurt today I could have screamed. He promised yesterday he'd help me get the Christmas tree out of the garage (it's the only help I ask for, I do all the rest of the decorating myself) yet when the time came he gave me that "anything I do is so much more important than everything you do" attitude, and said he was too busy.

Fine. Who needs you. I threw open the garage door and dragged the tree out by myself. I felt something funny give way in my shoulder when I did it yet kept going anyway, pulling and pushing the damned thing into the house and setting it up all by myself.

That shoulder, the right one, kept nagging me as the weeks went by. I couldn't lift the arm more than a few inches without a stab of blinding pain; getting dressed in the morning became an ongoing challenge and hugging anyone was completely out of the question. After the holidays I had the chiropractor look at it; tried nutrition and Jin-Shin-Do and Bowen massage, yet nothing seemed to do any good. Over time, I just stopped using that arm, because the injury seemed to tear afresh every time I lifted the elbow.

And before I knew it, I couldn't lift the arm at all even if I wanted to. I'd never heard of frozen body parts before, and now all of a sudden I was getting to be an expert on the subject. ❖

YOGA THERAPY

One sunny Sunday morning in May, the phone rang with an invitation from my friend Francy: "I'm starting a brand-new yoga therapy group in fifteen minutes. Someone just dropped out and there's an empty slot. Maybe this will help your shoulder. Do you want in?"

I'm not sure why I felt so deeply drawn to this suggestion; I'd never even heard of yoga therapy. Nearly half a year had passed since the injury had occurred and nothing else had helped my frozen shoulder, so why should this? Yet it was one of those profound, slowed-down, watch-yourself-out-of-body moments, and I said, "Yes absolutely," dropped whatever I was doing and threw myself in the car.

"Yoga therapy" turned out to be total truth in advertising—a serious primer in meditation, yoga postures and chakra work—and damn if it wasn't also highly effective group therapy. This small class of six participants proved to be the perfect thing at the perfect time.

I learned the basics of meditation, was introduced to the pain body (wow, I discovered how much my jaw hurt; I'd had no idea I kept it clenched all the time) and the emotional body. (Oh, no kidding… you mean it's rage that's stuck in my shoulder, preventing it from healing?) And over time I felt my unconscious mind slowly start to give up some of its dark, gloopy secrets.

My neglected first and second chakras found new life and seemed to start functioning afresh; maybe I did actually deserve to live and thrive after all. Gradually my all-black wardrobe stopped satisfying me and I began to crave *orange!* and then *sky blue!* as if they were air or food.

Then one day a few months later as I was art directing a photo shoot in a pet shop (and bitching to myself because the assistant I'd been promised hadn't shown up) I found myself perched on a ladder reaching high over my head to pick up large, fuzzy doggy beds one by one to move them out of camera range. And suddenly I realized *I was doing it with both arms.*

My shoulder had healed and I hadn't even noticed.

"Ok, I get it finally," I announced to the universe that evening as I chanted to the Gohonzon. "Enough with the weird ailments. From now on I'll pursue spiritual healing for its own sake, not just because some bizarro physical malfunction is forcing me."

The bargain seems to have worked. The opportunities for spiritual healing have been many, and I continue to welcome them all. And the health issues have faded away one by one, as my body happily minds its own business. ❖

From the outside my marriage with Kurt has always seemed perfect, at least to most of our single friends. Yet no marriage is ever really without its challenges.

ON MONEY AND WORTH

When Kurt and I first married, money was our—my—one huge hot button. The spending versus the saving; the superior earning power of one of us (him). When it became clear he couldn't be persuaded to spend any less, I reacted with panic and buried rage by spending nothing at all on myself for the first five years.

That got old when my socks sprouted holes and I ran out of makeup. On to Plan B, then, after much dramatic hand wringing and desperate prayer: I taught myself some sorely needed financial discipline and started doing the rainy day saving for both of us.

Yet the work-and-money thing remained a gaping, maggoty wound full of intertwined issues of safety and survival, competence and self-worth. Kurt always had plenty of jobs in the pipeline, but my work was more seasonal—hence the need for rainy day savings. Every time my business dried up, the same old argument reared its nasty head; each festering flare-up felt like a raw salt rubdown doused in acid and set on fire. *What was wrong with me,* he wanted to know.

Why couldn't I keep a steady flow of jobs like he could? I had no answers for him because I didn't know myself.

Convinced Kurt was the source of my pain, I was sure I could be happy if only he would stop criticizing me/value my contribution/be more supportive/treat me with respect. Then as I began to take responsibility for healing each of those issues one by one in my own prayers—as opposed to waiting for him to change—I couldn't help noticing that Kurt's behavior changed all by itself. When I started treating myself with respect, he automatically did the same. When I became more confident of my worth, so did he. And when I gave up the Bob Cratchit routine and started knowing I deserved good things, I discovered to my surprise that he wholeheartedly agreed with me. Slowly the unwelcome suspicion dawned that maybe the only person causing me pain was *me*.

Yet those financial sore spots kept reappearing, each one plunging me into that same familiar morass of fear and self-doubt. For over a decade I remained obstinately sure that my discomfort was all Kurt's fault because he wasn't understanding enough of my shortcomings.

Luckily for me, he's a very patient guy. Theoretically I knew how lucky I was to have Kurt in my life, of course. Not only is he my best friend and business partner, he's also my soul mate and spiritual mirror. Yet sometimes that "spiritual mirror" part is not so easy to swallow, and it's taken me a good long while to be properly grateful for it. ❖

HE AIN'T HEAVY

I began my Buddhist practice in the Mid-Wilshire area of Los Angeles, near Hollywood. Over time I began to feel very at home there, nestled in with a group of creative professionals who more or less shared my circumstances and worldview. Like me, most of the Buddhists I knew were chanting for things like a nicer apartment, a better job. Or, for the many under-employed actors in our midst, a recurring role on a sitcom.

I don't mean to imply these folks didn't have their serious sufferings; of course they did. Who doesn't? Yet by and large, we were a white-collar crowd chanting to make our already fortunate lives a little richer and more meaningful.

Then in '92 Kurt and I uprooted and moved to the Valley, the only place we could afford the mortgage on a house. There are some very upscale parts of the San Fernando Valley, but our little neck of the woods wasn't one of them. And my new Buddhist group wasn't anything like my old Buddhist group.

Lovely people, don't get me wrong, yet the cumulative weight of this crowd's karma staggered my middle-class suburban sensibilities. I'd never seen anything like the onslaught of issues they dealt with daily: Gangs, drive-by shootings, prison, SWAT teams, crack addiction and more.

These were my Buddhist members, and I tried sincerely to take good care of them. I chanted with, and for, them regularly; I visited them at home and tried to be as encouraging as I could. Yet I was repelled by the stark circumstances of their lives, and couldn't help holding myself a little bit removed from them.

Somewhere in the back of my mind I'd secretly tell myself, *This is not my real Buddhist group. In my real group nobody would have karma this heavy.* Because—and this was the part I never dared verbalize even to myself—if this were my real group and it was now my karma to practice as one of them, then that must mean some sort of terrible karmic cooties had rubbed off on me to bring my fortunes so low.

From time to time I'd join forces to help an individual or a family overcome whatever crisis they were currently facing, yet I could never extend meaningful support to the group as a whole. I was afraid if I acknowledged the full weight of the suffering I saw in all those eyes, it would surely crush me.

Then one sunny afternoon in August of 2002, I was chanting to my Gohonzon and hit that glorious zone where the universe is firing on all cylinders, and in that moment everything changed. Serene and filled with radiant light, I suddenly stepped back from myself and realized: *My attitude is upside down from what it should be. For the past ten years I've turned my face away from these peoples' misery. If I want to practice Buddhism as a Buddha would, I should be going out of my way to seek out and help the very people who are suffering most.*

Then, as natural as breathing, the decision formed itself: *I'll open myself completely and embrace all their sufferings as my own.*

And instead of crushing me, that fearsome karmic burden vanished altogether and was replaced by lightness and joy. I instantly fell in love with each of those members—young and old, felonious and law-abiding—and considered it a genuine privilege to spend every waking moment doing my best to help them overcome suffering and chart a course toward happiness.

Funny thing: In a way, I'd been right all along. This really *wasn't* my karma or my group, and mere weeks after I learned that glorious lesson of compassion, my life shifted completely once again. Out of the absolutely unforeseen whirlwind blue, Kurt and I left the Valley behind and moved to a wonderful house in a lovely little beach town up the Central Coast of California.

If I'd known a new and beautiful life awaited me as the immediate reward for opening my heart to the anguish of others…well damn, I'd have tried it a lot sooner. ❖

HALLS OF JUSTICE

The yoga therapy had seemed to unstick a whole lot of stuck stuff, and as a result all sorts of previously hidden information started bobbing up into my conscious awareness. One day in March of 2004, I was out in the garage doing the laundry when I very suddenly awoke to the constant stream of vicious, unconscious judgment I habitually used against myself.

It was a running critique of every thought, every decision, every action at every moment. *Everything I do is wrong. And no matter what I'm up to or where I am, I'm in the wrong place at the wrong time and I'm making the wrong choice. I'm supposed to be somewhere else earning my keep. And if I'm already earning my keep I ought to be someplace else still, being even more useful, earning even more money.*

I was shocked, although not really surprised, to reconnect with this awareness of merciless self-judgment. Although I hadn't been consciously in tune with it, I now recognized that this nasty chorus had been scratching away just beneath the surface throughout my life.

I dubbed it the Halls of Justice.

At first I could quiet this incessant judge and jury through chanting, or by climbing into bed at the end of a solid billable workday. Later as I started forging a deeper commitment to my spiritual path, the unforgiving jurisprudence became more insistent in response. Manifesting as an uncomfortable ever-present sandpaper anxiety, it brought with it a constant knot in the stomach that no amount of prayer or money in the bank could alleviate.

Which was a total drag. Yet on the plus side it was also an excellent motivator, because it never let me forget for even a moment how far I still had to travel on the road to peace and happiness. ❖

It was during this "Halls of Justice"period that I began to really notice Christ and Christianity for the first time. Even as a kid when its evidence lay in every house on the block except ours, I had never given Christianity much thought. As far as I was concerned, it was just that eight-hundred-pound religion other people practiced. Later when I thought about it at all, it was with mild annoyance at its cultural dominance, or stronger annoyance at its inroads into conservative American politics. Yet something about Christianity had always seemed to yank on mysterious strings deep within my life. Witness the following oddball and otherwise unrelated examples of its influence:

CHRIST IN ART AND FASHION

Most of what little I know about Christianity I learned in art history class. Annunciations and visitations in gilded egg tempera on wood; life-sized depictions of bloodied saints and martyrs, their eyes rolled up in exquisite religious ecstasy; and above all, lots and lots of translucent, white-marble grieving for the dead body of Christ.

It was in these college courses that I got my first real exposure to Christian history, and to my surprise, I adored the look of the whole thing. Christian art and architecture spoke to me so deeply I'd have lived the rest of my life inside a Gothic cathedral if I only could. Nothing to do with what goes on in there, you understand; I just couldn't get enough of that strange and gorgeous ambiance.

Even more than the art, it was the clothes that got me going—or rather, the accessories. I had no interest in those little gold crucifixes people wear to express actual devotion, yet back when bejeweled punk-Gothic crosses first came into fashion in the early 80s, it damn near killed me not to be able to wear them. My nerve endings ached to touch those big baroque badboys, to put them on and feel the weight of them against my body.

But no. Born a Jew, and now a practicing Nichiren Buddhist— an iconoclastic branch of Buddhism that avoids devotional imagery altogether—it was a lifelong taboo I couldn't bring myself to break. ❖

Speaking of exquisite religious ecstasy, apparently it can show up in the unlikeliest forms, and when we least expect it.

EPIPHANY

In July of 1997, Kurt and I were in Paris, wandering around a gray and unfamiliar neighborhood of hardware and restaurant supply stores when suddenly we saw it: A shirt in a shop window, and not just any shirt. A button-front Hawaiian the color of a brilliant Western sky, imprinted with doughnuts and crucifixes, pickup trucks and beer floating serenely through its puffy cloudscape. And there on the back, right in the middle, the huge cartoon face of Christ with an inscription that read: *Australian Jesus.*

I swear, light emanated from that shirt and we heard the angels giggling.

We entered the store, a kaleidoscopic wonderland; everywhere we looked was something to delight the eye. Scattered all around the shop were magnificently weird floor-to-ceiling kinetic sculptures that whirred and chattered busily as they moved up or down, in or out. I made my way past racks and rounders of fabulous new and vintage clothing, over to an inviting living room of ultra sleek white space-age pedestal furniture, circa 1969. Settling comfortably into an egg chair and scrunching my toes through the orange shag rug in sheer delight, I took in the dazzling scene all around me.

Everything about the place was so perfectly geared to my tastes, so thoroughly welcoming and richly satisfying, it was hard to imagine how it could possibly get any better than this. And then it happened: The opening sitar strains of *Within You Without You* wafted over the sound system. It had been years since I'd heard a Beatles tune, and this George Harrison number put me right over the top. Time glided into a glorious underwater crawl-stroke and I blissed out completely, the room dissolving into what I would many years later come to think of as "joy sparkles." Kurt appeared in front of me, beaming, as he modeled his new shirt.

And my Voice said: *Every moment of your life is supposed to be like this.*

I dimly recognized it as the truth. *Hey yeah, that's right. Every moment would be filled with pure delight, if I could only remember what to do.*

I did not consider this a spiritual experience at the time, even though I did refer to it afterward as an epiphany—but an epiphany in a *Today is the first day of the rest of your life* kind of way. The sort of thing you might see on an inspirational poster in the employee cafeteria. Several more years would pass before I would look back on this event and wonder at its true meaning.

Anyway, Kurt still has the shirt. From the back of the closet, Australian Jesus shines his awesome rayon light undimmed upon the world. ❖

The two previous brushes with Christ or Christianity seemed silly and sartorial, and therefore easy to dismiss. This one caught my attention.

ELAINE PAGELS

In November of 2003 I heard a radio interview with Elaine Pagels, the author of those books about early Christianity* and she sounded so interesting I ordered both of them right away from Amazon.com.

Ripping through these books back to back, I was a little surprised by how deeply the material hooked me. I had always known there were giant gaps in my knowledge of Christian history, yet was nevertheless shocked to learn there used to be lots of gospels floating around before the later leadership decided to keep only the Big Four, destroying the rest.

Actual conversations between Jesus and the apostles were scattered liberally throughout these books, which also startled me. I'd always assumed the gospels were written centuries after the fact, not realizing they contained any authentic quotes at all from the man Himself. As I read of His exchanges with those nearest and dearest disciples, I was surprised to find myself getting increasingly frustrated and impatient with Him, like: *Could You BE any more obscure and confusing in Your teachings? It's clear from the questions they asked that even Your own disciples didn't have a clue what You were talking about, so imagine how hard it must be for the average Christian on the street.*

Even more surprising, though, than my strange annoyance with Jesus and His teaching methods: The emergence of a sort of slightly tender *fondness* for the guy.

I confessed this unexpected newfound affection a few days later to my friend Leatrice, a seeker of various spiritual disciplines who enjoys a very comfortable and familial relationship with Christ.

* *The Gnostic Gospels* and *Beyond Belief: The Secret Gospel of Thomas*

"I'm feeling kind of a funny warmth toward Him, a sort of faint friendship, even," I admitted sheepishly.

"Oh!" she exclaimed, genuinely surprised. "How could you *not?*"

I stared back, uncomprehending at first. How could I not? *(Excuse me, was that an earthquake, or just all of my relatives turning over in their graves at once?)*

Perhaps you meant to ask: How *could* I? ❖

CHAPTER NINE

CLIMATE CHANGE

April 29, 2005

This is the strangest thing, and I don't know what to make of it. I was chanting very hard this morning, with all the lovely juices flowing, and I had one of those rare vow/epiphany moments. The kind where you spontaneously agree to stand up and be something bigger than you normally are for the sake of the whole world, even if only for a minute. Just then I glanced out the window to the right of my altar and in that same instant the sun broke through the clouds, shining down from a tiny square patch of blue sky.

That wouldn't be so odd, I guess, except the weather's been solidly socked in for the past two months without a break. Week after week, no sign of the sun underneath all that persistent white cloud cover. And now here it was, showing itself suddenly through a tiny hole in the sky and streaming glorious golden sunbeams directly into my living room window.

I don't know, it probably sounds insane, yet I had the very strong impression it was me—or rather, my vow—that changed the weather. ❖

THE WEIRDNESS

May 1, 2005

I can't figure out what's going on with me lately. First there was that thing with the weather the other day. And now seemingly for no reason, the supernatural terrors are back with a vengeance. The other night it was the old familiar thing, having to force myself to leave the protection of the magic covers so I could get up and make that dreaded trip to the bathroom. Being in a darkened room without the magic covers can still scare the bejeebers out of me even though it's been decades since I've encountered anything on those nighttime sojourns that could be considered genuinely disturbing.

Yet this time, genuinely disturbing doesn't even begin to describe it. The air felt thick, dense, like there were lots of versions of my bedroom crammed into each other, all occupying the same exact space. And I had the horrible, ick-filled impression I was walking straight through other people. Not ghosts, although for as much dread as I was feeling, they might as well have been. No, these seemed to be actual people in some other time or dimension; they were going about their business and didn't even know I was there. Ugh, my cells still shrivel up at the awful memory of it.

Then yesterday in the supermarket parking lot, yet another bizarre thing. As I was getting out of the car I looked down and noticed a little black bird, head cocked to one side and staring up at me with its bright yellow eye. And I don't know what happened. All of a sudden something shifted, causing a kind of radical, split-second change in perception. Nothing was different, except now I was looking at that bird without the slightest shred of normal human emotion and thinking to myself, Wow, look at that bright yellow eye—I'd like to poke that bright yellow eye right out.

I snapped out of it then, of course, horrified my mind could hold such sick thoughts of casual violence. Yet now that I've had a chance to think about it some more, I'm not so sure those thoughts were coming from my mind at all. In that sudden shift, I had become sharp, inquisitive, and utterly without human sentiment or morality. Not only didn't I feel like myself, I really didn't feel like a person at all.

I suspect, in other words, that I temporarily slipped into birdy consciousness.

I don't know what the universe is up to these days, but I wish it would cut it out.

Heralds, harbingers, whatever you want to call them; maybe none of these random, freakish occurrences had really been omens in the usual sense. Still as I later looked back on this period, I realized all these unrelated events had indeed been pointing the way to something big. And very soon nothing would be the same again. ❖

It was Stephen, the chiropractor, who first told me about Sedona, way back in 1986. He talked about the medicine wheels, the vortexes (that would be "vortices" to you, me and the Oxford English dictionary), and the legendary spiritual power in those rusty red rocks. I didn't understand most of what he said. Sixteen years later, one of our clients moved to Sedona and flew Kurt and me out there several times to consult on his new project, a small luxury inn. I tried to find evidence of vortexes then, yet really didn't know what I was looking for.

WATER AND POWER

One day during construction of his new Sedona inn, our client Steve ran across an ancient hand-drawn map of his property. And there, plain as day, were two lines running through the site, one labeled *Water*, the other marked *Power*.

"What's this?" he asked the guy from the city planning office. "I've already started excavation, I thought you told me there were no utility lines on my property."

City Guy carefully rechecked all his records on that parcel. "Sir, I don't know what those lines are, but they are definitely *not* utilities."

It's a fabulous place, the inn. The retirement project of Steve and his wife Connie, El Portal is a handmade, twelve-room beauty harking back to the turn of the last century. If a Pasadena Craftsman mansion and a sprawling Arizona hacienda had a love child it would be this place, a charmed amalgamation of river rock and adobe; of flagstone, reclaimed timbers and stained glass.

Even more remarkable than its roughhewn, built-to-last elegance and comfort is its strangely refreshing vibe. No matter how frazzled I might be on my arrival in Sedona—and no matter how much work I might be expected to accomplish while I'm there—after a couple of nights at the inn I typically feel as balanced, peaceful and relaxed as if I'd been lounging at a spa the whole time instead.

Must be something in the water. Or maybe the power. ❖

THE DAY THE EARTH STOOD STILL

It was a routine client referral, courtesy of Steve and Connie. A logo design for a new start-up business, a Sedona-based spiritual tour company.

"This process of logo development will probably be slow and tricky; I think I'd better fly out to meet with you in person, so you'll better understand what I'm looking for," warned the new client.

"No problem," I replied. "I'll design a few logos before you come, just so we have a starting point for discussion."

Fran arrived at the house a week later, on a beautiful day in May of 2005. The moment she walked in the door it seemed as if we'd known each other forever, and by that I don't mean I instantly took a liking to her—I mean it felt like the deepest reunion with somebody I only now realized had been missing all these years. Our business meeting suddenly took on an unexpected luminosity, a deeply burnished otherworldly glow. Seating ourselves at the dining room table, which doubles as a conference table, we got right down to business.

"Oh…yeah, that's perfect," Fran said almost offhandedly, as she glanced at the first logo I showed her. Pushing the stack of artwork aside, we instead spent the afternoon immersed in spiritual conversation.

She regaled me with stories, like that of her recent dead-of-winter climb up snowbound Hatu Peak high in the Himalayas, having been urgently summoned there by Spirit. And she showed me unretouched photos of things that defied logical explanation, like a startlingly un-cloudlike cloud formation of three perfectly nested concentric triangles, a symbol of personal significance to her, sent as celestial reassurance that she was on the right track.

"Show me a sign," she had implored, and there in the sky the answer had immediately revealed itself.

A Spirit that issued travel instructions and created symbols in the sky? We were clearly not in Kansas anymore, yet to my surprise

I was neither scared nor scornful of the turn the conversation had taken. Seemingly apropos of nothing, I felt compelled to tell her the story of my long-ago reiki experience; how it had reawakened my childhood terror of the supernatural, and the reiki master's odd response:

"In earlier times, healers used to be burned at the stake as witches."

Fran gazed at me as I talked, a faint smile on her lips. When I finished, she leaned forward, locked eyes with mine and spoke these seemingly innocuous words: *"I am guided to be in the presence of wounded healers."*

What happened next changed my life forever.

Time stopped… and then gently drifted away as if it had never existed in the first place. Something, not quite a memory, had been resurrected by her words, and that something felt at least five hundred years old. It was as if an alarm clock had sounded and some ancient and unknown part of myself had flung out an arm, groping blindly for the snooze button before reluctantly remembering: *No. I promised. This is my time to get up.*

In that same moment I became aware of infinite eternity, which seemed to emanate from within my being, expanding limitlessly outward to encompass the entire universe. My mind now soared far beyond the limitations of regular thought. I remember being puzzled, surprised this wasn't a joyous feeling; up until now, my spiritual leaps had always felt filled with light. By contrast this experience was profoundly melancholy, albeit with a secure foundation of serene peace and wellbeing underlying all.

The whole time this was taking place—seconds? eons?—Fran had continued to talk, in an effort to explain what that mysterious sentence, *"I am guided to be in the presence of wounded healers,"* had actually meant. She said she used to wonder whether she was supposed to do more than just locate people and wake them up; she couldn't help feeling that seemed too simple a task. But no, Spirit had made it clear over and over that her presence is all that's required. Just find those wounded healers and remind them who they are.

I shot her a glance. Although I was still capable of processing human language as if from an unfathomably great distance away, I really didn't want to. My mind had opened onto an undiscovered realm of limitless and effortless communication, totally unlike the inadequate stone-age squawks we humans employ. I wanted to revel in the pristine silence, to get a taste of true communion without all the distraction. I wished, in short, that she would shut up. Some of us were trying to have an awakening here.

Fran finished speaking and gazed peacefully at me across the table. The hoped-for silence enveloped me, stretching out uncomfortably without beginning or end until I couldn't stand all that untethered freedom. Disappointed, I realized I wasn't equipped to stay any longer in this remarkable state of awareness. Reluctantly I pulled myself back into time, into speech, into my body and my dining room. My hands and feet buzzed. I felt lightheaded.

"What is it you do, exactly?" I inquired faintly, wishing I could go lay down.

She hesitated. "It's hard to explain. All I can tell you is: I know I've done this many times before; I always go first; and I'm very good at what I do."

I nodded. I had no idea what she was talking about. Then, as if this would clarify things, she made an infinity symbol with her hand, beginning the loop at herself, sending it out toward me and then back to herself.

"I do this."

"Uh huh," I said.

Fran confessed then that she'd been delaying the launch of her company for months—years, even—afraid to set up her website for precisely this reason. She felt it was completely beyond her ability to describe or explain the spiritual experience to anyone. To put that which transcends words into words.* (see next page)

"Oh! Piece of cake," I said, "I'll help you write your website. That's what I do."

She looked at me as if I had just offered to lasso the moon.

And so began a most unusual collaboration. Our relationship is not quite client/vendor, not exactly teacher/disciple; nor are we precisely friends or sisters, although it holds elements of all of those. Fran's description comes closest: Bookends. Opposites in nearly every way, yet two indispensable halves of one mystical whole. ❧

---

* Now after a few years of seeing her in action, I can better describe for you what Fran "does" when she takes people on her InnerVision journeys.

Like most deeply gifted spiritual intuitives, she's sensitive in a variety of ways; information and experiences are seemingly always coming at her from all directions. She might surprise you with a message from your dead uncle Phil, for instance. She's also a synchronicity magnet, routinely drawing profound spiritual connections into her life, which then manifest as divine coincidence in the physical world.

These are useful talents to be sure, yet there is another way in which Fran is of invaluable service to others: She is able to receive messages from the highest Self of the person she's with, then tap into her own aspect of that same highest Self to relay the messages back to the person in the manner most appropriate to him or her.

Here's what that InnerVision thing feels like when she does it for me: It's as if a vast, mighty bridge opens up to another realm, and then waits in patient non-judgment while I decide whether or not to cross. Most of the time I accept the invitation to cross that bridge, and whenever I do, it's an absolutely awesome experience.

I Googled "wounded healer" the next morning, yet only found Amazon books about psychiatrists who abuse the doctor/patient relationship (surely that wasn't it), and Wikipedia references to a Greek myth about a centaur and a poisoned arrow (surely that wasn't it either).

I didn't ponder the mystery for long. Other things were vying for my attention.

EMERGENCY

Bob was sick. He'd already been to the vet more than once in the past month and the tests showed nothing out of the ordinary; now he was scheduled for a late-afternoon ultrasound at our nearby veterinary surgical hospital. The day after Fran's life-altering visit, we dropped him off at the hospital and came home to await the results.

At eight o'clock that evening we received the call: They still weren't sure what was causing his symptoms; they wanted to perform a colonoscopy while they had him under anesthesia. And by the way, the ultrasound had turned up a few benign growths on his liver— these weren't causing any of Bob's problems, but did we want to have them surgically removed while he was hospitalized?

"Absolutely not," I replied, appalled at the suggestion. "He's an old man. Under no circumstances would I put him through a surgery unless it was absolutely necessary." I agreed to the colonoscopy, and we settled in to wait for the diagnosis.

The phone rang at ten o'clock.

"We just began Bob's colonoscopy," reported the surgeon, "and the scope has accidentally punctured the unusually fragile tissue of his colon."

"What does that mean?" I asked uneasily.

"It means he either needs emergency surgery right this minute, or else we'll have to put him down."

I sat up chanting all through that long night. *Bob absolutely cannot, will not die. Not now. Not like this.* If we were to lose him as a result of this pointless accident I knew I'd never be able to forgive myself. Bob—and to a lesser degree our other cat, Morgan—was the default repository for all my animal guilt. I did everything in my power to make sure his life was as happy and carefree as possible. I might have been unable to change the plight of the suffering animal masses out in the world, I reasoned, yet I vowed my own pets would have the best quality of life I could give them. Bob also safely carried the unguarded love I dared not bestow on human beings. All in all a heavy burden for one small cat, yet he bore it with grace. And I could scarcely imagine my life without him in it.

As Bob got older, I worried more and more about his eventual death. Would he become ill and linger, forcing us to have him euthanized? I wondered whether I could ever feel whole again after his passing. And how would I find the strength to go on without him, my one true soul-kitty?

As it turned out, these questions were all for another day. Bob didn't die. He made it through the surgery and spent the next five days in intensive care. I spent those same five days in front of the Gohonzon, chanting like my life—and his—depended on it.

On day two after the surgery, we were allowed to see him. As the nurse brought Bob into the visitation room and he saw us waiting for him, I spied the relief on his face and understood immediately: He'd thought we were never coming back. That we'd left him to die alone and unprotected in this terrible place.

Kurt and I sat together in a big beanbag chair on the floor as our poor, bedraggled boy was delivered gently into my waiting arms. He looked awful; stitched from stem to stern, drugged up, dazed and clearly in pain. We both broke into tears at the sight of him, sobbing uncontrollably as we stroked his little head. Yet the moment Bob's weight was safely transferred from the nurse's arms into my own he scrambled angrily away from me. Unsteadily and with tremendous effort he half-walked, half-crawled into Kurt's arms instead.

It was like a knife to the heart, and I knew exactly what he meant by it: I was his great love, his unfailing protector. All his life he'd trusted me completely, and for what? This deadly betrayal. (A little animal guilt, anyone?)

Day four of his incarceration. We'd been coming by the hospital every afternoon during the visiting hour, bringing Bob his favorite "people foods" at the doctor's suggestion. Refusing to eat anything the hospital staff tried to feed him, he would gamely take a few bites of turkey breast or shrimp from us. Although he had little appetite, he couldn't help enjoying the special attention.

Every day I had been chanting for three, four, sometimes five hours at a stretch; it still wasn't clear whether Bob would pull through and this terrible fact alone pushed everything else from my mind. I couldn't concentrate on billable work, preferring to spend every available minute in front of the Gohonzon.

On this particular afternoon we arrived to find him lying listlessly in his cage, his long, usually lustrous fur looking greasy and limp. Not good. As I lifted him gently onto the table next to me I wished I could do more to help him. Something pinged at the back of my mind like a distant dream not quite remembered, a faint, hazy recollection from long, long ago:

Healing. Something to do with healing. What was it again…?

I had completely forgotten the extraordinary events of Fran's visit five days earlier, the unearthly awakening wiped from my memory as surely and thoroughly as if it had never happened. I groped at the cobwebby crevices of my mind, trying to will the experience back into focus.

…Oh. Right. Wounded healer.

I'm supposed to have some kind of mysterious healing abilities, I reminded myself vaguely, laying my hands uncertainly onto Bob's little belly. Closing my eyes, I inhaled deeply and exhaled what I hoped was healing energy into his body. To my astonishment he leapt to his feet, turned in a circle and sat down to briskly begin bathing himself.

"Did you see that?" I asked Kurt. "I just sent him healing energy, and look what happened."

"That's silly," said Kurt.

Bob bounced back like a cat half his age. On his arrival home from the hospital the next day, he wanted desperately to return to his normal routine; instead he was forced to endure two dreadful weeks of additional cage confinement in our bedroom. Between that and the endless rounds of shots and medicines he received three times a day, he was, understandably, quite pissed about the whole situation.

I sympathized, yet I didn't care. We were going to follow the doctor's orders to the letter for as long as it took. We had our precious Bob back, and that was all that mattered. ❖

CHAPTER TEN

HANDS OF LIGHT

Spooky, how close I had come to putting that life-changing awakening out of my mind forever, as if Bob's crisis had somehow stricken me with spiritual amnesia. A few days after I managed to remember that "wounded healer" business at the surgical hospital, my new hairdresser Claudia surprised me by handing me, not a fashion magazine, but a big blue book on spiritual healing to look at under the dryer. *Hands of Light*, by Barbara Ann Brennan. The moment I touched it I knew this was the book for me; that piece of information had somehow been transmitted right into my fingertips via some kind of unearthly electrical impulse.

I flipped through it and froze as my eyes came to rest on an illustration: A woman stood with beams of light emanating from her hands, which were positioned over a patient lying on a table. And just behind her, two ghost-y, light-filled entities stood, one on each side, and seemed to reach their hands in to merge with the radiant hands of the healer, all three of them working in unison for the benefit of the person on the table.

I sucked in my breath. Those ghost-bodies…they looked familiar. My childhood flooded back, in all its luminescent creep-show glory. *This* was the book for me?

May 22, 2005

My God. This is the book for me. The right teaching at the perfect time, it feels like every precious word is getting injected straight into my veins, the nutrient-rich teachings feeding my deepest hunger. All these questions about how the universe works, how energy works—questions I didn't even know I had—are all beautifully answered here. I love this stuff. And the ghosts? Well, reading about them seems totally benign now. Harmless, almost.

My very favorite part so far: She recommends an exercise as a method for opening a communication pipeline with one's spiritual guide. Which is basically to focus very clearly on a question you want answered, then write the question down and sit still to meditate. The words or images or physical sensations will start to flow; you write them all down, beautiful messages and gibberish equally, and worry about whether any of it is making sense later on.

Most of what I've scribbled down is heavy on the gibberish. Yet a few things have seemed really noteworthy, and they've stuck with me in a pretty powerful way.

The other night I asked, "How do I blend this healer stuff with my Buddhist practice?" And these were the images I got:

- *A large cross floats on a black background, possibly the night sky. Suddenly my viewpoint shifts to the side and I see this 3-D cross is actually a vehicle, a ship with many souls on board. And I'm stunned, because it honestly had never occurred to me that Christianity might be for real; that it might have any authentic healing power or spiritual validity to it.*

- *A beautiful white lotus blossom with a golden Buddha seated in the center; the petals keep unfolding and unfolding endlessly around Him.*

- *A fluffy animal seen from above: I think it's a lamb. Or wait, is it a dog? Lamb or dog? And I laugh out loud in mid-meditation because I realize it's trying to get me to say "Lamb of God," a phrase that would not otherwise spring to mind.*

None of these vignettes actually answers my question—at least not in any way I'm able to interpret—still the images seem important and I can't get them out of my mind. I've been doing the exercise every night, so we'll see whether I manage to get any better in the communication department or not.

I continued to study *Hands of Light*, eagerly trying every exercise it recommended. I wasn't what you'd call a natural, exactly, yet I got a decent enough result each time to encourage me to keep going.

May 28, 2005

Little shaved-belly Bob is finally out of the cage, although not yet free of his thrice-daily medication regime. Poor guy, he really hates it. On a happier note, there is one form of healing he really seems to enjoy. When I'm on the bed quietly practicing Hands of Light *energy healing exercises on myself, he'll drop whatever he's doing elsewhere in the house, gallop into the bedroom and leap onto the bed as if to say, Ooh! Do me next!*

And he'll push my hands off my own body and try to make me touch him instead.

The first time he did it I thought I might have been imagining things, yet he kept repeating the same behavior every day. I can take a hint, so now Bob gets daily "healing sessions," much to his apparent delight. I can't imagine he's getting any serious health benefit since I have no idea what I'm doing, and yet it seems to make him happy. ❖

Damn that constant knot in the stomach, the permanent state of unease. No matter what I tried, I never seemed able to find a moment's peace, and after the Dinner Table Awakening the anxiety became noticeably more acute.

DOING IT WRONG

June 5, 2005

Weird, how anxious meditation makes me. I can't seem to get past that feeling that I'm doing it wrong. I know that's only the Halls of Justice talking, yet knowing it and making it go away are two different things.

I get into a meditation and the visuals start to flow, but instead of leaving well enough alone I strain to squeeze out each image as it appears, then rush in to identify it, categorize it, slap on a label and assign it meaning. Gripped with fear all the while that I'm totally misinterpreting the message and missing the whole point.

Good God, no wonder I'm tired all the time. ❖

Despite the diligent efforts put forth by the Halls of Justice to make the meditation process as uncomfortable and unrewarding as possible, now and then some glorious, unadulterated bliss found its way into the proceedings anyway.

BE NOT AFRAID

June 15, 2005
Wow, what a beautiful meditation this morning, full of brilliant diamond facets sparkling and catching the light in every color. It was breathtakingly gorgeous.

Oh! And I heard from my Voice again. Before this I've only seen pictures every time I've done these exercises. It was nice to hear it speak. I had been starting to get scared in mid-meditation because my guide seemed to be taking me somewhere deep that felt too supernatural for my liking. So the Voice said: Be not afraid.

Which startled me for a second because it sounded so hokey-bible—this from the same Voice that said 'Long time no see.' Then I figured it must've purposely chosen an unlikely phrase so I wouldn't think I imagined it. And the strategy worked. I listened to it, I believed what it said and wasn't afraid.

I told Leatrice about it afterward and her face lit up at the news.

"Oh, Carrie! That sounds like it could have been Jesus talking!"

Please. Like nobody else was alive in biblical times.

June 21, 2005
Another vocal communiqué. Late last night I was lying in bed, needing to get up to go to the bathroom and yet too afraid to leave the protection of the magic covers behind. Story of my life. Anyway, I was lying there trying to pep talk myself into it when

*the Voice said: **The magic covers go with you wherever you go.***

*I liked that idea and decided to believe it. Then as I got out of bed, it added: **You are the magic covers.***

Wow. I am the magic covers?

Man, this could really change some things.

June 27, 2005

Here's an odd one. Late last night I was meditating, minding my own business, when a prayer popped in seemingly of its own accord, almost like a commercial interruption:

"Let my life be in perfect alignment with Divine Will."

I found this pretty startling, since it had never before occurred to me there might be any such thing as Divine Will, let alone that I might want to align with it. * ❖

---

* In much the same way it never occurred to me Christianity might be an authentic religion, it had also never dawned on me that any form of Divine intelligence might exist. It's not as strange an oversight as it may sound, despite the twenty years of devout religious practice already under my belt. Buddhism speaks mostly of universal laws and doesn't address the Western concept of God as we know it, so I had simply never bothered to ponder the possibility. Hey, I never said I was deep.

LAND OF THE MIDNIGHT HIKE

It was July of 2005, and a big client conference had brought Kurt and me back to Sedona and El Portal. Our group's mission: To find creative ways to dramatically reverse the downward attendance spiral of an ailing industry tradeshow, and set it back on the road to success.

A tall order, and I knew I'd be busy brainstorming with those guys. I also wanted to find time to steal away with Fran; we hadn't spoken much in the two months since our first meeting, and I was looking forward to seeing her in her native environment, the powerful energy sites in and around Sedona.

Client meeting number one began just as we arrived in town. Kurt and I quickly joined the gathering already in progress and hit the ground running, brainstorming for the rest of the afternoon. That meeting broke up at half past six, and plans were made for a group dinner. I excused myself as unobtrusively as I could, and called Fran instead.

The sun was already starting to sink below the hills as she picked me up in her four-wheel drive vehicle and we hit the road. Sedona's best-known vortexes are generally not among the places with which Fran feels an authentic energetic connection. Instead we turned off the highway and onto the red dirt roads heading out of the city.

I was a little nervous about the lateness of the hour, yet wherever she wanted to go was ok with me. I was starting to notice that whenever we were together I received a sort of contact high from her tremendous spiritual connectivity, and felt swept up into a heightened trance-like state where everything seemed more luminous, more deeply dimensional and drenched in spiritual meaning.

She told me there was a particular site she'd intended to take me, yet "I" had overridden her suggestion, requesting another spot instead. It was in Loy Canyon, a good fifteen miles from the inn. We tore over the dusty rutted roads as the sun sank still lower in the sky.

"I'm being guided to tell you about a story I read in one of Gregg Braden's books," Fran said. "And whenever I'm trying to convey a message from Spirit I have a very hard time putting the information into human language, so it helps if I use my hands when I talk. So if you see me talking with lots of hand flourishes, you'll know it's because I'm attempting to translate messages from Spirit."

Okaaay, I thought uneasily as the vehicle bounced and flew over the deeply pitted trails, her hands making graceful curlicue motions in the air, *But who's driving the car?*

"This is the story," she began. "There was a shaman who'd been called to a small village that was suffering from a terrible drought. The villagers had sent word asking for his help in bringing the rain. Gregg Braden happened to be there with the shaman at the time the request came in, and was invited along for the trip to the village.

"Expecting to see some sort of elaborate rain dance or ritual, Braden was surprised when the shaman walked out to a parched area of land, stood quietly for a few minutes and then turned and walked back to the car.

That's it? Braden wondered.

The rain started shortly after, slowly at first, drop by drop, building momentum until it drenched the countryside.

'What exactly did you do?' he asked the shaman.

'First I felt the rain pour down onto my head, wetting my hair, soaking my clothes. Then I felt the mud squishing up between my toes. And I gave thanks for all this water,' the shaman replied.'

That's it. That's the story," Fran concluded.

It's hard to describe the degree to which this information rocked my world. Throughout my years of Buddhist practice I'd searched tirelessly for the key to unlock the mystery of manifestation—what was the best, the most efficient, attitude with which to pray and see those prayers answered? For two decades that had been my overriding desire, my main spiritual motivator. And now here it was, the simplest answer imaginable, tied with a bow and handed to me on a plate: *Feel as if you already have the thing you're praying for, and then give thanks for having it.* *

How had Fran's Spirit known that was my number one question? I wondered, awed that this unseen presence was being so nice to me.

We arrived at the trailhead. It was now completely dark outside, and by completely dark I mean pitch-freaking-black. Fran pulled out a tiny flashlight and led the way.

"Maybe a hike isn't such a good idea anymore," I said nervously, my eyes glued to the small circle of light that illuminated next to nothing as it danced on the ground up ahead. Hiking in general was not my strong suit; hiking in total wilderness in total blackness seemed like lunacy. What about coyotes? Or cactus spines in the butt?

We followed a trail bordered by a barbwire fence on our left.

"Don't worry, we'll be fine," Fran laughed, "I know these canyons like the back of my hand."

I strained to see the trail around me, searching for loose rocks, sharp thorns, for twisted roots across the footpath. Nature had always been my sworn enemy, and I hated giving it unfair advantage while I flailed around as if blindfolded. Gripped with anxiety, mind buzzing and stomach in knots, I followed reluctantly as she led the way to a clearing.

It was hard to put my finger on what made this clearing feel so otherworldly and strange. It…sucked? Gravity seemed to behave differently here. I felt pulled strongly downward, along with all the grasses and fences. It was a somber and reverent feeling, as if I had joined with the Earth itself, enfolded as one in silent prayer. And although the night had previously been black as tar, I have a brightly lit and sharply detailed memory of that clearing. I'm not sure how that's possible; there was no more than a sliver of a moon that night.

I stood trying to quiet my mind, to relax my stomach, and was having no luck at all. As usual I felt worried and ashamed that I was

* Now that The Secret and the Law of Attraction are so widely talked about by so many people, it seems funny to think that only a few years ago this information was virtually unknown to the general public. In July of 2005, The Secret was still more than a year away from its release. Clearly some people had been clued in to the Law of Attraction long before that time; I just wasn't one of them.

missing most of what I should have been experiencing, certain I was doing it wrong.

We looked up at the luminous stars, and Fran pointed out Venus. As if in acknowledgement, Venus appeared to grow much larger as we watched—a radiant ball that hung shimmering in the sky a long instant before reverting to its previous size.

"Did you see that?" I whispered, awestruck. This business of spiritual phenomena showing up in the tangible physical realm was brand new to me.

"Welcome to my world," said Fran.

Intrigued, I made the decision right then to stick my toe down the rabbit hole just a little; to crack open the door to the unknown and see where the journey might lead me.

We turned around and headed back the way we came, this time with the barbwire fence flanking us on the right. We walked in silence as I pondered everything I'd heard and seen and felt that evening.

"That's odd," Fran said presently, "I can't figure out where we are."

We walked in circles for a long time, crisscrossing the trails and each time coming back to the barbwire fence. The night had grown completely black again, punctuated only by our rapidly waning flashlight battery.

"If I were here by myself, I'd just lay down right where I am and wait until morning to find my way back," said Fran amiably. "Don't worry," she added, sensing my horror, "that's not what we're going to do. I really can't imagine how I could've gotten us lost; this is such an easy trail and I've been here a thousand times. I'm sure we'll find our way back soon."

We didn't. I grew tenser by the minute. Then something crept into my awareness: I realized this was some sort of lesson. I was being asked to leave the anxiety behind and put my trust in Fran. No, wait…not in Fran. I was being asked to trust in Spirit as manifested *through* Fran. My heart sank; I wasn't sure I was capable of putting aside my anxiety no matter who was doing the asking, and

I understood Fran wasn't going to be able to find the way back to the car until I succeeded.

We tromped around for another half hour or so, while I tried to wrestle my anxiety to the ground. Finally, exhausted from the effort and hardly caring anymore, I did manage to release a tiny sliver of angst and hand it over to Spirit.

"Oh! Here we are," called Fran a moment later. "And look! There's the car."

We grabbed a quick dinner in a cafe. At the table she told me more about my mission as a healer. That I was supposed to be finding a way to do something big, something wondrous the whole world was hungry for.

"Come on," I scoffed, "how can *I* be some big ridiculous healer? There's nothing remotely healing about me. Small dogs and babies fear me. Hell, I can't even keep a house plant alive."

"Uh, hello…*wounded* healer," Fran replied.

I couldn't take it in. She seemed to be describing some completely unknown future version of myself, not the me that sat opposite her at the table, pushing my lettuce around.

It was ten thirty by the time I got back to the inn. Kurt was already in bed, lights out. He cracked one eye open as I got ready to slip under the covers.

"Seven o'clock breakfast meeting," he mumbled drowsily. "Get some sleep."

As if. I was wide awake and buzzing. I couldn't stop thinking about everything Fran had said over dinner. What *was* a wounded healer, anyway?

And there was plenty more to think about: The evening's luminous visions and lessons aside, I couldn't get over how safe I'd been out there in the big, scary canyon. Ninety minutes of marching around in total darkness, and I'd never once tripped or stumbled, never brushed a sharp thorn with my hand, never encountered so much as a bug bite. This was not the behavior of the natural world as I'd always known it. This was something altogether new.

I lay staring up at the ceiling. Before long I noticed I wasn't alone; something was staring back. Not the sort of ghost I was familiar with, as it had no recognizable physical form, no telltale glowy outlines. This thing seemed to be some kind of entity made up of only energy. At first I thought it might have followed me back from Loy Canyon, but it wordlessly corrected me, letting me know it was a local being with an interest in this property. It had merely stopped by out of curiosity to see who was streaming such wide-open energy in Room 6.

I acknowledged it cautiously, with a nod of my head.

How's it goin'? was the casual feeling behind its nonverbal response.

Damn. I had to pee. Taking a deep breath, I threw aside the magic covers and padded barefoot into the bathroom.

"If getting up-close-and-personal with ghosts is part of my path, then so be it," I said to Spirit, "But in the future we're going to have to take it a *lot* slower than this."

The entity and I lay awake together most of the night; eventually I nodded off. As I woke in the early morning light of dawn, the whole thing seemed silly. Had I imagined it? I looked up at the ceiling again. The overhead light seemed to be on, yet I couldn't be completely sure of that, as sunshine was beginning to filter in through the room's uncovered clerestory windows. *That's strange. I'm sure that light wasn't on last night.* I kept my gaze glued on it, trying to decide whether my eyes were playing tricks. Finally I couldn't stand it any longer; I turned away to glance at Kurt.

"Hey. Wake up. Is that overhead light on?"

He squinted up at it. "No. Go back to sleep."

I turned to look again and sure enough, now the light was off. Hmm.

I ran into Steve on my way upstairs to the breakfast meeting.

"Has anyone ever mentioned having, um, unusual experiences in Room 6?" I inquired cautiously.

"Oh, you mean the ghost?" he replied.

We'd stayed at the inn at least a half-dozen times; I'd had no idea it was haunted, and was horrified no one had ever thought to mention it to me. Yet at least now I knew I hadn't imagined the overhead light. The entity came back and messed around with the TV a few times (leaving it chattering away inside the closed armoire for us to discover upon returning to the room), but other than that made no further appearances.

Grabbing a Krispy Kreme and a coffee on the way in to the meeting, we started working at seven o'clock sharp and kept the ideas flowing nonstop until noon when the series of meetings officially ended.

We all split up to pursue our various spare time interests, agreeing to meet again later that evening for dinner. I called Fran.

We had arranged to meet and begin our web writing project together. The tradeshow brainstorming had left me with precious few brain cells by this time yet I did my best, concentrating hard with her for the next four hours.

A strange feeling overtook me as the afternoon progressed, and it wasn't altogether pleasant. This symbolic description is the best I can manage: It felt as if Spirit, working through Fran, approached me with some sort of phone jack attached to Fran at one end, with the free end shown to me as an unspoken invitation. When I reluctantly agreed to a hookup, it then found a port on my being that was configured perfectly to receive it, plugging in gently with a solid click. It was an icky sensation.

I was not accustomed to such humbling acts of submission, and found the whole idea disturbing. And weirdly intimate. Yet I knew it was the right thing to do.

That evening our group got together for dinner under the stars in the courtyard of the inn. Unrelenting workaholics all, we promptly turned the conversation back to tradeshow business and held a third, unscheduled brainstorming session until the wee hours of the night.

Time to go home. Despite the inn's restorative properties, I awoke early the next morning completely fried; my brain felt swollen inside my skull.

The flight home was a blur. As Kurt maneuvered our car out of the Burbank airport parking lot in preparation for the ride back up the coast, I sat limp and empty in the passenger seat, watching dully as a silver Mini Cooper made a left turn at the light in front of us.

That's the car, said my Voice, which I had decided to call Spirit from now on.

"Really? *That's* the car?"

A few months earlier I'd considered trading in my ten-year-old Taurus for a new Prius or maybe a Honda Element, but had finally concluded there was nothing wrong with the car I had. During that brief shopping phase I had never even considered a Mini, yet now that I looked at the car I had to admit it really was pretty damned cute.

And then, conveying a whole series of complex concepts without actually speaking any of them, Spirit caused me to understand that I should apply the Gregg Braden lesson on manifestation—*feel as if you already have the thing you're praying for, and then give thanks for having it*—by manifesting myself a Mini Cooper.

Paid for upfront in cash, I decided simultaneously, with no dealer financing. It sounded like an outlandish quest, but I accepted the challenge. ❖

BEYOND RELIGION

CHAPTER ELEVEN

LEAVING BUDDHISM BEHIND

July 17, 2005

*T*here's no denying it, I'm seeing everything differently these days. It's been building up ever since the awakening back in May. Something changed forever that day, and now nothing about my spiritual life feels the way it used to. Outwardly I've continued my normal routine, staying active in the Buddhist organization, going to all the meetings. Yet increasingly, Buddhism no longer seems to be in sync with my spiritual path. It just doesn't feel like it fits anymore.

The people in this organization are like my family; I don't know where I'd be without their help. And I'm used to feeling only gratitude toward my Buddhist practice for all the gifts the Gohonzon has given me. I don't know what to think, now that I seem to be at odds with Buddhism itself.

Up until May I was serenely certain I would be practicing Nichiren Buddhism for the rest of my life, so this turn of events has been pretty surprising. Confusing. Disturbing. Who the hell am I to contradict a Buddha?

And yet, there it is.

Despite all efforts to preserve it, my sincere connection to Buddhism seemed to be slipping away as I became increasingly disengaged at meetings. Did I no longer belong with this group? Or any group? Lonely as the prospect seemed, I was starting to feel the need to forge my own spiritual path; it no longer seemed appropriate to follow in the well-traveled footsteps of others.

I was also becoming increasingly concerned for the Buddhists in my care, and knew I needed to do what was best for them. Since I was no longer a sincere practitioner, maybe my presence wasn't a good influence on them; maybe I shouldn't be entrusted with the care of members if I didn't honestly believe in Buddhist practice anymore.

It took a couple of months to face the situation squarely and scrape up the courage to bring a previously unthinkable question into my nightly meditation:

"Should I leave Buddhism behind?"

Answer: *Image of a rocket taking off and heading into space; as it moves beyond the denser Earth atmosphere, the big, fuel-heavy booster falls away, leaving the faster, lighter stage-two rocket to continue its trajectory alone.*

" So…organized religion was the booster rocket and I'm meant to go on without it now?"

Answer: *Image of a diamond twirling, throwing off rays of multicolored light, followed by a close-up image of a broad toothy smile.*

"What? That's not specific enough. I don't want to misunderstand, this is too important; for all I know, I could be manipulating or distorting these answers. I'd love to be able to stay home at night and not have to go to meetings anymore if that's truly an option—but only if it's honestly the right thing to do. I don't want to misinterpret Your responses just so I can spend more quality time in front of the TV every evening, so I need You to be absolutely clear."

Answer: *Image of the "thumbs up" signal, followed by a shining star in the night sky.*

I hesitated, unconvinced. And then these words were spoken aloud within my mind: *Come now.*

So this was it. I hadn't misunderstood.

Come now. Part invitation, part gentle command. I felt lightheaded at the thought of leaving behind everything and everyone I knew, of striking out all on my own.

"Ok, I'll come now…Can I bring my Gohonzon with me?"

Of course, bring anything you like.

Just come now. ❖

ENDINGS AND BEGINNINGS

August 5, 2005

It's hard to walk away from Buddhism altogether after so many years of habit, so many beautiful relationships forged through hell and high water. Even though I'm not chanting much anymore, I've still been saying yes to the monthly world peace prayer meetings. Selfish reasons, really. It's bittersweet-nice to get together with everybody, even though no one here is comfortable with my decision to move on, and they'd all love to talk me out of it if they could.

I was chanting with the whole group at this morning's meeting, when all of a sudden I got sort of infused with light, involuntarily rising up to become infinitely bigger than my usual self. It's happened before, yet nowhere near as powerfully as this. And in that illuminated instant I was delighted to take full personal responsibility for the happiness of the entire world.

Ironic, since I've spent the last twenty years hiding from that responsibility.

That was an understatement. Nichiren Buddhism was all about standing up to accept one's larger mission for the sake of all humanity; Daisaku Ikeda* never missed an opportunity to urge each of us on to greater heights of selflessness, asking us to grow limitlessly in faith and surpass him in our efforts on the world stage.

I never wanted to hear about that. Although I enthusiastically went through the motions of helping others, it was always just as a means to an end. The Buddhist rule of thumb is: The harder you work on other peoples' behalf, the more you see your own personal goals realized. So I chanted my ass off for the sake of others, only because I was determined to make good things happen for me. It did

---

* President of the worldwide Buddhist organization.

134 Long Time No See

feel great to help other people, of course, yet ultimately I was in it strictly for the cookies.

Now here I was, with both feet out the door, and newly discovering a deep, unstoppable desire to do exactly what I'd been resisting all these years. Without wanting anything in return.

So all those lovingly patient Buddhist efforts to raise me had apparently paid off at last—just seemingly not in any way that was ever going to benefit Buddhism. ❖

Well, there *was* one last piece of manifestation business to sort out before moving into the kind of practice in which spiritual transformation would become its own reward.

MINI COOPERS, MANIFESTATION, AND COMMUNICATION

I had agreed to manifest a Mini Cooper back in the middle of July. It took me seven months to actually take possession of that car, yet most of the delay was caused by blind circular stumbling *(Should I be entering contests and trying to win a car for free? Or should I be saving up windfall cash?)* and by fits of darkest doubt. Although some days I did feel able to give thanks for the new car I already owned, there were plenty of other times when the whole endeavor seemed painfully ridiculous.

Three months into the process, Kurt asked what I wanted for Christmas and my birthday; only half-joking, I said I'd like a Mini. So we ordered the car over Thanksgiving weekend. Periodically after that, the dealership would call to give me updates: The factory is swamped, they haven't begun production yet; the car is built, it's sitting on a dock somewhere in England; the car is still sitting on the dock; and still sitting, and still sitting.

The delay was fine with me, since I still wasn't sure how I'd pay for it. And as long as I remained unsure, the car remained in transit. One day in February of 2006 I was looking through our bank records and noticed with great surprise that over the past several months our minimal savings balance had somehow swelled beyond the full price of the car. How had that happened?

A few more weeks went by, then one day I thought, *I really should go transfer that money into the checking account, just in case the car comes in.* So I went to the bank, and on my return Kurt said, "The dealership called. They have your car."

All that Law of Attraction stuff is great, don't get me wrong. I do love my little car. Yet here's the genuinely noteworthy thing about the Mini: It became a communication channel.

Because I had Mini Coopers on the brain—looking at least once an hour at the car photo tacked to my computer; meditating daily on the feel of the steering wheel in my hands; the gratitude I felt for such limitless abundance—I noticed each and every Cooper I saw on the road. Not only noticed it but got a small electro-jolt of spiritual connection.

And before long I started to observe an intriguing phenomenon: Often, when I was out driving and silently pondering a spiritual question, a Mini would appear beside me on the road as if in answer. And along with that Mini's presence would come a wordless sensation that seemed to apply perfectly to the question at hand. Every time a Mini Cooper appeared it would deliver its electrical pulse of spiritual communication, and through that pulse managed to somehow transmit a lesson or reassure me I was on the right track.

On one particularly hard day I was out running errands and feeling very raw and alone, uncertain where my spiritual path might lead me next and not knowing where to turn for comfort or guidance. As I tumbled these thoughts over in my mind I glanced to my left and was surprised to find a white Mini driving quietly beside me. Instantly I was flooded with gentle feelings of warmth and support. There that car stayed, matching my speed perfectly for the next ten minutes or more until finally I couldn't help but smile, my loneliness forgotten.

Yes, I know Mini Coopers are weird instruments for communication. And who knows how all those Mini *drivers* fit into the equation? Yet I was starting to realize that Spirit is endlessly creative and ingenious at using whatever tools are available at the time. I was looking to learn better communication skills, and given the nature of my seven-month quest, the Mini Cooper was the perfect vehicle. So to speak.

And then it was over, as abruptly as it began. As I left the dealership after taking possession of my new car I saw another Mini on the road and noticed immediately that the electroshock spiritual connection was gone; now it was just another car. I understood then that I had graduated from this particular language course and would soon be embarking on the next. It had been a strange curriculum; I couldn't help wondering what lay ahead as I eased onto the freeway in my shiny new Mini Cooper and headed for home. ❖

As the months of meditation progressed, my communication skills gradually seemed to strengthen along with my trust and confidence in this peculiar process of discovery. Some experiences tested that trust and confidence more than others.

DEATH WATCH

September 18, 2005

The other night in meditation I felt something big that seemed to be asking to come into my awareness. Not wanting to push me, it sat outside the gates of perception, waiting patiently for permission to enter. I felt a little heart-pounding sick at the thought of it—who knew what sort of frightening lesson this might turn out to be—yet I agreed to let it come.

The next thing I knew, I was in three places at once. Part of me was reliving my own murder from a previous lifetime, a brutal rape and strangulation. Yet it wasn't nearly as scary or disturbing as you'd expect, because a second part of me was peacefully watching it unfold from a detached bird's-eye viewpoint and the third part of me knew I was safely lying in my own bed the whole time.

I'm being shown this for a reason. *This was the thought that filled my mind, and I knew it was the truth.* I'm supposed to forgive this guy.

Yet it didn't seem to require forgiveness in the usual sense of the word. I didn't get that I was supposed to be saying, "Oh, there, there, it's ok that you're murdering me."

It seemed I was being asked to remain open-hearted and peacefully present while he did this awful thing. So I did. And as I made the choice to do it, I dimly sensed that this decision to stay loving in the face of hatred was having a big effect, shuffling the deck on my own past or future timeline, although I couldn't begin to say how. ❖

CHAPTER TWELVE

VISION TEST

October 11, 2005

The Barbara Brennan Hands of Light *workshop in Los Angeles is coming up this weekend. I've really been looking forward to this. Even though it's a little bit repulsive to think these instructors will be able to read our minds and see our energy and all of that creepy, invasive stuff.*

I don't know which will be worse: Having them read my thoughts, or see whatever trouble my energy is getting itself into. At least I know what my own thoughts are, but my energy could be doing its own unconscious thing, telling truths about me I don't even know myself. Gives me the willies, just thinking about it. Yet I guess that's the nature of the beast. And if I'm really supposed to become a healer, I'll have to learn how to read minds and see invisible stuff, too.

I knew I'd be a fish out of water at the workshop; most of the other participants seemed to be healing arts professionals of one kind or another, and many of them already had deep natural talents in the "I see dead people" department. So all in all, I was feeling slightly remedial since I knew I wasn't noticeably gifted at any of that *Hands of Light* stuff. And also kind of lonely because as far as I could tell I was the only one there for purely spiritual purposes.

Fifteen or twenty people had signed up for this workshop, all women except for two guys. One of those men a very handsome young thing, the other quite big and clearly self-conscious about it. As for the women, within the first ten minutes three of the blondes had automatically banded together in that Darwinian selection process known to highschoolers everywhere: Survival of the cutest.

And my inevitable knee-jerk response: *Oh hell, unpopular again. I'll be the last one picked for basketball.*

Did I really pay good money to spend the weekend doing *this?*

Day one – Morning session

First exercise: Opening our chakras through music and movement. Mainly we all kept our eyes closed as we were guided through this novel and interesting form of moving meditation. Every so often I'd crack mine open to catch one or two of the blondes pirouetting on tippy-toes like princess ballerinas as we listened to celestial upper-chakra melodies.

And then a moment later, as Barry White crooned *"Let's get it on,"* we'd all plummet back to Earth, grinding our hips in an attempt to get those base chakras cooking.

"You may find that some of these workshop exercises will press your buttons," one of the instructors called out, "so please, come see us and we'll talk about it; don't ever just run out of the class—"

Too late. Big Guy bolted for the door and never looked back. I guess the struggle to get in touch with his inner lap dancer had been too much for him.

After a morning devoted to opening both our chakras and our "high sense perception" through different kinds of meditative exercises, we broke for lunch. Five or six of us ambled toward a nearby vegetarian restaurant. To my surprise, Cute Guy zeroed in like a laser beam, falling in step beside me as I walked.

Striking up polite conversation, he asked general questions about my work.

"I see from your website that you're a designer..." he began.

"You *what?*"

I knew these people could see auras and energy, but how the hell did this guy end up with psychic wi-fi? And if he could pull up my website at will, what else could those spooky x-ray specs tell him about me?

"Oh! No," he laughed good-naturedly. "I saw your email address on the signup list, so I Googled you before I came here today."

"Oh." I couldn't decide which explanation was creepier.

He was a life coach, he explained over lunch, and he'd researched me because he was on the lookout for new clients.

"Thanks anyway," I replied, and we chatted about other things instead as I pushed the strange vegan meatloaf around on my plate until the hour was up and it was time to return to class.

Day one – Afternoon session

More high-sense-opening exercises and a quick tour of the human energy field, and then we got down to business, pairing off to try a "chelation," a sort of energy-clearing and aura-balancing technique real Brennan practitioners perform as a prelude to actual healing sessions.*

Half the students lay down on massage tables; the rest of us stood beside our recumbent partners and followed the step-by-step procedures called out by the instructor from the back of the room. Beginning at the soles of their feet, we allowed ourselves to be celestial conduits for unblocked energy flow. Slowly working our way up the body, we continued to merge our own energy fields with those of our "patients," allowing them to channel whatever nourishment they might need directly from the universal energy field, through their opened connections with us.

---

* The healing is what Brennan students spend four years in school to learn. Apparently the basics of chelation can be picked up in a weekend.

Hey, this was kind of fun. Even though it made my brain hurt to concentrate so hard, and I was sweating like a mill worker from the unexpectedly strenuous physical labor, still the process felt surprisingly satisfying.

I grew increasingly blissful as I worked my way up toward the head. Somewhere around the sixth chakra, I was seeing brilliant facets of pure diamond light through my closed eyelids and feeling more right, more radiant, more completely at home than I'd ever felt before.

This must be it, I thought. This must be what I've always been meant to do.

"This is the fulfillment of your soul's deepest longing," announced the instructor, apropos of nothing, from the back of the room.

Excuse me? I opened my eyes and glanced furtively around at the other students, none of whom seemed to have noticed the strange pronouncement. We finished our work on the seventh chakra, ending the chelation with an encircling grid of glowing golden light, and stepped away from the table.

Afterward I sought out the teacher at the back of the room and asked where that "soul's deepest longing" remark had come from.

"Oh," she said nonchalantly, "you were feeling it so I said it."

I was fortunate to be borrowing the lovely Wilshire Avenue penthouse apartment of some out-of-town friends during the weekend of the Brennan event; it was located a block away from the workshop space. Wonderfully convenient, yet cold and lonely without Kurt and the pets. After a peculiar night's sleep I woke early, still buzzing with heightened sense perception. Gazing out the window as I began my morning chanting ritual, I was delighted to see the sky turn a beautiful rose pink in response to my prayers.

It was one of those marvelously effortless chanting sessions where everything feels very switched on and alive. A prayer sprang into my mind of its own accord:

Whatever lessons today might hold for me, let me be open to all of them. I don't want to miss a thing.

Day two – Morning session

A little meditation and then straight into another chelation exercise, this time with roles reversed.

Oh, hooray! I thought. *This'll be fun to start the day by receiving bodywork.* Yet I was half a beat late in stepping forward to choose a partner, and nearly everybody was already paired up.

Oh no! Basketball!

Or maybe more like musical chairs. I looked desperately around the room at all the happy couples. Then I spotted her: There, way on the other side of the room was a lovely young woman I hadn't spoken to at all the day before, a professional massage therapist with a gentle, reassuring manner. I beelined toward her, noticing another girl determinedly heading her way at the same time.

Oh God. We got there simultaneously and stood gazing despairingly into each other's eyes, neither of us stepping forward to claim the massage therapist as a partner. Even I, with my nearly nonexistent high sense abilities could plainly see what was going on with this girl's chakras and energy; she was chronically unable to verbalize her needs, and her quiet shyness covered a simmering rage at having been overlooked and undervalued her whole life. I knew she wasn't capable of asserting herself in this situation, and I felt sick with shame at the thought of whisking the prize out from under her nose just because I could.

"You need to step forward and learn to get your needs met."

It was that same instructor talking, this time in a very stern voice. All three of us turned toward her, yet to my great surprise she was staring fixedly at me. At *me?* Was she talking to my rival, and looking at me to warn me to back off? Or was she telling me to disregard that other girl's feelings and take what was supposedly mine? I hesitated a long moment, shaken and confused, then claimed my partner at last and walked back to the waiting massage table. I still didn't know whether I had done the right thing, or whether I'd misunderstood and steamrolled over that other poor girl. I climbed onto the table gratefully, glad for a calming and restorative hour in which to regroup.

Or not.

That table was really hard. My skin itched, my joints ached. *Is it cold in here, or is it just me?* Man, this was boring. *Hurry it up, honey; I need to use the restroom.* By the hour's end, every nerve ending felt like it had been sandpapered off.

When it was over at last my partner smiled blissfully, thanking me sincerely for the experience.

"Your anger was present," she told me.

I nodded, repeating it pensively. "My anger was present." That made sense, sort of. It would explain why I'd been so intensely uncomfortable the whole time.

"No, no!" she corrected me. "I said *'Your angels were present.'* They stood behind me on either side and wrapped their arms around me, reaching in to touch you through me. They gave you all of their love and support," she continued. "It was one of the most beautiful things I've ever experienced."

Angels were sticking their hands into me? Like the illustration in the book? I shivered at the thought. *Those were no angels, lady. Those were ghost-bodies.*

…Weren't they?

Too disturbed to participate in the workshop, I skipped the next chelation exercise, curling up in a fetal ball instead in the corner of the room.

Whatever lessons today might hold for me, let me be open to all of them…

We broke for lunch. This time I'd brought a sandwich so I stayed in, along with a couple of other students and the teaching assistant. After lunch I joined the assistant and one of the women in conversation. She and I were feeling deeply connected, and before long she began pouring out her heart to me, describing painful family dynamics surrounding her mother.

I listened intently and then almost without thinking, slipped into Buddhist leader mode, having counseled hundreds of members over the years. Out of the corner of my eye, I could faintly see the assistant's energy start to grow agitated as he became increasingly angry with me—freaky, the things that become visible when you do all those high sense exercises—and I didn't care. He hadn't liked me from the start, and I felt it was more important to try to help this woman than to back off so he could maintain control of the conversation.

I ignored him and focused all my attention on her, although by now I could see the long strands of my own energy reaching out to meet his in a violently sloppy slap-fest taking place halfway between us.

Too distracted by the Moe and Larry action going on between us to continue with the counseling, I changed the subject back to the *Hands of Light* books. Not surprisingly, given the battle going on, the conversation turned to energetic defense patterns and which of these one might typically employ, based on one's chronic emotional issues and weaknesses.

"Yeah, I'll tell you what *your* energy pattern is," the assistant sneered, then accurately described my most secret emotional weaknesses and their corresponding energetic defenses, before spitting out his diagnosis at me.

It felt a little bit like getting all my skin torn off.

Note to self, I thought a half hour later when I could breathe again, *remember exactly how that felt, and vow to use fledgling superpowers only for good, never evil.*

These are the lessons today holds for me… Yeah, all right.

Whatever.

Late that afternoon I retrieved my trusty old Taurus from the parking lot and gratefully headed for home, winding my way up the beautiful Pacific Coast Highway. The road was completely deserted. I felt thoroughly beat up and raw after the experiences of the past two days.

Pulling up to a red light, I sighed dispiritedly. *I could really use a Mini right now,* I thought to myself.

And then immediately took it back.

No, cancel that. I'm sorry to be such a big baby. Just this morning I received that message of love and support from my "angels," or whoever they were. That ought to be enough reassurance for anybody for one day. I really don't mean to be so needy—

And then I glanced out the window to my left.

A Mini Cooper sat quietly beside me. ❖

CHAPTER THIRTEEN

HOW MANY COINCIDENCES DOES IT TAKE TO SCREW IN A LIGHTBULB?

For the first twenty-seven years of life I was proud to be a hardcore cynic, believing in nothing at all. Unless, of course, you count unwavering faith in the horrifying unchecked power of a malignant universe. *That* I believed in totally. Everything else, every other possibility of a world beyond our five senses, I dismissed as bullshit.

Then I stumbled onto the Gohonzon and began chanting. And the moment I did, the manifestations of benefit began rolling in. Chant for a job: Get a job. Chant about finances: Get a check in the mail.

Hmmm. Coincidences, probably.

Chant for a better boyfriend: Meet a new guy who was, indeed, incrementally better for me than the previous one. Chant for my rust bucket car not to break down until I could get to a service station: Absolutely.

Four, five, six chance occurrences. Which begged the question: How many coincidences did it take to transform a cynic into a skeptic? Seven? Seven hundred? If I could now rely on coincidences to appear like clockwork, at what point did they stop *being* coincidences and start being prayers answered?

I made the leap to cautious skepticism fairly quickly back then. And for the next two decades I remained open yet skeptical toward all things mystical, unproven or unseen.

"Show me that it's real, and I'll believe in it completely," was my rule of thumb. "If not, then not."

That attitude had served me well for a very long time. And yet, here I seemed to be, suddenly leaping into the deep end of the pool without so much as a pair of floaties to hold me up. I no longer found myself prejudging things the way I'd habitually done before. I no longer automatically rolled my eyes at angels or vortexes or past lives.

From cynic to skeptic to what? I used to assume the progression was cynic to skeptic to gullible rube, yet now I wasn't so sure. Opening up to a wider reality didn't mean I couldn't still smell a fraud from a half-mile away. Cynic to skeptic to…maybe there wasn't even a name for it. ❖

There may not have been a name for it, yet I was finding plenty of opportunity to exercise my newfound open-mindedness, especially when a certain Sedona resident came to visit.

WAKEUP CALL

October 17, 2005
Fran is here, staying with me at the house while Kurt's in Japan on his annual Buddhist pilgrimage. It's kind of great having her here, doing her InnerVision thing night and day; on the one hand I'm comfortably at home on my own familiar turf, and on the other, everything about my little world takes on a much deeper glow while all this extra-dimensional stuff is flying around between us.

We worked on Fran's website project that whole first day—or, rather, we meant to. One thing that happens when we get together in our Vulcan mind-meld mode is that I seem to lose most of my linear left-brain abilities and go floating off with Fran on a dozen adventures at once. So although we worked for at least ten hours that day, probably no more than four of them were devoted to the website itself. The rest of the time was spent receiving InnerVision messages, some of which contained reading list recommendations from Spirit. (*The Isaiah Effect: Decoding the Lost Science of Prayer and Prophesy* by Gregg Braden and *The Spontaneous Fulfillment of Desire* by Deepak Chopra were two of the suggested books. I ordered them from Amazon that same day.)

After dinner, we moved into Kurt's office so Fran could print a stack of research she'd done online earlier in the day. I chose a cozy upholstered chair in the corner while she worked at the desk. Shortly after I sat down, little Bob padded into the room and jumped up on my lap. Craning his neck upward to meet me, we reverently bumped foreheads in greeting, and then I planted a lingering smooch on the top of his head. Satisfied, he curled up for a nap.

"It's so beautiful seeing the two of you together," said Fran. "Your relationship is so pure." I looked up, startled. I hadn't realized she'd been watching.

"He's very tired, you know," she continued quietly. "And he's thinking about going home."

Oh please God no.

"Is he in pain?" I asked.

"No, he's not in any pain. His body's just worn out. And he doesn't want to leave you until he's sure you're strong enough to go on without him."

I looked down at Bob, suddenly quite blurry on my lap, as I struggled to make sense of this new information.

"Please don't stay on my account," I whispered to him at last, with as much sincerity as I could muster. "Do whatever's best for you."

The next day, Fran and I were out having lunch at a little bakery around the corner. As we waited for our sandwiches I told her all about the Barbara Brennan books, about the weekend workshop I had recently attended, and that I was mulling over the idea of taking the BBSH four-year program to become an accredited full-time Brennan healer.

"I don't really want to do it; I don't feel drawn to that school or even that line of work," I added, "but at least I'd be fulfilling my mission, right?"

"No. You're not here to follow in somebody else's footsteps, to be trained in an existing discipline. You're supposed to invent a brand-new form of healing—and it may not even be physical healing we're talking about, I don't know—but it will be something totally unique to you that the world hasn't yet seen."

I stared blankly at my lunch plate. "What the hell new kind of healing could I possibly come up with?"

Fran took a bite of her sandwich. "You'll figure it out."

Ten o'clock that evening. We were sitting in the kitchen talking, when I suddenly remembered I'd promised Kurt I would feed the fish while he was away. They'd been expecting their afternoon snack at five o'clock.

We grabbed the food and headed outside, yet as we approached the fishpond I sensed uneasily that something wasn't right. Straining to see in the darkness, I gradually realized that nearly all the water had disappeared, and our rather large population of fish was darting around in only about an inch-and-a-half of water. My stomach twisted with fear. *What could have happened? How long had it been like this, under my negligent care?*

I refilled the pond about halfway with the garden hose, careful not to add too much chlorinated city water all at once. Although the fish were Kurt's pets, not mine, I'd learned a few dos and don'ts over the years, including how not to kill all of them at once by shocking their systems with too much tap water. I threw in a handful of salt to help them adapt to the new environment, and then fed them their snack. They seemed none the worse for wear, splashing this way and that as they nipped at the food pellets.

Poking around the pond's perimeter, I searched in vain for the cause of the problem. Had the pump suddenly sprung a leak? Was there a hole in the liner? Nothing seemed out of place so I resolved to wait until morning to try and figure it out, when I'd be able to see more clearly.

Fran and I said our goodnights and I went off to bed. I'd been badly thrown off balance by the pond incident; although the fish seemed unharmed, it had brought up a host of old unresolved feelings: *Kurt will find out I'm a poisonous screw-up and I can't be trusted to keep anything alive. I let him down like I always do…and those innocent fish are paying the price.*

I drifted into an uneasy sleep. Some time later, I was awakened by Kurt's voice shouting my name: *CARRIE!*

"Hm? Wha?" I said out loud, squinting around me at the empty bedroom in a daze before glancing at the clock: 1:29 in the morning. Good God.

Getting up, I threw on a robe and began to follow Kurt's wordless instructions. Opening the cabinet by the back door where he keeps his pond supplies, I peered into its dim recesses. I pushed aside other containers as he directed me to a tall shaker can of water detoxifier; the salt had been ok as an emergency measure, he wanted me to know, yet this was the appropriate conditioning agent for neutralizing the harmful chemicals from the hose water.

Armed with the detoxifier, I went out to the pond. I was shocked to see it had once again been drained of all the water I'd added only a few hours earlier. This was no slow leak. Refilling the pond to its brim, I added a good dose of chemical neutralizer at the same time.

There, I thought to myself. *That should buy us at least an hour or two.*

Inexplicably I felt a direct connection now, not only with Kurt, but also with the minds of all the pond fish.

"How are you guys holding up?" I asked. "Little ones: Show yourselves."

A representative handful of tiny black mosquito fish swam out to greet me, before heading back under the blanket of pond plants.

"Big ones: Show me."

Two or three of the larger orange goldfish swam out toward me, then turned and disappeared beneath the plant cover.

We're all ok, was the nonverbal message they communicated to me, *We trust you and we're not worried at all.*

I gazed up at the luminous stars overhead. Suddenly I felt a tremendous whoosh of reassurance and love coming from Kurt; he wanted me to know I'm *not* a screw-up. That I'm trusted and altogether worthy. The fish and I stayed out there together a long time, enjoying the quiet company and basking in our group hug with Kurt.*

---

* When he got back from Japan I asked him whether he'd been aware of any of this. He smiled and said no, although he agreed I'd done exactly the right thing with the water detoxifier. Interestingly, right after he diagnosed and fixed the pond problem my temporary psychic bond with the fish disappeared completely as if it had never happened.

The next day, unable to find the source of the problem, I simply shut off the pump. No waterfall, no aerating bubbles, but at least the fish had plenty of water until Kurt came home to fix it.

On October 21, 2005 at 7:33pm Fran wrote:
To: Carrie
Subject: Send off

A funny thing happened when I left your house this morning: As I merged onto the freeway, two of the strangest-looking little cars I'd ever seen pulled up on either side of me and they kept me company for the next ten miles before they both peeled off and went their own way. At first I couldn't figure it out, and then I realized: They must be Mini Coopers!

It was kind of like being escorted to the borders of Munchkinland. Thanks for the royal sendoff, Glinda! ❖

BURNING QUESTIONS

For the past six weeks I'd been trying to think of a Halloween costume for my friend Deb's big annual party, and kept drawing a blank. That was kind of odd, because I can usually conjure up half a dozen different costume options yet this time I was out of ideas.

On the first Saturday in October I had an appointment with a Brennan practitioner down in Los Angeles. It was my third visit, and this time she decided to perform a spinal clearing on me. I couldn't say what transpired during that hour on the table, yet I knew it was deep; it felt as if hundreds of years' worth of trauma and drama had been cleaned out and healed, all in that one butt-kicking bodywork session.

I awoke the following morning, knowing with perfect clarity what my costume would be:

I want to be Joan of Arc for Christmas.
I mean Halloween.

And I felt an indescribably deep satisfaction—reverence, almost—at the idea of dressing up as someone who'd devoted her life unwaveringly to God.

Let's see—I'd get one of those unisex suit of armor costumes from the Halloween store, I decided, and retrofit it with a big, bejeweled cross in the center of the chest (finally, an excuse to wear a great big cross on my chest!) and a gold-leafed Renaissance halo behind my head.

But how to handle that whole "burned at the stake" thing? This costume wasn't supposed to be a joke. It seemed to express something spiritually rich and authentic for me, and I wanted to treat it with respect. Dragging a flaming stake behind me didn't seem like the effect I was hoping for. On the other hand, I reasoned, if Joan ain't burning, nobody would be able to figure out who I was supposed to be.

As I sorted laundry I pondered the question, finally deciding two tastefully blazing ankle bands would do the trick. Heading out toward the garage with my laundry basket, I was concentrating deeply on how these flames might be constructed to give as authentic a death-by-fire impression as possible—and *WHAM!* Without warning, a split-second yawning terror blind sideways vertigo moment. Then just as quickly the door slammed shut on this horrifying abyss, my vision cleared and I was still standing in my sunny backyard, trembling with the laundry basket.

I'd completely forgotten what the reiki master had said:

In earlier times, healers used to be burned at the stake as witches.

Apparently she wasn't kidding. And judging by what had just happened, hundreds of years later while merely thinking about roasting on a stick, it must not have been a very nice way to die.*

Halloween night. The individual costume pieces had all turned out beautifully, yet I'd never bothered trying the whole thing on at once to see how it all came together. As I stood before the mirror and turned this way and that, surveying my St. Joan getup from all angles, something strange and unexpected was slowly dawning:

I looked kind of…*hot.*

From the front, the armor bore an uncanny resemblance to a form-fitting jacket paired with sexy thigh-high boots; and from the back—yikes, from the back, with the costume's black elastic bands strapped over the black bodysuit beneath it, Joan looked a hell of a lot more dominatrix than saint. Catwoman of Arc.

Somehow this was not at all what I'd had in mind yet we were already late for the party. I couldn't say for sure whether anybody figured out who I was supposed to be that evening, flaming ankles or not.

But I was popular. ❖

---

* No, in case you're wondering, I do not imagine I was Joan of Arc in a previous life. For what it's worth, I think I was probably an un-famous healer who got the extra-crispy treatment for running afoul of the local church.

CHAPTER  FOURTEEN

THE SPONTANEOUS
FULFILLMENT OF DESIRE

One of Spirit's recent book recommendations had been an interesting volume on synchronicity, *The Spontaneous Fulfillment of Desire* by Deepak Chopra.

The material grabbed me right away; I could feel from its telltale electro-jolt this was another in the long line of "right book at the right time" teachings that had been coming my way in rapid succession. One more piece of mystical homework assigned by a loving, unseen teacher whose aim it was to bring me up to speed ASAP.

I was reading a chapter about trying on different archetypes to find the ones that resonate most powerfully. The book listed several of these along with descriptions of what each of them represented; who they were, how it felt to embody the attributes of that being. The goddess Hera, symbol of regal power and beauty. Saraswati, goddess of wisdom.

Suddenly something caught my eye. An invisible movement at the left page margin, repeated over and over again, a bouncing motion that somehow seemed explicitly familiar. And then it came to me: This was the motion of the little dog icon from a software program called Fetch, and it was occupying the location it would have appeared if it were on my computer screen. It would be bouncing to tell me a file had been successfully downloaded and the information was waiting.

I followed the invisible icon to where it seemed to be pointing. It was bouncing opposite a paragraph about yet another archetype:

The redeemer.

Something joyous leapt out of my heart unbidden. *YES*, I thought, *that's IT! That's the one I want to be!*

And then I thought, *Wait, what? I'm not even sure what a redeemer is, but it sounds suspiciously Christ-y. And that can't be right.*

Can it? ❖

So many questions, so few answers. I didn't know it yet, but all questions—including the ones I didn't know I was asking—would very shortly be answered. In the meantime, a few loose ends required some attention.

JUNKYARD DREAMS

November 14, 2005

Last night I had one of those intensely evocative dreams, the kind that won't go away after waking. I was walking through a junkyard, and was surprised to find my beautiful altar there amid the discarded household appliances and rusty car parts. I was shocked to see it in that condition; it seemed alarmingly disrespectful to let that lovely thing sit surrounded by castoffs. The Gohonzon deserved better. I hadn't realized I'd let the situation get this bad without addressing it, and knew something had to be done right away.

When I woke, the meaning was clear. Although I'd stopped going to meetings and caring for members, at first I still chanted reverently to the Gohonzon twice a day as I had for decades. Yet within a surprisingly short period of time as my practice of meditation grew stronger and more vibrantly alive, my connection to the Gohonzon began to wane until I no longer felt any need to chant in the mornings. Soon I had no desire to chant in the evenings either, although I continued to go through the motions of the ritual together with Kurt as was our nightly custom.

Now, I had to admit, the Gohonzon seemed like just another piece of paper, albeit a pretty one. It was as if my intense connection, devotion and need for it had never existed.

I knew it was time to scrape up the courage to tell Kurt I wouldn't be going through the motions anymore. From that day on, I would officially be a non-chanter. ❖

FIRE WALK WITH ME

The warm Santa Ana winds came up full force on a Thursday night a couple of weeks later, softly clattering the bedroom blinds even after the windows had been closed. It was one of those no-sleep nights, and I spent hours floating in and out of delirious alternating half-visions:

Pouring rainstorms dissolved into dry, whispering leaves that swayed and rustled restlessly on the breeze. *I am the wind.* This was the feeling that accompanied me on my strange journey, weaving its way again and again through misty ocean currents and swirling desert updrafts. *I am the wind.*

Early Friday morning Kurt stepped outside to collect the newspaper.

"Oh my God, come look!" he shouted to me, "The hills are burning!"

I ran outside in my robe and fuzzy slippers. The foothills three blocks behind our house were aflame. The wind pushed roiling columns of billowy gray smoke high into the air, obscuring most of the area; the nightmarish scene looked almost as if a series of bombs had exploded just beyond the next-door neighbor's roofline.

It must have been burning unchecked for hours, yet although the inferno raged alarmingly near our housing tract, the wind was pushing it steadily and determinedly away from us. As a result, we could detect no hint of smoky smell in the air; not a speck of ash or any corrosive toxic compounds made their way into the lungs or onto the ground.

Spend any time at all living near California's open spaces, and you'll become enough of a fire expert to know this complete lack of "second-hand smoke" was absolutely *not* business as usual. The effects of local fires are typically experienced for miles beyond the actual conflagration, in the form of eerie orange-gray skies, snowy layers of ash and intolerable air quality. So strange was this current blaze with its pristine blue skies and sparkling fresh air, in fact, that if you didn't turn to look at the hills with your own eyes, you'd never have known there was a fire at all.

I couldn't shake that dreamlike and vision-y feeling from the night before; nothing about this situation seemed quite as it should. These were Santa Ana desert winds, fierce and warm and dry as a bone, yet they were blowing in from the wrong direction, seeming to come from nowhere near the desert itself. And although the fire raged out of control practically within spitting distance, I personally felt sort of peacefully safe, as if it held no threat to my family's wellbeing. I had the distinct feeling, in fact, that this whole semi-hallucinatory event had been invented just for me as a lesson of some kind. A piece of homework I was expected to accomplish.

And what could that lesson be, exactly? Was I supposed to put the fire out? Or throw some kind of protective shield over all the living beings and properties in harm's way? Or maybe I was supposed to just let it burn; maybe this was intended to be some kind of harsh group lesson in non-attachment?

I stood outside for a few minutes, watching the Fire Service planes drop load after load of water and fire retardant from high above those glowing red mountains; watched as the furious wind scattered each payload acres away from its intended target. Whatever I was meant to do about this, I decided, it probably wasn't going to be easy.

Back inside the house, heart pounding, I put the question out into the universe:

"What is the lesson? What, specifically, am I supposed to do?" I automatically picked up the Chopra book, *The Spontaneous Fulfillment of Desire*. I'd been performing a daily morning practice from this book for the past couple of weeks, a meditation utilizing seven principles. One principle for each day of the week. I opened the book to read that day's principle, then froze as the familiar electric current of recognition came when I read this statement:

Imagine that your thoughts affect the natural forces of the universe, that you can bring rain and sunshine, clouds and rainbows.

And put out fires, apparently.

So that was it, then. I was supposed to prove to myself that I was big enough and powerful enough to affect the Earth's natural forces. To put out this fire using my mind alone. I hoped I was up to the task.

"Ok," I responded, "I'll do my best. But I refuse to let any animals or people be killed just so I can learn a lesson. I'll figure out how to put this thing out, yet absolutely no harm can come to living beings or personal property."

And that became the number one focus of my prayer: *Nobody dies, nobody suffers pain or loss.* After an hour or so of this stubbornly protective meditation, I realized I'd better move on and try to do something about the fire itself. So, in my mind I made myself large— like, beanstalk giant large. I lay propped on one enormous elbow, sprawled out along the smoldering ridgeline, and extinguished portions of the fire with my huge hands.

Oddly, that actually seemed to work. As I stood watching, those fire areas under my "hands" invariably calmed down until they were reduced to glowing embers. Unfortunately, however, every time I went back into the house to try and get some billable work done (I was under a tight deadline that day), those same areas became rekindled by the wind and began to burn afresh. A couple of hours of alternating "giant" meditation and billable work went by before I realized I wasn't really getting anywhere.

Lunchtime. Some friends would be driving up from Santa Monica in a few hours to stay the night at our house and go hiking in the nearby foothills the following day. We were low on breakfast provisions, so I decided to squeeze in a quick trip to a nearby bakery.

As I walked outside to the car and glanced up at the ever-spreading wildfire, I knew I'd better ask for some help, since all my previous efforts at fire containment had gone nowhere. Spacey and trancelike, I started the car and pointed it toward the bakery.

"What am I doing wrong?" I asked. "What action should I be taking instead?"

Change the weather now, said Spirit.

Oh. Right. I guess I'd known it from the start, yet changing that furious wind seemed too daunting a job for someone as inexperienced as I. I'd been hoping the task could be accomplished in some other, less challenging way. Pulling into the bakery parking lot, I floated underwater into the building, feeling thoroughly out-of-body and dreamlike. Choosing a handsome assortment of pastries, I watched as if from a distant hilltop as the girl boxed them up.

"That'll be forty-eight dollars," she said pleasantly.

Damn, I thought vaguely as I handed over my credit card, *Those are some expensive baked goods.* *

"How do I make the wind stop blowing?" I asked Spirit, stowing the bakery box in my car, "I don't feel like I'm strong enough to force it to change."

The moment I asked the question I was wordlessly given the answer: I didn't have to force it. I only needed to become one with it. Returning home, I fell immediately into a deep, meditative vision, letting myself merge with the wind.

It turned out the wind wasn't angry at all; it was just single-mindedly caught up in its own dervish-like momentum. It yielded easily to my guidance, and together we slowed gradually, gently, finally coming to rest in stillness and peace on the desert floor.

I opened my eyes and looked out my office window. The trees still moved in a moderate breeze. Damn. For a minute there I really thought I had successfully changed the weather, yet clearly must have imagined it. The stillness of the wind had felt so real…but by the looks of those trees it seemed I'd failed. Apparently I just didn't have what it took to get the job done. I returned my attention to the deadline project without bothering to investigate further.

Kurt came into my office a moment later. "It's the strangest thing," he remarked. "The wind changed directions all of a sudden a

---

* Later that evening I looked at the receipt; she'd accidentally charged me twenty-nine dollars for a two dollar-ninety-cent baguette. I received a refund on Monday.

minute ago. Now it's a damp, cool ocean breeze. I'll bet now they'll be able to put that fire out in no time."

By the time our guests arrived in the late afternoon, no evidence of fire remained except for the telltale blackened hills directly behind our house. According to the news reports of the following day, not a single human or pet had fallen victim; not one building had burned. (As they keep no record of wildlife casualties, I can't make the claim that no animals died. Yet my belief is that no mortality of any kind— other than vegetal, of course—was associated with this fire.)

Saturday morning's hike took place high in the hills several miles northeast of our house; the panoramic views showed the previous day's burn area and beyond, stretching all the way out to the ocean. Although the newspapers would later report that it took several days to fully contain and then extinguish the last remnants of that fire, we found no visual evidence of it. Apart from the slight blackening there was no hint of flame, no wisp of residual smoke to be seen in any direction. The sun shone in a clear, cloudless sky, the water shimmering brightly in the cool, still air. ❧

ALL THE WORLD'S A STAGE

Maybe it was a long time coming. One night while deep in meditation, I abruptly got fed up with living in fear of the unseen things lurking out there in the big bad universe.

"Enough already, with fighting to keep out the unknown terrors," I said to Spirit, "I've spent my whole life doing that. It's a battle I never win anyway, so let's open the door once and for all and get it over with. Whatever the universe is really made of, it's time for me to know."

And the more I meditated on it, the more I really, *really* wanted to know. All that week I thirsted, hungered, to learn the true nature of reality, asking for it again and again in my prayers. Probably it would include all kinds of ghosts and monsters, I reminded myself, yet at this point I didn't care. I was sick of running away. It seemed to me whatever the universe actually turned out to be, knowing had to be a whole lot better than not knowing.

Then a few nights later in mid-meditation came an abrupt change of scene, a vision that felt as real as anyplace I'd ever been.

I slowly woke up to myself standing on an old wooden stage in a small, slightly run-down theater; dust motes drifted in the late afternoon sunlight that streamed in through high windows. I held a script in my hand, and was dimly aware I'd been droning on for I don't know how long—eons, maybe—reciting my soliloquy to a nearly empty house. And no one was listening. The few who sat scattered nearby were too busy rehearsing their own lines to pay any attention to me.

And then Spirit spoke: *Put down the script and walk out of the theater.*

"What?"

Putting down the script was a revolutionary idea, yet admittedly it made sense. I'd been shocked to discover myself unconsciously play-acting, and could see the pointlessness of continuing to recite my lines. Especially since nobody was listening anyway. But walk out of the theater? Did I dare? I'd never been outside, didn't know there *was* an outside. I tried to picture it, and only came up with a terrifyingly bright void.

I understood that this theater and script were being shown to me as symbols of the "reality" I'd unthinkingly accepted until now. Scary as it was to contemplate leaving it behind, I knew it was time to find out whatever might lay beyond.

Will you agree to put down the script and walk out of the theater?

I hesitated, falling out of the vision and back into bed as I said it: "Ok."

And with that agreement to step beyond the world of unconscious play-acting (in which each of us is the star of our own production), I embarked on a new phase of accelerated learning, a Mister Toad's Wild Ride of dreams, visions and recommended reading that would ultimately lead me to my answered prayer: A teaching designed to guide my wobbly baby steps toward the true nature of all reality. ❖

CHAPTER  FIFTEEN

REALIZATION OF ONENESS

April 11, 2006

Leatrice lent me a book almost two months ago, a dog-eared paperback called Realization of Oneness *by Joel S. Goldsmith. I didn't like anything about the look of it. The grimly earnest, band aid-colored cover positively shouted, "Eat your alfalfa sprouts!" circa 1973.*

She'd said I'd probably find it interesting, yet as it turned out I just couldn't get past those visuals. (Yes, I am totally that shallow.) So I slipped it discreetly to the bottom of the homework stack, where it languished for at least six weeks. And then the guilt of keeping the book too long finally got to me. I pulled it out and began to read.

Wow. This ugly little volume turned out to be jam-packed with electro-buzz recognition, even as it spoke of completely alien concepts like: God is real and the world isn't; (Really? Seriously? God is real?) And: We are not separate people who live in separate bodies. In truth we are one Being.

And then there was this one, which seemed the total opposite of everything I'd ever been taught: It doesn't matter what we do (or do not do) in this world, because none of it is real; only God's

perfect unconditional love is real. And nothing can exist outside of God, because God is everything. So only unconditional love exists. Therefore, this world can't be real because nothing in it qualifies as perfect unconditional love (which is changeless and eternal), so, by its very definition, this world doesn't really exist.

Yet this final one was the kicker: Instead of trying to change the world, one should strive instead to become a redeemer—there was that word again—offering only the infinite, healing reality of God's divine love to the world.

It was a brand-new set of messages I'd never heard before, and I knew instinctively the entire previous year of study had been preparing me for this. I needed time to absorb all this information; as it happened, Kurt was off for one of his Buddhist pilgrimages to Japan, so I had the house to myself for five days. I spent it in seclusion, reading and meditating (instead of earning a living) hour upon hour, for each of those precious days.

I developed an odd eye condition over the course of those five days: Random sparkles of light started to appear in my peripheral vision. These were not like joy sparkles, which are essentially invisible and seen with the inner eye, and which mainly act as carriers of spiritual bliss. These new sparkles were visible pops and flashes of actual light.

I was fairly sure (hoping, anyway) the phenomenon was spiritual in nature. As opposed to, say, the early warning signs of glaucoma. The general feeling that accompanied the sparkles was always warm and reassuring, which led me to believe they were probably a good thing. But really, who can you ask about something like that? Certainly not an eye doctor. I mentioned it to no one.

Sparkles aside, those five days of concentrated meditation cleared up a lot of things. Now I knew for sure what a redeemer was. I just didn't know how to admit to anybody that's what I wanted to be when I grew up.

April 21, 2006

Leatrice came by today to pick up her book. We had a lovely conversation about it, and although I hadn't intended to speak of it to anyone, I wound up confessing to her that I think I want to be a Christ. Surprisingly, she didn't laugh at me. In fact she seems to think it's a perfectly natural choice, although to me this oddball ambition doesn't seem natural at all.

I mean, besides the general weirdness of the whole idea, I can hardly believe I'm volunteering for a job that is pretty much guaranteed to end badly. What's up with that? Some sort of holy death wish, maybe?

"You should take a look at what A Course in Miracles *has to say about that," Leatrice advised in response to that question. "It claims otherwise."*

A Course in Miracles…I vaguely remembered having heard about that once, way back in 1982. Something to do with Marianne Williamson. I think somebody told me she wrote it to help the gay community of West Hollywood in its fight against AIDS.*

All well and good, yet what could that possibly have to do with this? ❖

---

* Ok, so I was a little confused. Although she is best known for her lectures on its teachings, Marianne Williamson did not write *A Course in Miracles*, and there is no connection whatsoever between *A Course in Miracles* and Marianne's fine work on behalf of AIDS patients in Los Angeles.

THE DISAPPEARANCE OF THE UNIVERSE

One day shortly after finishing *Realization of Oneness* I was poking around on Amazon, looking for another Joel S. Goldsmith book to read. After buying a handful of volumes by authors I knew and liked, an intriguing recommendation popped up for a book I'd never heard of: *The Disappearance of the Universe,* by Gary R. Renard. On an impulse, I bought it.

The Amazon box arrived a few days later, and it was instantly clear which book should be read first; pretty little eye sparkles flashed and popped all around *The Disappearance of the Universe.* It looked like a fun book by an interesting guy, so I happily settled in for what I thought would be some enjoyable, light reading. Until I got to the second page, where Gary suddenly mentioned seeing little flashes of light around objects in his peripheral vision.

I froze. *Good God. He's talking about eye sparkles.*

My heart seemed to stop beating, time slowed to a crawl and the book came alive in my hands, pulsating dizzily with light and energy: *This is it, this is it, this is it.*

I put the book down carefully and stared a long while as it lay innocently in my lap. All of the previous homework books had announced themselves in one way or another, each one letting me know I was about to read the right book at the right time. Yet none of them had packed this kind of wallop. *Am I really ready for this?* I wondered.

I took a deep breath and prepared to start the book over again from the top. *Here we go,* I thought. *Fasten that seatbelt, kiddo.*

It was probably a good thing this whole *Disappearance* event began so momentously, because honestly, I don't know if I'd have finished reading the book otherwise. *The Disappearance of the Universe* kicked my butt. Again and again it blew my mind apart, then carefully reconstructed the bits and pieces of my metaphysical worldview only to nuke them once again fifty pages later:

Only eternal love is real; everything else is illusion. (Yes, ok, I'd heard that recently.) Yet now the shocking implications of that teaching were becoming much clearer. Not only was it the three-dimensional world of bodies and houses that didn't really exist.

The past year's homework had been all about learning the spiritual dynamics of chakras and auras, the powerfully transformative possibilities of energy healing. Naturally I'd assumed these teachings reflected spiritual truth. According to this book, however, all these phenomena and many others actually belonged to the false world of the ego mind (the mind that causes us to believe we're separate bodies living in a fake world), and they possessed no spiritual reality of their own.

Manifestation? Synchronicity? Forget about it. Clever inventions of that same ego mind, designed to keep us recirculating inside the closed loop of the illusory 3-D world while we mistakenly believe we're getting somewhere on the road to enlightenment.

Holy cow.

Ok then, what about sacred energy sites like Sedona's vortexes? Surely those were real spiritual places—I'd felt their power firsthand. Nope, according to this teaching, there was no such thing as a "real spiritual place." All places were one, and none was more special or spiritual than any other. Everything we knew or thought or perceived about the universe was all part of the same ego dream, and none of it had any reality. *The universe itself* had no reality.

Shocking as all these revelations were, they weren't the main reason I almost put the book down. I did dimly realize, upon reflection, that all the spiritual concepts I'd learned this year (each of which had been specifically brought to me by Spirit, only to be pushed aside now) had been offered as "expedient means," as the Buddhists would say. Each had been a temporary teaching, designed to deepen my understanding before being discarded in preparation for the next.

No, I was more or less ok with the expedient means. It was this next teaching that was giving me the willies. *The Disappearance of the Universe* is essentially a riveting, four hundred-page infomercial for *A Course in Miracles,* and I would never in a million years have been attracted to that particular curriculum if Gary and his ascended Teachers had not made such a breathtakingly persuasive case for it.

The *Course* seemed way too Christian for my taste, too bible-ish and hard to read, and most of all too damned long—I'm just not the "365-day workbook" type. Left to my own devices I would never have picked up *A Course in Miracles,* yet that's exactly what I was about to do. And, strange to say, I couldn't wait to get started. ❖

A NOTE TO YOU, THE READER

The remainder of this book is marked by a much more frequent and easy two-way communication with Spirit. Because I've been studying *A Course in Miracles* for the past couple of years, most of these in-depth conversations with Spirit take the form of lessons about various *Course* principles as they pertain, in real time, to events happening in my daily life.

Partway through writing this book I realized that because we delve so deeply into *A Course in Miracles'* subject matter, it might be helpful to include here a brief synopsis of the *Course* itself for those who are unfamiliar with its teachings. So I've written a short summary of the *Course* called *The Crash Course,* which is included at the back of this book.

The rest of the book can be enjoyed whether one is familiar with *A Course in Miracles* or not. Yet to derive optimal richness of meaning from Spirit's gentle lessons, one may find it helpful to peruse *The Crash Course* in order to gain a better understanding of the context in which these lessons are presented. ❖

A COURSE IN MIRACLES

May 27, 2006

Wow. That's pretty much all I have to say about it. When I picked up the book, there were no eye sparkles, no pulsating light shows. Just the strong, sure knowing that this is the last teaching I will ever need.

So much richness, so much eye-opening clarity and beauty. It's funny, because I was initially afraid I wouldn't be smart enough to understand the Course. *I had to read, re-read and re-read again every paragraph of the* Course *that was quoted in* The Disappearance of the Universe, *because I found its bible-meets-Shakespeare style of writing so hard to follow. Eventually I started praying about that, asking for more and better brain cells, or increased wisdom, or whatever it was going to take for me to absorb and understand the meaning of the* Course. *And that prayer seems to have been answered in spades; now the depth and brilliance of the* Course's *text takes my breath away.*

Sometimes I can only read one paragraph at a time. Not because it's hard to understand, rather because it contains such a vibrant world of information I need to stop and meditate on it, to take it all in. And now, well, somehow a year's worth of workbook lessons doesn't seem like nearly enough.

Now if I can just get over the persistent Christian-ness of it, especially the weird unfamiliarity of that Holy Spirit business, I'll be all set. ❖

CALL IT WHAT YOU WILL

Maybe this would be a good moment to pause and clarify what I mean when I use the word "Spirit."

Certainly Fran has influenced my choice of that title. She tends not to use religious sounding words like "God," preferring general terms like "Spirit" instead. I've never asked her precisely what she means by "Spirit," yet over time I adopted the word too, for ease of conversation.

What I meant by "Spirit" back when I first began using the term was a sort of cross between what the Buddhists call the Mystic Law of Life* and what Barbara Brennan calls the Universal Energy Field, with maybe a pinch of Divine Intelligence thrown in. Sort of an ecumenical and highly ingenious life potential that likes us an awful lot.

And my Voice, the spokes-being for that energy field/law/intellect—well, having moved on from the earliest days when I thought it was the Gohonzon talking, I was later content to think of that Voice as my Guide. Somebody else in a similar situation might prefer to call such a presence an angel, if they're into that sort of thing.

Yet after embracing the *Course*, with its strong focus on the communication role of the Holy Spirit, I quickly began to perceive my Voice as that of the Holy Spirit (or "Spirit" for short) and that role seemed to suit it better and more authentically than any other.

"Holy Spirit" can be a tough name to get comfortable with; it certainly was for me. If that title bothers you as you read on, feel free to substitute. Call it your own highest self, if that helps. It's as good a description as any other.

Because whatever we choose to call it, that beautiful, gentle Voice will always answer, no matter what name it's given. ❖

---

* AKA Nam Myoho Renge Kyo.

The more I studied *A Course in Miracles,* the more the information contained within it surprised and confounded me, upending all my previously cherished notions about spiritual progress and the road to enlightenment.

BUMMER

June 6, 2006

The Course *talks a lot about the state of being that is Christ, or full enlightenment, and offers clear instructions on how to get there from here. That's the good news.*

The bad news: Who knew that forgiveness of others would be the mandatory prerequisite?

Apparently, it doesn't matter how much we work on our own spiritual growth. We can strive for self-perfection until hell freezes, yet if we want to become enlightened, we first have to recognize the perfect holiness and innocence that exists in the other guy. In all the other guys. Until we manage to sincerely render a "not guilty" verdict on the world, in other words, our own enlightenment is simply not in the cards.

Damn it. I just don't like people that much.

And it seems like such a Catch-22, besides. I mean, wouldn't you have to already BE enlightened, before you could manage to overlook everyone's smelly faults and see the world as perfect and holy?

I guess that's why there are hardly any Christs running around. If it were easy, everybody would be doing it. ❧

YOU'LL WRITE BOOKS

July 12, 2006

A little while ago I was reading a passage from the Course *that says we have to choose either the thought system of the ego or the thought system of Spirit; that it's impossible to have both. I decided to stop reading and meditate on that.*

It was really hard to concentrate, my mind full of distracting nonsense chatter, yet I persisted and eventually found a tiny window of split-second clarity, so I took advantage and grabbed the opportunity to choose the thought system of Spirit.

It's weirdly quiet now inside my mind; the old familiar chatter is gone, I'm all alone and I don't know what to do with myself. It's so strange to suddenly be without that constant mental noise. I can't quite put this feeling into words. Beautiful but uncomfortable, I guess. Serene, yet boring. Lonely. I've mostly just been walking around the house, touching things.

Something else changed, too, besides the removal of the jibber-jabber. It feels like I have a super-enhanced communication channel now. The connection somehow seems to have become bigger and more "solid" than it was before.

I was sitting in the living room, just looking around at stuff when Spirit made this pronouncement, clean and clear as a bell: **When you're ready, you'll write books.**

It was unexpected news. I understood from the wordless concepts surrounding this statement that we were talking about the writing of spiritual self-help books, of all things—a job for which I knew I was ridiculously unqualified. Yet I was surprisingly ok with it. Even though I also understood that we weren't talking about me hiding myself away to write books in solitude, much as I loved the hermit-ish idea of that.

No, this new job description seemed to carry a much higher profile, as if I might be traveling around to talk publicly with strangers about all this stuff. Which normally would have seemed repellent. The thought of losing my privacy, of letting strangers look at me—the idea of reaching public prominence had always profoundly creeped me out. Actually, it was more than that. The notion of celebrity wasn't just creepy; it felt deeply unsafe. Terrifying, really. Almost like being exposed to the public was the same as death.

Yet I was pretty sure I wouldn't have to write any books until after I was enlightened anyway—because who'd want to hear anything I had to say until then—and by that time I surely wouldn't be afraid of strangers anymore. And, God knew, there would be oodles of time before any enlightenment would be coming my way.

So I quickly decided to buckle down and work extra hard on the "getting enlightened" part and forgot all about that silly book writing business. ❖

CHAPTER SIXTEEN

FORGIVENESS AND GUILT

July 19, 2006

I'm supposed to offer the Course's form of "forgiveness" exercises every time someone pisses me off. Instead of spewing anger, I'm supposed to silently remind myself (and them) that they're not really guilty at all; they're actually perfect immortal Spirit, eternally pure and radiant and entirely innocent of whatever crime I imagine they've committed.

Yet what if the opportunity for practicing those exercises hardly ever happens? After all those years of Buddhist prayer on the subject, I'm no longer the hothead I used to be. Nowadays I sometimes go a week or more without any flashes of irritation. Not like that's such a big improvement over the old days of fiery rages and silent ice storms; I seem to have traded the outward anger for constant low-level anxiety instead, and while it seems like it would be comparatively easy to apply forgiveness exercises to somebody outside myself who momentarily makes me mad, I don't really know how to offer forgiveness to something that's so big, dark and sludgy on the inside.

Spirit weighed in: *Don't wait for a reason. Offer forgiveness to everyone you see.*

"Even if I'm not mad?"

That you believe you're a body living in this 3-D dream world is proof that you unconsciously perceive everything around you as guilty. The belief in separate bodies is part of the ego's thought system, and that thought system is based on guilt. So everyone and everything you think you see is an equally suitable subject for your forgiveness exercises.

The more often and more sincerely you can remember to practice forgiveness, the sooner that internal sludge will begin to melt away of its own accord.

I looked forward to the idea of melting that internal sludge, and spent the next several days asking to become more aware of the unconscious thought system of guilt that held sway over my 3-D life, reasoning that I couldn't hope to start cleaning up what I didn't know was there. ❖

WAR AND PEACE

July 26, 2006

Well, I seem to be getting my wish. I'm starting to see the unconscious thought system of guilt, and it isn't pretty. It also isn't what I expected. I thought I was asking to understand more about the way I perceive guilt in others, and instead I've been developing a painful awareness of the silent, underlying viciousness that lurks behind my own every thought and action. Even my most seemingly benign or loving behavior turns out to be driven by deeply rooted, unrelenting rage. Not a very nice thing to realize about oneself. According to the Course, *everybody has this same hidden motivator, yet I guess for most people the internal ferocity stays safely out of conscious awareness unless they specifically ask to see it.*

I began to meditate about all this rage a little while ago, when suddenly I felt dragged into another place:

*I was out-of-body, watching myself on a battlefield. Mud and blood and mano a mano mayhem galore. I saw my grimy, tear-stained face, matted hair, my armor smeared with everybody's blood including my own. I felt fragile, scared, convinced I was being attacked from all sides and hell bent on defending myself at all costs. Yet I couldn't help noticing on closer inspection that although the other warriors looked ferocious in their battle gear, they weren't actually doing anything to hurt me. I seemed to be the only one lunging again and again to attack each one who came near. That realization stopped me cold. And then, sort of like the episode when I was shown the symbol of the theater a few months ago, Spirit said: **Put down your weapon and leave the battlefield.***

And this time I was only too happy to do it. Stripped off the armor and walked away without a backward glance, feeling immensely relieved to be free of the burden.

The anxiety sandpaper is gone, at least for now, which

leaves me feeling kind of almost peaceful. I hope this lasts, yet it probably won't. This kind of vision seems to just be a teaching tool, not a permanent breakthrough. Still, I'll enjoy the peace and safety while I have it.

God, I could sleep for a week. ❖

HOW DO I KNOW IT'S REALLY YOU?

As wonderful as this new and improved communication channel seemed to be, I wasn't entirely sure I could trust it.

"These conversations are great," I said to Spirit, "and it's always a pleasure to hear from you, yet I have to ask: How can I be sure it's really you talking and not my ego mind? We both know the ego is a master impersonator, and it's capable of slipping in to hijack any discussion without me realizing it."

It's very easy to tell the difference, My dear. Just listen carefully to everything that's said. If what you hear is loving, gentle and designed to lead you toward ultimate freedom, you'll know it's Me talking.

If you hear the slightest judgment, or a single word that lacks pure unconditional love you'll know it hasn't come from Me, for I'm incapable of anything less than total love for you. Be vigilant in each of our conversations, and soon you'll be able to trust wholeheartedly in your ability to tell the difference.

Following that advice, I taught myself to pay close attention to the meaning behind every word, and soon found it easy to tell each time a bogus thought or idea was planted within our conversations.

And as I learned to trust in my own ability to recognize the words of Spirit, I also began to relax and trust more deeply in the lessons being offered. ❖

Should I be treating the Holy Spirit like a respected family friend? Like a college professor? This new, more familiar relationship with Spirit was bringing up some unexpected issues for me to examine.

TEACHER'S PET

I've always felt a need to please authority figures. That's not necessarily a bad thing; cops and school principals have always liked me, reliably finding me innocent even when caught red handed. And I can't even count how many traffic tickets I haven't been issued over the years, just because I'm so respectful and pleasant each time they pull me over. This behavior isn't a cynical ploy; it's just how I am. I want them to like me. Yet as much as it's had its advantages, overall I don't think this desire to win approval from those in power really serves me.

Especially when it comes to spirituality. Being *perceived* as a sincere and devoted Buddhist practitioner by my leaders was at least as important to me as actually being one. Don't get me wrong, I practiced with great resolve whether anyone was watching or not, yet often for no better reason than to impress my leaders with the awesome purity of my trustworthiness and devotion.

Old habits die hard. I still found myself doing "good girl" things now and then in an attempt to curry favor with Spirit, knowing full well my efforts meant nothing at all.

And Spirit concurred: *What you do in this world, whether in your daily life or in your spiritual practice, does not affect My love for you, which is total and complete. You could not possibly do anything to make Me love you more than I already do.*

By the same token, nothing you do or fail to do could ever make Me love you any less. You are loved wholly and unconditionally, dear one, whether you can accept the reality of this love or not. ❖

Spirit's statement of unconditional love was a wonderful thing, so beautiful and reassuring. Yet I soon discovered that accepting the reality of what that unconditional love actually means can sometimes be a lot more challenging than it sounds.

DEATH STARE

July 30, 2006

This morning Kurt and I spent an hour or two at the outlet mall for some concentrated wardrobe updating. Nothing too exciting. A much-needed pair of jeans, some socks. Afterward we went to lunch at a nice brewpub.

A ballgame played on the big screen behind us, and most of the folks in our section were watching it. I was busily enjoying my sandwich, when I suddenly looked up and locked eyes with a guy who wasn't watching the game at all. He was giving me that look, that bone-chilling "you don't deserve to take up space" stare of death. I froze in mid-bite. I've been getting that stare all my life. You'd think it would get less shocking or less painful with time, yet somehow it never does.

As I stared back at the guy helplessly, Spirit spoke: *Many have shown you the Death Stare. Yet every time you misinterpret its true meaning, and thereby miss its value.*

Each one who stares at you in this way offers you the loving opportunity to wake up and be released from your self-made prison of ugliness. Instead of fear or anger, try feeling gratitude to this man who stares.

"Gratitude? Are you kidding?"

I'm not. And while you're at it offer him forgiveness, as taught by the Course. *This guy who seems to be separate from yourself is actually one and the same as you. You find him guilty of terrible judgments against you, and yet he really only reflects your own debilitating self-judgment. Thank him for being the one to bring this fact to your attention, and let him off the hook for his supposed crime. I assure you, he is completely innocent.*

I looked at Death Stare Guy once again. His eyes hadn't moved. I felt an unexpected rush of...what? Not gratitude, exactly. Almost friendship, or tenderness. For, although I had ignored hundreds or thousands of prior wakeup calls, something within this guy had gone out of its way to try and reach me anyway. And, in some very small way, succeeded. ❖

CHAPTER SEVENTEEN

FREAKOUT

It was a perfect summer afternoon and I was outside, meditating in the garden. Of course, I would never enjoy the beauty of nature in quite the same way again, after the *Course* had so gently yet firmly asked me to really *see* the things I unthinkingly perceived as beautiful; the bees buzzing on the backyard lavender, the golden mustard-covered hills beyond. By following the *Course's* gentle logic to its inevitable conclusion, I had been forced to admit that everything I celebrated as beautiful was actually nothing more than an exercise in fear, reeking of death and decay. I was grateful for the wakeup call, but really, kill a pastoral mood why don't you?

I'd been re-reading *The Disappearance of the Universe*, and it was interesting to note the effect it had on me the second time around. It still kicked my butt, yet for completely different reasons this time.

The thing I found most disturbing on the second read had completely escaped my notice the first time: The four stages of perception, starting with dualism (the total belief in separation, which is where we all start out), proceeding to semi-dualism (a fence-riding foot in both camps, not believing fully in either one), non-dualism (a recognition of oneness) and finally on to pure non-dualism, or perfect oneness with God, the divine love which is all that is.

It was disturbing to read that each of these stages typically took years, maybe even decades or lifetimes. Up until then I'd blithely assumed my accelerated homework program had meant I was on a fast track to enlightenment (maybe a year; two or three years, tops), and that I would find each step of the journey more beautiful and natural than the one before it.

Yet as I reflected on this book's description of the enlightenment process, I suddenly understood what those steps actually entailed: Not only to give away all attachment to my body and to the world it seemed to inhabit, but to give away my whole personality. All my likes and dislikes, my talents and quirks. My individuality. My identity. Every last speck of the person I thought of as *me*.

"Oh, *HELL* no!" I yelled, catapulting out of my Adirondack chair.

Mind you, I'm no stranger to "karma attacks," as we called them in Buddhism. Over the years I'd learned it was always best to face these meltdowns head-on, since they could immobilize even the most sincere practitioner for months if left unchallenged.

Yet this, the imagined prospect of voluntary spiritual suicide, was scarier than any karmic blowout I'd ever experienced before. Never mind that I wasn't so in love with the person I thought of as "me," and realized I'd probably be better off without my anxiety-ridden personality-self hanging around. The alternative was just way too frightening to contemplate.

The next few days oozed by in a fight-or-flight blur; I could find no relief from the panic, no answer to the unknown terror that might be waiting to get me after I shed the protective coating of my distasteful ego self.

On Day Three of this mess, Spirit weighed in: *So what will you do now?*

"Oh, God, I don't know!"

Will you go backwards? Will you stop studying the Course *and forget all you've learned?*

"I've thought about it, believe me. But no, I could never go back now. My eyes have started to open; I know too much to want to close them again."

So...does that mean you want to stay as you are?

"No! I can't stand being spiritually stuck. It feels awful. I need to keep moving forward."

So you don't want to go back and you can't stay where you are. Well then, My dear, your only other option is to trust in Me. Put yourself in My hands and let Me carry you forward to a greater understanding of the truth.

"I so completely don't want to do that right now. Yet I can't think of any other way out, so I guess I'll have to try."

By the end of that week, the panic subsided. Putting aside my initial reluctance, I found I was able to take that small leap of trust in Spirit, and was rewarded with a new sense of warmth, of being unconditionally cared for. And in response, a new feeling grew within me, something inappropriate and bizarre.

"I'm so sorry, I know this is dumb and I promise it'll be very temporary—*I seem to have developed a crush on You.* I know it's crazy (not to mention weirdly insulting to my actual husband), yet there it is. I've never experienced gentleness like Yours, and falling for You is the only way I know how to respond. I'm sure I'll come to my senses soon. In the meantime, is it ok?"

Of course. No worries.

And so, for a thankfully brief period of no more than a week or so, the Holy Spirit became my Boyfriend.

A few days later we took off for Sedona, just me, my husband and my Boyfriend; this trip was more about pleasure than business, and we'd been looking forward to it. Kurt had made plans to spend the first full day at the inn with Steve, so Fran picked me up early that morning for what would turn out to be a marathon daylong InnerVision journey.

Heading up the long, rocky dirt road to the top of Schnebly Hill, Fran and I stopped at last on its broad overlook to take in the majestic view that lay spread out before us. I'd been feeling very out-of-body all the way up there. I could tell we were in for some powerful stuff that day.

"Am I safe?" I asked my Boyfriend nervously as I inched toward the cliff's edge to get a better view.

Perfectly safe.

Silently I took in the raw beauty of the towering red rock cliffs and scrub canyons far below. Still anxious despite Spirit's assurances, I felt lightheaded and queasy, my heart pounding a little in my throat.

Allow, said Spirit.

I closed my eyes just for a moment, and reopened them to a vision: Literally a bird's-eye view as I swooped out over the canyon, coasting on air currents, my winged shadow trailing me as I scanned the ground far below.

I gasped in pain at the sharp, matter-of-fact ruthlessness of my gaze. *I was hunting for prey.* Waves of sickened animal guilt washed over me. At that same moment my perception seemed to widen slightly and I became aware of myself making small, frantic movements on the canyon floor; I realized I was also some kind of desert rodent, scrambling to hide myself in the sparse vegetation.

Suddenly I understood. I was not just the murderer, the guilty abuser as I'd always assumed. Somehow I had gotten stuck in an endless feedback loop, predator and prey, victim and victimizer simultaneously. And I knew it had to stop.

Allow, Spirit repeated.

I closed my eyes against the breeze and the tears, and agreed to open the festering wound of animal guilt, exposing its dark secrets to sunlight for the very first time.

We headed next to an area known as the Heartwell. Normally it held a fairly sizable body of water, Fran explained, home to all kinds of fish and wildlife. The summer drought had dried it up entirely, causing concerned locals to step in to rescue and relocate the stranded fish. Recent cloudbursts had partially refilled it. As we approached, we saw it was once again teeming with life—strange, disturbing, prehistoric-seeming life.

I was still reeling from the prey-and-predator lesson on Schnebly Hill. As we moved closer to the turbulent water's edge as if in a slo-mo dream, it became clear we were witnessing a terrible life-and-death struggle on a similar theme: Three large, slug-like creatures were locked in a desperate underwater dance, two of them apparently attacking and eating the third. Jesus.

Thousands of these slug creatures thrashed and swam beneath the water's murky surface, while above it buzzed a multitude of not-really-dragonflies; big, alien winged things the likes of which neither of us had seen before.

I understood intuitively that the black and busy waters of the Heartwell held a tangled connection to my own anxieties; that the strange creatures lurking beneath that surface were being shown to me as stand-ins for my own uneasy guilt and shame.

As I peered into that dark water I experienced the second half of a powerful vision I'd had a few nights earlier, concerning a pompous consultant who had been hired by one of my clients. This consultant was a complete pain in my ass. The week before, he'd arranged a conference call for no other purpose than to spank me in front of my clients for an imaginary mistake I'd made; the "mistake" being that I'd dared to hold an opinion (on a subject within my own field of expertise) that happened to be different from his own.

Anyway. Not for nothing do I practice *A Course in Miracles*. I drowned that guy in forgiveness exercises for a solid week, in an attempt to free myself from the compulsive internal viciousness I fell into every time I thought of him.

After scores of these forgiveness exercises in which I struggled to perceive his perfection through the eyes of ultimate truth—instead of seeing him as the infuriating sonofabitch he certainly seemed to be—the consultant had appeared to me in a vision a few nights earlier.

"See *through* me," he had implored in an ethereal, underwatery voice. And my heart had gone out to him, his pain so clearly evident.

Now, standing at the Heartwell and gazing into the restless black waters, I saw him again. And again those same words, yet with a subtle change of inflection that lent an altogether new and far deeper meaning: "*See*, through *me*."

It was an invitation to perceive the perfection in all of Creation by first perceiving the perfection in this one very imperfect guy. He was urging me to look beyond his transient ego-self to the limitless beauty of his true nature, so I'd be able to take that same lens and use it to see the reality of Heaven everywhere, in everything. I knew he was offering me nothing less than a key to unlock ultimate truth.

Too bad I wasn't anywhere near being willing or able to reach out and take that key. It was all I could do to stand still and accept the fact that this annoying bastard had been the one to offer it.

From the Heartwell Fran and I drove to the Shaman's Cave, a strange and wonderful mound of bright orange slick-rock sitting all by itself in the middle of nowhere. We chose to get to it by the most direct route, via rarely used Forest Service roads, rather than the usual red dirt highways. The rains had left some of these narrow roads nearly impassable, yet our trusty four-runner took us up one boulder and down into the next gully with ease.

Arriving finally at the Shaman's Cave, we hiked our way down a long scrub slope and up the trail on the other side. The cave itself sat high on that patch of slick-rock, inaccessible from almost every side.

"Keep an eye out for rattlesnakes," called Fran over her shoulder. "This is their time of day for sunning."

"Safe?" I asked Spirit urgently.

Safe.

Reaching the aptly named slick-rock, Fran demonstrated the proper way to shimmy across the smooth rock face, placing her toes into shallow indentations etched by the generations of bare feet that had come before. I eyed the rock reluctantly. What the hell had I been thinking, coming way out here? This was not at all like me, to get involved in some crazy extreme-sports challenge. One clumsy move and I'd surely tumble to my death on the canyon floor below.

"Still safe?"

Still safe.

I took a deep breath and hurriedly scrambled across the rock face, then followed Fran into the cave mouth itself. The cavern was large and clean, showing very little evidence of modern human activity. At the far end was a round hole in the wall that overlooked all of Loy Canyon below.

"This is a very powerful spot," Fran informed me. "By sitting in this round opening with one foot inside the cave and the other foot outside on the rock ledge, it's possible to straddle two dimensions at once. Go ahead and try it," she suggested, climbing out the hole to meditate on the ledge overlooking the canyon.

I positioned myself in the opening, yet couldn't relax. Although seated very securely with my back supported against the curved opening and both feet planted on solid rock, every time I closed my eyes I had the uncomfortable sensation of falling sideways out the hole, jerking myself upright over and over again. I tried and failed to meditate for at least ten minutes before giving up in exasperation.

This is a complete waste of time, I thought crankily, *I don't know what we're supposed to be doing here.* I climbed out the hole and joined Fran on the ledge. This felt a little better.

Closing my eyes, there came an immediate invitation: *If you let Me, I'll show you what you are.*

I considered for a moment. Even though the offer was plenty frightening, I probably did want to see what I was.

"Yes. Ok."

Soon we were flying hand in hand over the canyon, me on the left and Spirit (a vague and non-specific entity) to my right.

What are we supposed to be wearing? I fretted. *Shouldn't we both have some kind of white robes or something, flapping in the breeze?* And a moment later we did.

Looking to my right, I saw Spirit's free hand dissolve into a shower of shimmering light, like a gentle, glowing birthday sparkler. The ball of light climbed up the right arm, dissolving as it went, across the body and down the left arm until only sparkling light remained. It paused where our hands met, asking wordless permission to continue. I could see where this was going and didn't like it a bit, yet after a long hesitation I agreed.

The light dissolved my hand, arm, body, other arm, hand. I jerked away reflexively and we became two individual balls of glowing, sparkling light. My ball sped crazily around the other, repelled yet drawn like a maddened bug to a candle flame. As my ball zigzagged its agonized orbit, the other ball remained absolutely still, waiting patiently.

I knew what was being asked of me—I just didn't want to do it. The game wore on for another excruciating minute before I finally hit my limit, unable to stand the discomfort of resistance any longer.

"Oh, all *right*," I said testily, pausing at last to allow our two balls of light to merge gently, softly into one.

Later that evening, Fran had planned a midnight hike to the ancient Honanki Ruins with her friend Terri. Although I was pretty sure I'd already received all the otherworldly lessons anybody could possibly need for one day, I agreed to go along.

Built by the ancient Sinagua Indians, the crumbling Honanki cliff dwellings stood eerie and majestic in the moonlight. As we picked our way respectfully around the perimeter of the ruins, first Fran and then Terri became overwhelmed by the grief and sadness they felt there. Tears rolled silently down their cheeks as they mourned the Native Americans who had long ago built these structures.

I watched them quietly, feeling the stagnant stuck-ness of the grief they'd connected with. I didn't know what to do or say to relieve it.

No resistance, said Spirit.

No resistance to what? I wondered. Suddenly I gasped, threw my head back, and as I did I felt some kind of communication connection shoot through me from Heaven to Earth or vice versa.

"They don't need your tears," I informed the two women gently, the words not my own. "They have plenty of tears already. Your tears keep them stuck in their grief. What they need from you is the courage and strength to move beyond your own raw emotion. They need you to bring them joy instead. Only your joy can heal them truly."

Fran and Terri gulped and nodded, brushing away the tears.

Although I had dutifully passed along the message, I remained largely unmoved by the Native Americans' plight. No surprise there; like me, they were guilty humans, not innocent animals. Yet I saw the unmistakable correlation to my own animal guilt. Like these two women with their Sinagua connection, I now understood my solidarity with the animals' suffering was doing the victims no good at all. I wasn't sure what it meant, yet I knew I too was being asked to step up and let go of my unholy connection to the brutality. It was time for acceptance and transcendence. And, God help me, for forgiveness. ❖

CHAPTER EIGHTEEN

IF THE WORLD ISN'T REAL,
DO I STILL HAVE TO RECYCLE?

August 20, 2006

*O*k, let's say for the sake of argument that I buy the logic of A Course in Miracles. That our true state is limitless immortal spirit, which has no measurable characteristics of any kind. That the world as we know it isn't really real; that if something has weight and mass and vibrational energy and solidity, that's automatic proof that it's imaginary, precisely because it is measurable and solid.

The whole argument seems wildly counterintuitive (especially after stubbing one's toe on the bed frame in the middle of the night) and more to the point, it brings up some troubling questions about proper behavior here in the 3-D dream world.

It's a slippery slope, in other words, deciding where personal responsibility begins and ends when you've recently learned the world's all fake and you made the whole thing up. Saving the planet seems like a pretty pointless exercise if there's really no planet to be saved. And what about lending a hand to those in need? Is charitable behavior still an appropriate response to the world's imaginary ills?

I put the question to Spirit. "If helping outwardly is more useless than rearranging the *Titanic's* deck chairs—since neither the chairs nor the iceberg exist in the first place—does it even matter how I treat the homeless guy on the bus bench?" I asked.

Yes, dear one, it matters because you and the homeless guy are exactly the same thing, and you can't know Heaven without him.

"Yeah, so You've said. Yet according to You, his suffering isn't real and I'm not perceiving him as he truly is. He looks hot and thirsty to me, but am I just reinforcing his belief in illusion (and my own) by trying to alleviate what isn't really there?"

It's true that his discomfort is an illusion, as is any worldly remedy you may offer him. The illusory actions you choose to take within this dream world have no real effect on anything. Give him a dollar and a bottle of water if you want to, as you did the other day. There's nothing wrong with compassionate action.

Just remember silently as you do so that his perceived suffering isn't real. In truth he is safe and infinitely abundant. He is perfect, immortal spirit, holy and innocent and forever untouched by poverty, heat or thirst.

By sharing some small recollection of this truth between your minds, you and the homeless guy will both return to the memory and the very real experience of Heaven's limitless joy that much sooner. And what could be a more compassionate action than that? ❖

Opportunities for forgiveness lessons present themselves everywhere we go. I discovered those lessons are not always hard work; now and then they can turn out to be a real treat.

HOTEL FORGIVENESS

The time had finally arrived for our client's big Vegas tradeshow. We'd spent the past year diligently implementing the strategies that had emerged from that marathon brainstorming session in Sedona the previous July, and now, in mid-September of 2006, we were anxious to see the results of our efforts. Leaving home hours before dawn on the first day of the show, Kurt and I drove to Las Vegas under starry skies that gradually brightened into hot desert sunshine as the morning wore on. Sticky and exhausted, we found ourselves at long last in the lobby of the Mandalay Bay Hotel. As I stood with our luggage in the long check-in line I amused myself by looking around listlessly at all the other people, reminding myself vaguely that each and every one of them was holy and innocent, and not at all the dreadfully guilty bastards they appeared to be.

Suddenly Spirit spoke within my frazzled mind: *There's no such thing as unforgivable sin.*

I was startled to realize I already knew it was true. The *Course* had been talking about this very subject lately, and in wonderment I recalled the gist of its teaching: That all "sins," from the biggest to the smallest, were equally imaginary; that Heaven judged no one; that you and I, the only ones actually doing the judging, were wasting our time and effort on fantasy damnation where none was required. It wasn't our job to keep any special grudge alive, stronger than all the rest, because no sin was ever held apart in any special category requiring our eternal condemnation.

A giant weight seemed to lift off me, and I felt momentarily disoriented by my own lightness. I looked around, blinking at the joy sparkles that now danced everywhere in my vision. We were at the front of the line now. I gazed serenely at the hotel clerk, who smiled radiantly back.

"You've been upgraded to a suite at THE Hotel," she said. "Enjoy your stay."

THE Hotel, despite its pretentiously goofy name, is by any standards a swell place to stay. Mandalay Bay's sleek, swanky answer to a chic New York boutique hotel, every room at THE Hotel is a suite, every suite a whole lot bigger than my first half dozen apartments. As I drew back the living room curtains and gazed out the floor-to-ceiling plate glass at our spectacular high-rise view of the strip, the joy sparkles made everything that much more glorious.

This free hotel room is merely a symbol of the joy, the freedom, the abundance that's really mine, I told myself blissfully. *This hotel room is not real, this body is not real, this world is not real. Only eternal love is real.*

I smiled, Buddha-like, at my reflection in the glass. ❖

And then there are the forgiveness lessons that aren't so much of a treat. The ones that require, well, forgiveness.

HOTEL FORGIVENESS, PART II

A few weeks later. Funny how it goes when the shoe is on the other foot.

The previous month's tradeshow success had confirmed that our turnaround efforts were paying off. Attendance was up; the show floor looked and felt far more vibrantly alive than it had the year before.

Kurt and I decided to celebrate with a little post-show getaway to Santa Fe, a town we both love. I searched carefully for a hotel online, finding it strangely difficult to get a room at any of the familiar places we knew.*

After hours of research I chose a small hotel complex that offered charming little casitas, situated just a couple of blocks off the main plaza. From the photos and the TripAdvisor reviews, it seemed ideal.

It was not ideal. Our casita turned out to be a rundown, decomposing, putrefied horror, yet there was nobody to complain to and nothing to be done about it; the place was staffed by indifferent nineteen-year-olds and all rooms were non-refundable, paid in advance. And the town was booked solid for the festival. *Oh, your room smells like a sewage leak? You're welcome to go look for another.*

On a 3-D world level, we dealt with the situation by never going home to our room. Out the door every morning at first light, we'd return as late as possible in the evening, too exhausted to stay away another minute. And Kurt, never a crunchy-granola type of guy, surprised me by buying a sage stick and matches on our first foray into town. He didn't like that casita's vibe any better than he liked its smell, and so made a point of performing a thorough smudging

---

* We found out later that our trip coincided with the annual Albuquerque Hot Air Balloon Festival; balloonists in the know apparently prefer to stay in Santa Fe and drive the sixty miles in butt-freezing pre-dawn cold back to Albuquerque each morning for the races. Who knew.

every night to cleanse both its energy and its sewage stink before hopping reluctantly into the awful bed.

On *A Course in Miracles* level, I knew what I had to do: Each day from morning 'til night, I offered forgiveness exercises to the absentee owners, the minimum-wage employees, the intentionally misleading website and that stanky little casita itself, marinating the whole place in holy innocence until I felt temporarily better about it. Or until the margaritas kicked in, whichever came first.

We were four days into the trip, having a drink in an upstairs patio bar overlooking the plaza, when I suddenly remembered my blissed-out realization in front of the plate glass window in Vegas: *This hotel room is not real, this body is not real, this world is not real. Only eternal love is real.* I snorted with laughter, sending my drink down the wrong pipe, the tequila blazing a fiery trail.

Coughing fits aside, that beautiful realization was every bit as true now as it had been back then. Funny how it ain't quite so easy once a little sewage gets flowing. ❖

WHAT'S THE FREQUENCY, KENNETH?

Every now and then I get one of those difficult, disconnected days when the extraordinary events of the past few years seem like nothing more than pointless episodes from somebody else's fever dream. And on days like that, it's hard to believe those events have anything at all to do with me.

November 7, 2006

I feel lost and completely off the track today. I have no idea what I'm doing or where I'm supposed to be going. Over the weekend I thought I knew exactly where I was headed. So in tune, so connected with Spirit. So sure I'd be enlightened by next Thursday. Yet today I can barely remember what any of that confidence and exuberance felt like.

Sometimes I half wonder if I'm making it up, this "I hear a Voice" thing. Or if I really do hear what I think I hear— well, maybe it just means I'm an incredibly well-adjusted schizophrenic, so good at functioning in society that I haven't realized I'm crazy yet.*

I mean, other than that whole "My dog tells me to kill people" business, is there really that much difference between somebody like Son of Sam and me? I'm sure that guy would swear his voices were totally real, too.

Nah. Chances are pretty good that I'm not nuts or pretending.

I know my Voice is real because it brings along with it the undeniable physical sensation of peace, and a kind of all-encompassing gentleness I've never experienced anywhere else on Earth. And which I'm totally incapable of conjuring on my own.

When push comes to shove, I guess it's that loving release from pain, that sense of perfect anxiety-free safety it brings that convinces me it's the real deal. Even on dark and foggy days like today. ❖

---

* Isn't that supposed to be one of the signs? That you don't realize you're crazy?

TIME OUT

You'd think after all these years I would've been more able to suppress the quirky time-bending antics of the universe, much as I used to do with the supernatural stuff. Issues with time had been dogging me since childhood, and although I'd long since mastered the art of showing up promptly for appointments, I never did manage to make the clock behave the way I knew it was supposed to when no one else was looking.

November 19, 2006

Time slipped this morning, as it sometimes still does, but this time unfortunately not in my favor. There's nothing nicer than lying in bed for an extra hour while the clock says only four minutes have passed, yet this morning it was the opposite experience.

Today I was intending to meditate for a bit and then study the Course *for the rest of the hour, so when I opened my eyes after only two or three minutes I was shocked to discover that the whole hour was gone. It hadn't been a particularly deep or tuned-in meditation; I know I didn't even come close to experiencing the no-time state of awareness where it all seems to pass by in a single moment. And I certainly didn't drop off to sleep. No, the damned clock was just doing its slip 'n slidey thing again, and this time my early morning peace and quiet got swallowed up in the process.*

I hate when that happens. ❖

CHAPTER NINETEEN

CORPORATE RETREAT

Kurt and I were back in Sedona, this time because Fran had asked me to help her put on an InnerVision corporate retreat. Twenty people would soon be taking over the inn to soak up a few days of luxury bonding and paradigm shifting, along with a pinch of that certain spiritual *je ne sais quoi* that only Fran can provide.

I was nervous about it for a number of reasons. These people were from an entertainment industry company, for starters; I'd done enough work for the movie studios over the course of my career to know they're not exactly a hotbed of harmonious interpersonal relationships. Yet in the case of this Sedona retreat, I wasn't worried about backstabbing politics or high-maintenance personalities. My fears were fixed mainly on my own complete lack of legitimacy in the role of assistant spiritual facilitator. I felt sure this young and trendy group would spot me as a fraud immediately. Or worse: A fraud that wasn't pretty enough.

On a different yet somehow related tangent, I was also worried because Fran had asked me to drive one of the three big off-road tour jeeps each time we were to caravan out into the land. And that was just not my thing. It's not that I was unwilling; it was simply that I'd spent a lifetime denying that I live in a body (or at least *this* body), and as a result I lacked confidence or mastery when it came to propelling said uncoordinated body through space. Even walking sometimes seemed like an alien and hazardous proposition.

For the same reason, I avoided operating machinery. Especially a machine like this one: A big, loose, rattling heap with a mind of its own, made for bouncing over rutted dirt roads at top speed as it carried its payload of passengers up and down the mountainsides. The thought made me sick with dread. Hell, I didn't even learn to drive a car until I was twenty-three, and only then because my job demanded it.

If only I could manage to get myself enlightened before this retreat takes place, that would solve everything, I daydreamed wistfully. *No spiritual credibility issues, no body-self-hatred, no equipment phobias. It'd kill all birds with one holy stone.*

Yeah, best of luck with that. So my only other option was to dig deep with prayer and forgiveness exercises, over and over until my fears and judgments were gradually replaced by a genuine glimmer of compassion for this group of people I hadn't even met yet.

December 13, 2006
First day in Sedona: I made myself useful. Good thing I'm an organizer by nature, a calm eye to the hurricane that is Fran. Together we took care of all the last-minute details, running errands, stuffing backpacks, working our way down the "to do" list until late into the night.

Fran seems greatly reassured by my participation in this event. I hope to hell I don't let her down.

The following day, a Sunday, Fran took off early with the tour bus to meet the group at the airport in Phoenix. I stayed at the inn to set up a casual late dinner that would be ready for them when they arrived. It was hard yet enjoyable work, getting everything prepped and ready for the tired and hungry members of the group as they straggled in off the bus.

And what a lovely group it was. The company's owner, a generous and impulsive man, had decided to bring his entire organization, from the gray-haired senior executives to the young interns. Far from being the jaded and cynical fashionistas of my fears, many of these charming kids had never before visited a luxury hotel and were shyly starry-eyed at the prospect.

I spent most of that night in meditation and prayer: *Let me rise to the occasion and support this group in whatever way is needed, that they might have the experience they're meant to have here. Let my own fears and insecurities never get in the way of their experience or my own.*

I awoke early the next morning, and suited up in cold weather gear. The group gathered after breakfast in our respective vehicles, Fran in the lead, my jeep in the middle and a third driver bringing up the rear. Off we roared up Schnebly Hill.

To my utter astonishment, I found the unpredictable bucking, leaping and clattering of the jeep as we flew up the bumpy dirt road to be...*fun.* My passengers shrieked with delight, and occasionally alarm, as they bounced around like so many rag dolls. The sharp, cold air felt exhilarating as I chased after Fran's jeep that was fast disappearing in a cloud of red dust up the road ahead of me.

I knew intellectually I'd always been terrified of exactly this sort of precarious driving situation, yet for the life of me couldn't remember why. It was an extraordinary feeling, to suddenly find a debilitating lifelong phobia simply *gone.*

Halfway up Schnebly Hill, we stopped the jeeps. The group, having had a hand in marketing the recent opening weekend of *Apocalypto*, was required to participate in a rain-or-shine Monday morning conference call with Mel Gibson and the studio. The executives all clustered around the speakerphone to dissect and analyze the box office numbers. The rest of us leaned quietly against our jeeps, enjoying the serenity of the wide-open sky and spectacular rock formations surrounding us on all sides.

Mel came on the line to complain about *Apocalypto's* unfair reviews; the thin, scratchy voices droning on the other end of the speakerphone sounded strange and incongruous in this majestic setting. A few of the younger employees peeled off for a short hike, cameras in hand. I needed to pee, and hadn't yet decided what to do about it: Wait a few hours until we hit civilization, or play Nature Girl right now? As the minutes dragged by and the conference call showed no sign of ending, I took Fran aside to ask her advice. She pointed across the road to a dry creek bed.

"Follow that creek bed until you're safely out of sight," she whispered, handing me a tiny plastic capsule containing some sort of baby wipe. "Bring the trash back out with you."

I did as she instructed, walking a few hundred yards to get away from the group. Just before reaching an appropriately secluded spot, I stepped unexpectedly in a hole and wrenched my ankle.

"Oh bloody hell," I gasped out loud, seeing stars. Skip-hobbling the final few yards, I moved to hide myself behind a big boulder. *Great*, I thought. *How am I going to drive a jeep and hike for two days on a sprained ankle?*

Yet I felt strangely at peace about the whole thing, and noticed that only a few moments after that first blinding stab, I was feeling no residual pain. That seemed odd. I zipped up and stood, rotating the offending ankle experimentally: Nothing. No discomfort, no swelling, no weakness. Full range of motion. It felt no different, in fact, from the other ankle. I hiked back up toward the jeeps, lost in thought. It hadn't even occurred to me to put my healing intention on that ankle, yet somehow *it had automatically healed all by itself.* That would make two spontaneous healings (one emotional, one physical) within the last hour. In the middle of this corporate retreat, I seemed to be having my own private InnerVision journey. It was shaping up to be an interesting couple of days.

When I reached the jeeps, I found the group gathered in the same position with Mel still yakking about reviews on the speakerphone; it was like I'd never left. Half an hour later we resumed our expedition to the top of Schnebly Hill, the place I'd had my bird of prey experience the previous August. As everyone piled out of the jeeps to snap scenic photos of each other, I moved toward the rim to admire the view. I stopped ten or fifteen feet short of the cliff's edge, mindful of the strong, intermittent winds that were pushing in the direction of the canyon.

Trust more. Come closer to the edge, said Spirit.

I took five or six hesitant steps, and then stopped; this was as far as I wanted to go. The wind drove at my back, urging me forward to the edge of the precipice.

You cannot fall. I have you.

"Oh, sure, my eternal Self can't fall, but this mortal body can definitely crash down into the canyon."

You cannot fall, Spirit repeated patiently. *I have you.*

I considered for a moment, risk-averse as ever. Reluctantly I picked my way out to the edge, the wind gusting fitfully at my back. As I reached the cliff's edge and closed my eyes, the wind abruptly shifted. Instead of pushing me forcefully toward the canyon, a gentle breeze now played lightly against my face.

I guess I should have known Spirit would never ask me to do anything truly harmful, I realized sheepishly.

And when will you put your trust in Me?

"I'm working on it. I swear."

December 15, 2006

I'm so pleased for Fran. This retreat has been working out just the way we hoped it would. Those who came for employee bonding in a nice setting have been getting what they came for; those who hoped to identify a more spiritually nourishing way of doing business are finding that as well. And although I had my doubts it could happen in a corporate setting, the ones who have felt called to experience Fran's unique gifts are managing to each have an individual InnerVision journey within the larger format of the group retreat.

On the final hiking day, a large group set out to scale Bear Mountain, one of Fran's favorite peaks. I'm not a big elevation climber; halfway up the hill I'd had enough. I wanted to rest. Besides, there'd been precious little opportunity for quiet reflection in the last couple of days, and this seemed like the perfect chance to steal a little quality meditation time.

I sat down on a wide rock ledge overlooking the flatlands below. An unseasonable December bee kept me company as it buzzed around and around a small patch of green scrub. I closed my eyes, anticipating a delicious meditation session.

But no. My knee itched. My eye twitched. My butt quickly got sore on that hard rock. I shifted positions and tried again. The bee buzzed. My nose was cold. The wind whistled in my ears. Finally I began to slip into a meditative state, yet as I did it seemed as if I were being sucked right off the ledge, pitching forward headfirst off the mountain. I tried again—and again felt myself being dragged forward into space. I opened my eyes each time to check whether I was in danger of falling, and there I was, still seated safely on that big wide ledge.

It reminded me of the discomfort I'd felt at the Shaman's Cave the previous August, when I kept jerking myself upright over and over again to counteract the sensation of falling out the hole sideways. What was going on here? I felt restless and sort of cranky now too, similar to my feelings at the Shaman's Cave just before agreeing to allow a major lesson to unfold.

Ah. Ok. This was finally starting to make some sense.

"All right," I said to Spirit, "whatever the lesson is, I'll stop resisting and allow it to come in now."

At that same moment, the first of the returning hikers called out to me as they made their way down the hill.

Oh well, I thought, disappointed. *I guess there'll be no lesson for me today after all.*

Back at the inn, I met up with Kurt. On his own each day while I worked with Fran's group, he'd been having a great time exploring the neighboring towns. The previous day he'd been poking around in nearby Jerome, a copper mining ghost town-turned-tourism Mecca, and wanted to show me a painting he'd seen in one of the curio shops there. I liked Jerome, and wasn't needed for the rest of the afternoon, so why not?

Once on the road, Kurt stopped to fill the gas tank. I was alone inside the car. I closed my eyes, and as I did so the wind whistled loudly in my ears. My eyes flew open. The interior of the car was silent, the windows rolled up.

That was weird, I thought, and closed them again. Again the wind whistled and moaned, as it had earlier on Bear Mountain. *Ok, this was not right.*

Open eyes—quiet car, Kurt visible through the window as he pumped gas. Closed eyes—the car's interior began to ooze, merging somehow with the big, flat rock I'd been sitting on earlier in the day. Open! I'd just keep my eyes wide open, that's all.

It worked for a few minutes, and then the weirdness began to overtake me whether my eyes were open or shut. By the time we reached Jerome and parked the car, I was simultaneously sitting on Bear Mountain *and* walking up the hill with Kurt to the row of shops, fighting down sick panic with a studied outward nonchalance.

We strolled around for what felt like a week, heading back toward the car as the December twilight fell. The dual realities hadn't abated, yet they hadn't gotten any worse, either. *Maybe I can keep a handle on this until it passes*, I reassured myself hopefully, *and everything will be ok.*

As he started the car, Kurt popped in a CD of the *Beatles' LOVE* soundtrack. Normally this choice of music would've delighted me, yet under the circumstances this kaleidoscopic mashup of Beatles tunes, familiar yet disorientingly new, became the final stitch pulled from my rapidly unraveling security blanket.

Now all space—and all time—gently slipped their moorings. I was simultaneously sitting in the darkened passenger seat of Kurt's car; fidgeting on sunlit Bear Mountain; and lounging in my 1974 bedroom, of all places, wearing out the grooves on *Sergeant Pepper* and the *White Album*. Each of these "realities" seemed distinct and completely authentic, yet was separated from the others only by a clear, oozy Jell-O wall of perception. I inhabited all three, and it was way more than I could wrap my mind around. The ride back to Sedona was one long, silent scream.

Back in familiar surroundings, the terror slowly faded. I even enjoyed having dinner with the group, our last one together.

Later that night, safely in bed, I picked up the conversation again. "What was that all about?"

It was the lesson you requested on Bear Mountain, of course.
"Which is?"

The lesson is that time and space are illusion. You made them up, and they seem very real to you. Yet they exist only in your perception, not in reality.

In truth, "Always" is the only time, and "Everywhere" the only place. In truth, you, yourself occupy Everywhere and Always. Put aside your faulty perception and trust in Me to show you the truth as it really is.

"You're asking me to let go of my lifeline, and I just can't."

What you perceive as a lifeline is really the chain that keeps you shackled. Let it go, My love, and put your trust in Me instead.

Remember, you cannot fall. I have you. ❖

CHAPTER TWENTY

SOMEWHERE IN THE SEQUOIAS

I like to get in a good solid hour of meditation every morning along with my workbook lesson, and on vacation that doesn't ever happen. So on the first beautiful snowy day of our weekend getaway to the Sequoias I got up early, read quickly through the *Course's* workbook lesson and then took my act on the road. The gist of this particular day's lesson: I judge everything the way I want it to be.

We'd covered that concept before, yet until then I'd always misunderstood it as "I choose to engage in wishful thinking." As in: *I judge all things to be made of lollipops and moonbeams, because that's how I'd prefer to see them. I will ignore the world's ugly reality and pretend that everything is swell on Earth as it is in Heaven.* Although I was beginning to suspect that my bleak worldview might not be entirely accurate, still it seemed foolish to willingly lay aside all judgment and condemnation—my protection, my armor—in favor of potentially delusional rose-colored glasses.

Yet I decided this time I wouldn't jump to my usual dark conclusions. I let the lesson's real meaning sink in: *I have the power to judge everything the way I want it to be, because this world is made of nothing at all; it's an empty, neutral series of projected images with no inherent qualities of its own. I'm the one who unconsciously fills it up* with my beliefs about what's good and bad. I can choose to keep filling it with fear, hatred and guilt, or I can choose something else altogether.

At this point, Spirit offered an idea: *As a way of practicing today's workbook lesson, why not stay neutral and let Me interpret everything you see? You can perceive the world and everything in it as pure divine love.*

"What? No way."

Just for today. It'll be fun.

"Fun?" It didn't sound like fun. It sounded dangerous. And more than a little irritating.

Sure. Perfect love, perfect safety, divine gentleness—it's great fun. You'll see.

Kurt and I were in the forest by now, hiking the glistening, snow-covered trails as the majestic Sequoias towered silently all around us. It was a magnificent setting, yet as always I felt ill at ease in the natural world.

"I don't dare see the world as being full of gentleness and love. Nature is cruel and harsh, it's all about death and survival. I could get eaten by bears."

Says you. Consider for a moment that you are completely wrong about everything. Every tree, every bird, every scrap of moss, even every rock is a wholly neutral symbol you made for the purpose of projecting your own fear and guilt onto it. Of themselves, they are nothing. Just as "you" are nothing and "your husband" is nothing. You and your husband are not these bodies you seem to inhabit. In truth you are pure love; you are perfect, radiant light.

The unseen bears you're so afraid of right now are part of that same divine light. I assure you, you are completely safe out here in the wilderness. Why not forgive it? Why not see it as the gentle, holy truth it really is?

"I can't bring myself to do that. But thanks for explaining. It helps to know I'm protected."

When I promise you safety, you imagine that Spirit—a

separate entity—is protecting you from that slippery ice, those hungry bears. You're quite wrong. No separate entity exists to intercede on your behalf, and besides, there's no need to protect you from a dream. The truth (or as much of the truth as you can grasp right now) is that the bears and the ice are one with your holy Self. In perfect gentleness they support you and keep you safe within this dream world just as the cactus and coyotes functioned to keep you safe during your pitch-black Sedona hike. Your one Self, which includes all bears, coyotes, and prickly desert plants, supports you in your lesson plan as it lovingly awaits your awakening.

This was a lot to take in. *Ice is part of my one Self? And cactus supports my spiritual path?* Surely I'd misunderstood. We'd been hiking for hours by now; I was growing tired and my heel was starting to ache. I really was trying to do as I'd been asked, yet still couldn't help being a little unconvinced about letting Spirit take over to reinterpret the world for me.

You feel fatigue yet it doesn't have to be so. Your body is nothing. Why not drain it of all meaning, all purpose, all pain, guilt and fear? Drain it of all the weakness, strength, beauty and ugliness you think it holds. Empty it of all pleasure, all anxiety, all weariness and shortness of breath. By agreeing to do this you could realize the truth about your body right now, and let me carry you instead.

"I'm still new at this. Is that something I'm even capable of?"

It is. It's something everyone is capable of. I speak to you of Heaven's truth, dear one, and this information is not meant for you alone. What is true for one is invariably true for all. Everyone can realize the truth at any moment. All it takes is willingness.

Try setting aside all your beliefs about bodies right now. See Kurt hiking the trail up ahead of you? You could take this opportunity to perceive him as perfect divine light and love. Why not leave your body awareness and join together with him and with Me as one immortal Holy Spirit? Just for a little while?

The idea startled me, and I didn't like the sound of it.

"Because he doesn't deserve it."

Oh, you're wrong. Divine love is what he is.

"Well then, because *I* don't deserve it."

Again, quite wrong. Divine love is what you are.

"Whatever. I can't make myself let go of all meaning from my body. Even if I wanted to."

Oh, I see. Not done enjoying the pain and tiredness, yet?

"No. I mean, yes! I'd love to have You carry me. I just can't seem to figure out how to make it happen."

I'm carrying you now, dear one; I have been from the start. Yet as you know, you'll be unable to feel the limitless love and strength that I Am, until you completely release the dream of fear. And to do that, you'll have to set aside your belief in separate bodies and be willing to recognize the oneness of all things.

"Yes. I know. And I want to, I really do. But ego's got a grip on me and it won't let go."

Ah, My darling child. You're so wrong. Ego has no grip on you. It's you who grip the ego, unwilling to leave its dark illusions behind even for a moment.

I considered these words carefully and at this point I did try to drain my body of meaning, without much luck. So instead I focused my belief on seeing Kurt, the other hikers, the trees and rocks, birds and sky as a single column of holy, gentle light. And I seemed to feel the faintest glimmer of safety, support and quiet perfection in response. But my heel still really hurt.

Back at the lodge I made a long-awaited beeline for the ladies room. As I headed into the stall, Spirit spoke once more: *Every moment of every day, the truth awaits your memory. Why not make it today?*

"You're asking me to give up everything I know, yet why should

I listen to You? You're just an imaginary Voice in my head." Kidding. Sort of.

Oh, My love, think again. I'm the only truth you've ever known.

"What does that mean? What are you exactly?" It had never before occurred to me to ask.

I Am the memory of God in you. ❖

SEQUOIAS, PART II

It snowed that night and all the next day, a Sunday. Several travelers were stranded without chains, unable to head down the mountain. The drifts lay a foot high in places, a slick layer of ice coating the road underneath. Kurt and I weren't planning to leave for home until the following morning, so we were free to enjoy a cozy day snowbound at the lodge.

Theoretically, anyway. Kurt is never one to stay cooped up for long; he had the trail maps out as he sipped his morning coffee. After breakfast we drove carefully through steady snowfall to the Giant Forest and hiked around in perfect quiet, spending quality time alone with the monumental trees. It was lovely yet exhausting. In an attempt to keep feet and ankles dry, I lifted each leg high above the snow like a cantering pony, which made our twenty-minute hike feel more like an hour on the elliptical trainer.

We returned to the lodge to relax in front of the fire, yet after an hour or two of reading and sipping hot chocolate, Kurt was itching to get outside again. Back on the road, we made it as far as the Lodgepole area; the sky had turned a deep, forbidding gray, the snow now falling with much greater force. We left the car in what we had reason to believe was the parking lot, and soon found ourselves trudging through alternating patches of deep slush and deeper snow, the stinging sideways flakes pelting our faces.

Kurt was delighted. As a California boy, he'd never seen this much snow before. But I had. Snow held no romance for me, no happy reminders of ski holidays and hot drinks around the fireplace.

For me, childhood snow memories were all about waiting in blizzards for the bus that never came; about trudging home from school in leaky Wellies that bathed my feet in icy slush. I remembered my mother carefully peeling the frozen socks away from discolored, frostbitten feet and gently massaging the toes with her hands. The exquisite daggers of pain as feeling was slowly restored, mingled with uncomfortable awe as I watched while my mother displayed the only physical tenderness she'd ever shown me.

Snow—beyond the picture-perfect Christmas card variety, anyway—held a mixed bag of difficult emotions. As I trudged behind Kurt in ankle-deep slush, I relived the complicated discomfort of those long-ago childhood winters.

Snow doesn't have to hold the meaning you assign to it. You could give all past snow to Me and see it anew, each peaceful flake bathed in holy light. Yet to do so, you must be willing to leave your past "snow baggage" behind forever.

Standing on a pristine riverbank in drifts up to my knees, I gazed at the rushing black water as needle-sharp pinpricks of snow collected on my face. I didn't want to give up those painful memories, and felt a little bit outraged at the very suggestion. They were *mine*. Those memories were precious and had to be hoarded. Kept safely hidden, protected from theft. And then I realized how dumb that was.

"Why would I feel that way? What could possibly be desirable about hanging onto smelly old childhood baggage?"

Because your ego mind values it dearly, of course. Not only are the memories themselves of no value, the events they preserve never really took place. The school bus, your frostbitten toes— none of it ever truly existed. Only the pure and unchanging love of God exists. Decide now that you'd rather see the truth of Heaven reflected everywhere, than the terrible dream of vengeance that you made.

For the first time then I felt the small stirring of an honest desire to believe in the holy truth instead of my own bitter and twisted interpretation. Not that I was yet capable of any such thing. Yet this was the first inkling of willingness. The first dawning of the only sane conclusion anyone could ever hope to reach: Who in their right mind *wouldn't* want to trade in their worthless imaginary baggage for the perfect, safe, loving, peaceful, joyous, eternal truth? ❖

CHAPTER TWENTY-ONE

BOB SPEAKS

On January 11, 2007 at 4:49pm Fran wrote:
To: Carrie
Subject: Visit

Soon it'll be time for me to come and
visit you again at your place, if that
works for your schedule? I've been having
visions about you lately, much stronger and
more intense than any visions I've ever
experienced before.

Carrie wrote:
Oh yeah? Like what kind of visions?

Fran wrote:
It's hard to put into human language. This
is the best way I can describe the feeling:
You know those Indiana Jones type movies,
the ones where there's a powerful object

that's been broken in half, and two people
at opposite ends of the world each have a
half? And when the two halves are brought
together a really amazing thing happens?

That's the feeling I have. Like you and
I each have half of whatever it is, and
when we bring the two things together in
one place something big will be set in
motion.

Carrie wrote:
Wow! That sounds so cool. How soon can you
get here?

Fran wrote:
Soon. When the time is right.

After more than two months of breathless waiting, the time was
finally right. Fran arrived on our doorstep on a Monday afternoon
in March, suitcase and laptop in hand. It was good to see her.

I'm not here, Bob informed her as she crossed the threshold into
the house, and repeated it again as she put away her toiletries in the
guest bath: *I'm not here*. She wasn't sure what he meant by that, and
resolved to wait for an explanation.

She didn't have to wait long.

"So," Kurt said to her over dinner, "I'm sure Carrie told you our
little Bob died a couple of weeks ago."

"No!" she said, turning to me in shock. "She didn't!"

I looked down at my plate. "No, I didn't tell you. I didn't tell
anybody."

I hadn't felt like talking about it. I didn't want anyone to offer the
typical family pet condolences; didn't want to be asked if we planned
to get another kitten to take his place. As if anything ever could.

"Yes," Fran protested, "But why didn't you tell *me*? I knew the truth of your relationship. I knew what he meant to you."

I shrugged and shook my head. "I don't know why. I just didn't want to tell."

He had died on a Monday morning at the end of February. I heard a small commotion during my morning meditation, and didn't realize what had happened until I came upon him lying comfortably in the middle of the hallway about twenty minutes later.

That's odd, I thought as I approached to get a closer look, *This isn't one of his usual sleeping spots.* I guess I knew before I knew; before I saw his beautiful calm face, golden eyes opened wide and looking only slightly startled.

The folks at his surgical hospital were very sweet, giving me a box of Kleenex to take home in exchange for Bob's limp and unfamiliar little body. Kurt and I spent much of that day crying in each other's arms. Bob had been with us almost as long as we'd been together ourselves; it was hard to imagine our lives without him.

I was deeply grateful that Bob had engineered his passing to be as gentle and non-guilt-inducing as possible. On the 3-D level of form, he'd waited until we were all safely at home together, until I could be near enough to find him right away, yet not so near as to witness the seizure itself. There was no emergency trip to the vet, no drawn-out illness, no terrible decision to have him put down.

On a spiritual level, I knew he'd hung on until I was strong enough—just barely—to apply the *Course's* lessons on death and illusion. It was a hard and bitter thing at first, to tell myself that Bob had never been a body, that death doesn't exist; that Bob was, is and always will be perfect immortal spirit, joined with me in eternal oneness.

There was no solace that first terrible day. Then, curiously, by the middle of Day Two the pain had been gently replaced by a sad sort of peaceful resignation, a surrendered finality: *So be it.* I blessed my darling Bob once again for waiting—probably long past the time his frail little body would have preferred to go—until I was ready to find the lesson in his passing instead of getting hopelessly stuck in the grief. ❖

CARPOOLING

March 20, 2007

Whenever Fran comes to visit I always have the most vivid dreams. I had this really powerful one last night, and it's still on my mind:

I was riding with Fran in her car. We'd been traveling a very long time together down a midnight-dark rural road. As I looked out the window at the starry night sky I felt safe in the knowledge that she understood where we were going, even if I did not... Then my vision began to slowly clear until I dimly recognized, with mounting horror, that I was seeing hands—MY hands— on the steering wheel in front of me; that I was driving the car. That I had, without realizing it, been the one driving all along. In stunned disbelief I turned my head to the right, and saw Fran smiling at me peacefully from the passenger seat.

Holy crap. The car careened out of control on the darkened road, my toes too far away to reach the brakes. I woke up sweating, just before crashing us into a house at the top of the hill.

Fran laughed when I told her about it at breakfast. "That's so true! From the first time we met you've assumed it was me in the driver's seat, yet I could've told you it's always been the other way around." She studied me pensively for a moment.

"We've known each other before, you know," she continued at last. "You and I once belonged to a secret order of very powerful women..."

As she spoke I got a dim sensory flash of torch-lit rooms and roughhewn walls; of big, heavy crosses worn reverently around the neck.

"...The group was called Lamb of God. And you were its leader." She paused to let her words sink in. "Carrie, you *always* drive the car." ❖

THE INTERRUPTION

After cleaning up the dinner dishes the following evening, Fran and I sat talking in the kitchen awhile. I was whining, as I confess I'd been doing a lot lately, about how impatient I was for enlightenment. Not even the full Christ-y-ness that the *Course* promised. Who knew how long that'd take. I figured I could be happy for starters with just the partial enlightenment that comes from experiencing the oneness of all things. The kind where you still have to come back for one more lifetime to tie up the loose ends later on.

"It's so hard not knowing if it's coming in twenty years or twenty lifetimes," I lamented. "I'm trying to teach myself to be patient, to be ok with not knowing, to accept that I'll probably have to keep coming back again and again. The coming back part isn't so bad, I guess; what I really dread are the twenty or thirty years of groping around in the dark before stumbling onto a spiritual path. I finally found a beautiful two-way relationship with Spirit in this lifetime, and it doesn't seem fair to have to lose it again. The thought of starting all over from scratch, of going through those lonely decades of terrible messed-up blindness one more—"

"You're not coming back."

"What?" *That was awfully rude*, I thought, a little annoyed at the interruption. *I was just getting warmed up.*

"You're not coming back," Fran repeated patiently. "This is your last lifetime."

My last lifetime. Once again Fran had seemed to describe a completely unknown future version of me, somebody actually capable of attaining the state of Christ. As much as I wanted to believe in the idea, it just didn't seem plausible, knowing all I knew about myself. So I pretended the conversation never happened and threw myself into helping Fran instead, spending most of the following day working on her various projects.

Three different film and TV companies had been after her lately to collaborate on documentary projects. None of the proposals were quite right for her, yet it was clear that the universe was nudging persistently, letting her know it was time to step out on a larger stage.

I marveled at her courage. You couldn't pay me to go public with this "hearing voices" stuff, and yet there she was, getting ready to take her InnerVision thing and put it out there on the big screen for all the world to see.

"That's amazing," I said. "I'd be way too chicken to step out publicly if I were in your shoes. I've always hated the idea of being seen, of living a high-profile life where total strangers know my business. Thank goodness *I* won't have to step into the spotlight until after I'm already enlightened, because I'm sure by then I won't care who knows my personal stuff."

"What do you mean, you won't have to do it until *after* you're enlightened?" she asked in amusement, one eyebrow skyrocketing.

"Oh! Well, Spirit said 'When you're ready you'll write books,' so I figured 'When you're ready' means 'When you're enlightened.' Because after I'm enlightened I'll probably have something accurate and legitimate to say. And even if it turns out I don't have anything of my own to say, it'll still be ok because by then I'll be making hardly any mistakes in perception, so I can just be the secretary taking down the Holy Spirit's dictation—what's so funny? *Quit laughing at me!*"

"That ain't the way it works, girlfriend. You need to step forward *now*, and agree to write books exactly as you are. I hate to break it to you, you're in the same boat as I am."

Oh God not yet not yet not yet! She's wrong—that can't possibly be true. I looked around the room wildly, searching for an escape and seeing none.

It just can't.

Yet I knew damned well Fran was right; I'd felt the electro-jolt truth of the statement as she'd said it. But how could now be the time? And what the hell was I supposed to write? Let's face it. I was at best a so-so student of the Holy Spirit's teachings, kind of slow and only partially willing—and a walking bundle of fears and anxieties, to boot. How could somebody like that help even one other person find the way to happiness and peace?

I couldn't sit still. Stumbling out to the garage I hopped onto the treadmill, head down and staring sightlessly at my moving feet.

Agree to take this leap of faith and trust, dear one. As the process unfolds you'll understand what to write and how to write it.

"There's no way I'm ready. What if I misunderstand You and tell people the wrong things? I wouldn't even know the difference. No. I should wait and get enlightened first so I can be sure I'm passing Your messages along correctly…"

So what you're saying is: You can't write until you're enlightened, because if you're not enlightened, you can't hear Me clearly?

"Wait, what? No!"

Your enlightenment is not a prerequisite for this task. Will you trust in Me when I tell you that now really is the appropriate time for you to begin writing books? I would not lie to you, My love.

"I want to agree, really I do…"

But you won't agree yet.

"No, not yet. I just can't. But I will, I promise."

When?

"Soon."

I felt myself enveloped then in a gentle embrace that blurred away the edges of time and space. I relaxed for a moment in its quiet safety, even as my feet kept running.

The truth is, you've already agreed, My love. The books are already written—

I moved quickly, though not quickly enough, to slam the door on the frightening end of that sentence. Like a faraway sigh on the breeze I heard it: *And they've already helped more people than you can imagine.*

I stopped the treadmill in a daze. Suddenly I noticed what I'd been staring at blindly throughout the conversation. A stark white logo on the treadmill's black base, in huge extrabold letters it said: **TRUE**.

In the shower, the following morning:

"Ok. All right. I'll agree to write books *now*. Jeez. I'll need You to tell me exactly what to write, though. Nobody will buy me posing as the big spiritual know-it-all, offering shiny pearls of self-help to all the people of the world."

So don't be the big spiritual know-it-all. Be yourself, write about your own journey in your own words. And I'll do the rest.

Write about my own journey. So this wasn't supposed to be a spiritual self-help book after all. It would be an autobiography? A tell-all memoir?

Holy crap. Goodbye to life as a regular person; hello, woo-woo laughing-stock. Well, maybe it'd be ok. Maybe no one would ever read the damned thing. But that would defeat the purpose, wouldn't it?

Well, I'd just have to learn to live with public ridicule, then. This was going to take some work.

March 21, 2007

Well, it's been a pretty momentous visit so far. Hard to say if its revelations have been Indiana Jones-worthy, yet there's no denying it's been anything but dull.

Fran left yesterday to spend a few days with one of those documentary producers in Los Angeles. As great as it is to have her around, I'm enjoying the quiet while she's away. It gives me a chance to catch up on loose ends and let things settle back down to normal for a bit. ❖

Well, maybe "normal" was too strong a word for it.

GRILL GUY

Our old Weber grill had seen better days so I'd been meaning to shop for a new one before summer rolled around. Taking advantage of a free afternoon during Fran's absence, I found an awesome restaurant-quality grill on eBay—brand new, never used—the catch was we had to pick it up in the San Fernando Valley. No shipping or delivery. This would've been a deal breaker with my Mini or Kurt's little Audi, yet Fran was on her way back here after her L.A. visit, and she drives an SUV with a big, wide hatchback. She agreed to make a detour to pick it up.

From the start the seller seemed mistrustful and suspicious in the extreme. After careful negotiation we settled all the details, I paid for the grill and Fran set out to pick it up. Then a payment snafu caused the funds to be transferred from my checking account instead of my AmEx card as agreed upon.

Uh-oh, I thought, *I'd better let him know what happened right away, since he doesn't seem to like surprises.*

RRRING! Fran was on the phone. She'd arrived at the guy's house to find him in mid-meltdown: I was a *THIEF*, a *LIAR* and a *SCAM ARTIST!* He had half a mind to *CALL THE COPS!*

Kurt appeared just then in my office doorway.

"That grill guy just canceled your purchase and refunded the payment."

Yikes. I still wanted my beautiful grill, but did I want it this badly?

Kurt got him on the phone and straightened out the whole misunderstanding, then repurchased the grill according to the original agreement. The guy sheepishly apologized for jumping the gun, and set about helping Fran load the grill into her vehicle.

RRRING! This time it was Grill Guy. Turned out the thing was enormous, it wouldn't fit inside the hatchback even when partially disassembled. He must've been feeling guilty for his earlier behavior, because he surprised us all by offering to rent a trailer and drive the grill up the coast the following day.

I was glad the grill was coming, yet couldn't shake off the unexpected violence of the encounter. I made plans to be out when Grill Guy was scheduled to arrive the next day; I was having a hard time applying forgiveness lessons to him, and didn't want any further contact if I could help it.

Later that night, lying in bed I could feel a powerful lesson waiting in the pipeline, something I was supposed to learn about this guy. I knew it was time to stop resisting it.

"Ok, all right. Show me what this Grill Guy is really," I said to Spirit.

Suddenly I was transported.

It was night. I was standing high on a hill, gazing down into a valley obscured by dark, brooding clouds. I could hear the ominous sound of bombs going off in the distance and saw patches of cloud briefly lit from beneath by the explosions. I felt a sense of foreboding; it was obvious I had entered a war zone.

I seemed to glide down the hill and into the valley, and as I did so I saw to my surprise that there were no bombs. *The clouds themselves* were producing those harmless noises and flashes of light. Beneath the cloud cover, no violence was taking place.

And then I saw it. There, maybe fifty feet in front of me, a slender column of the sweetest, gentlest and most welcoming light imaginable, reaching up through the blackness toward Heaven. I found it irresistible; without conscious intention on my part I moved toward it and merged with it, not noticing until afterward that the whole valley and all its cloud cover had completely vanished, leaving only that perfect Heavenly light.

This is what the Grill Guy is really, said Spirit.

I wish I could find words to describe for you what it felt like to be in the presence of that magnificent light. No words come close to explaining its pristine qualities or how its holy presence made me feel. Let's just say it was really, really good. *Really* good.

Usually the feelings that accompany these visions fade away after a day or two, yet I can still recall the divine perfection and quiet safety of that light source even now, years later. I hope I always remember it. ❖

MORGAN

With Bob's passing it was as if little Morgan had simultaneously learned she was a princess *and* won the lottery. Having spent her entire life in the tyrant's shadow, she'd been banned from all the house's best places since kittenhood, and lived in fear of getting the snot beat out of her if Bob happened to spy me cuddling with her. I belonged to him, and there was to be no sharing. Ever.

Yes, Bob was king and Morgan learned that lesson early and well. As a result, she slunked through the house like a tiny furbearing ghost, allowing as little human contact as possible. It was just safer that way. Kurt and I often tried to extend kindnesses, yet it only made her nervous that Bob would find out. Sometimes toward the end of his life I'd catch her looking at him with an expression that plainly said, *Aren't you dead yet?*

And now it was slowly dawning on her: The whole house was hers. *We* were hers, to cuddle and kiss as much as she wanted. She'd been several pounds overweight for a long time, having stolen Bob's food at every opportunity; now the extra weight melted off as she ran joyously around her new domain.

As much as I missed Bob, I was really glad for her. It was a pleasure to watch her blossom into her new role. The first half of her life hadn't been easy; I resolved that she'd know what it was to be the cherished "only cat" for the second half.

It was Fran's final day here, filled with a hundred last-minute details. On her way out to the garage with a basket of laundry, she glimpsed little Morgan staring at her intently from the living room sofa, hazel eyes wide. This was highly unusual; in general, Morgan kept to herself and made as few communication overtures toward humans as possible.

"What, Morg?" Fran asked her aloud. "What is it, little Morg?"

A chill swept up Fran's spine as the odd choice of nicknames reverberated in her mind: Morg. *Morgue.*

The cat stared at her, wide-eyed. *I'll be leaving soon,* Morgan said. ❖

CHAPTER TWENTY-TWO

WEEPING PUSSY WILLOWS

On April 6, 2007 at 7:32pm Carrie wrote:
To: Fran
Subject: Déjà vu all over again

Tonight I looked out the garden window after dinner, and saw little Morgan lying peacefully on the ground, under a chair. It didn't seem right so I went out to look. She was lying on her side, eyes open. Still warm. Exactly the same way that I found Bob; she was dead two months to the day after his passing.

How can this be? It's all so strange and shocking. I thought she still had the whole second half of her life ahead of her. I thought I had time to make it all up to her, to try and make her happy and let her know how much she was loved.

Poor little one.

The next day passed in a painful blur. I was too sad and confused to make much sense of it. That night, lying in bed I couldn't help but uneasily wonder: *Did I cause this?*

I already suspected that I had somehow engineered Bob's 2005 surgical emergency, creating that terrible distraction in an attempt to put the Dinner Table Awakening permanently out of my mind. What if I had unwittingly done it again? What if Morgan had passed before her time because of the lessons I was now trying to teach myself about death and illusion? What if she knew I'd use her untimely death to learn lessons about deeper truths? If I wasn't so busy trying to transcend the cycle of life and death...might she have chosen to live a little longer?

Are you asking if she died for your sins? No, dear one. Believe Me, you are guilty of nothing.

Despite Spirit's assurance, I never did get any sleep that night. The following morning passed in a heavy daze. After lunch, Kurt and I decided a change of scenery might help, so we went to the mall and walked around aimlessly for an hour or two. On our return to the house afterward, we spied an enormous, oddly-shaped bundle of tree clippings lying on our front porch, wrapped neatly in brown paper and tied with twine. The thing had to be at least ten feet long and six feet around, stretching the entire length of the porch.

As we got closer, I could see the florist's card attached. Nine pussy willow stems, sent by Fran. Kurt and I laughed 'til we cried. Although we knew she imagined she was ordering nine individual stems, the florist had sent nine gargantuan branches sporting dozens of stems on each branch. A whole thicket of pussy willows, taller than our living room ceiling and wide enough around to poke your eye out.

On April 9, 2007 at 10:02am, Carrie wrote:
To: Fran
Subject: Pussy willows

Thank you so much, they're absolutely beautiful. Kurt is out at the nursery right now, buying a ceramic pot tall enough to put them in.

And thanks for your kind condolences. Somehow I wouldn't have expected Morgan's death to hit me as hard as it did. Everything remains terribly painful and strange; I'm getting weird trance-y death messages, and I don't know what any of it means. Tell me if you can shed any light on this:

At 1:11am Saturday night I woke up feeling clearer and much more at peace. So much so, that on Sunday morning I decided to keep my date with Kathy to go on a beach walk together at my favorite wilderness beach. It was cool and foggy-gray there; usually I love the beach when it's like that.

That beach experience turned out to be incredibly disturbing and surreal. Usually one or two dead things wash up on that particular beach yet that day we saw at least thirty dead seabirds along the shore, maybe more. Kathy counted fourteen pelicans alone.

Even beyond the high body count, everything seemed sort of wrong, and I was feeling very out-of-body and removed from it. The beach maintenance guy flew past us in his truck (they usually stop to chat, so

we were going to ask him what was going on)
and he looked like he was crying. No birds
at all were in their usual bird sanctuary
lake; instead they were all standing on the
beach staring out at the ocean. I could
dimly feel something very wrong coming from
them, yet I didn't want to know so made a
point of keeping it out of my awareness.

I don't know if it was coincidental or
part of the whole weird event, but the
river mouth was gone, with no sign it had
ever been there. That's normally where we
end our walks and turn around to head back
the other way, at that spot where the river
meets the ocean and cuts the beach in two.
Yet the river had completely vanished. So
instead without realizing it we walked and
walked, way past where the river should
have been, for at least a couple of miles
more. Then we turned around, and both of us
were suddenly so exhausted we could barely
move, dragging our feet all the way back in
lead weight underwater slo-mo mode. On the
way, a wedge of seabirds flew no more than
eight feet off the ground directly over our
heads and it wasn't right—the wedge was
short three birds on the left side. I knew
that meant something, that it was an urgent
message aimed at me, and I didn't want to
take it in.

Our supposed forty-five minute beach walk
took us three hours. Afterward, I couldn't
shake the weird dreamy essence of the whole
experience, and last night I had a feeling

the flying birds in the wedge were trying to show me how many of their group had died, how many were missing. I felt helpless and panicky since I couldn't do anything for those birds even though they were all reaching out trying to tell me about it.

I mentioned the dead birds to Kurt and he said, "Oh, yeah, there's a toxic algae bloom that's killing the seabirds."

Right now the whole thing is still one big whirly-swirly of leftover animal guilt mixed up with poor little Morgan's death. I'm sitting outside of it, kind of detached and numb.

This morning I tried to get some clarity about it in meditation, and so far I haven't got a clue. That's why I'm hoping you'll be able to help me figure out some of this stuff. I'm not thrilled that I chose this dead bird experience the same weekend as Morgan's death. Apparently this is some sort of lesson I really need to learn ASAP, and I'd better learn it now so I don't have to keep stumbling over it.
C.

Fran wrote:

Before we talk about your email, I'm guided to say this to you: Morgan and Bob chose to walk this path together with you. They each fulfilled their purpose perfectly, exactly as it was meant to be. To put what I'm feeling into human terms: It's as if they're both together now, dancing around with party hats on, saying, "We did it! We did it!" Then they notice your confusion and your anguish, so they stop their celebration and say, "What is it? What did we do wrong?"

Don't dishonor their contribution by losing sight of the lessons they came to teach you. You need to dig deep to find the joy and the true meaning in all these occurrences.

Which brings me to your email.

You said…"I'd better learn it now so I don't have to keep stumbling over it."
As I read those words, I knew they were in the wrong order. You really meant to say: I'd better keep stumbling over it so I don't have to learn it now!

Here's what I mean by that:

All the events of the past week are profoundly connected. Morgan's death, the toxic algae. Carrie, I can't emphasize it strongly enough: Find the courage to look beyond the obvious. Don't assume the signs you've been shown are negative. They are filled with joy.

One especially powerful message leapt out at me as I read your email, and it concerns the part where you "cross over" the river. The message it holds for you is this: Walk on water. Go beyond the boundaries that have stopped you in the past. This whole experience on the beach is very much about transcendence. And remembering.

I Googled some information about that toxic algae bloom. It doesn't kill in the way you might expect. It doesn't just poison the animals that eat it. Instead, it causes a form of amnesia, which leads to paralysis.

You're right about that wedge of birds. They were asking you to do something… and it isn't what you think. They were asking you to overcome your amnesia, and transcend your paralysis. They were asking you to remember who you are. They left three spaces open for you in their wedge—a "trinity", if you will—and they issued you their invitation. They said: Come join us anytime you're ready. ❖

ALL ACCESS

April 14, 2007

Fifty-nine more workbook lessons to go. Today's Saturday morning lesson was beautiful, and it inspired me to try and give today entirely to Spirit. On the way to the supermarket after breakfast, I was busy applying forgiveness exercises consecutively to each pedestrian I saw, when the "new" idea suddenly occurred that I should open it wider and try doing the forgiveness thing for everybody at the same time. All the drivers, passengers, shoppers and cashiers in the checkout line—all were equally innocent and holy, all were pure and perfect and united in oneness with me.

It's not like I never thought of trying this before, I'd just never been able to focus my mind or my willpower clearly enough to successfully pull it off. This time the barrier suddenly lifted; taking that next step toward peaceful unity seemed logical and easy.

This pattern of persistent blockage and sudden release is starting to be familiar. And when that release comes, it's never from the outside. It isn't because somebody or something "out there" decides to stop blocking the way. This is the best way I can describe the feeling: It's like trying repeatedly to get backstage to see your favorite band, and each time the big, burly security guy bars the way. Then suddenly, on the forty-seventh try, you look down and notice you forgot you're holding an all-access pass.

So that's what it felt like. You could say I noticed that pass in my hand and temporarily remembered that nobody had the power to stop me from going wherever I wanted to be. So I sailed past that egoic gatekeeper and for the first time was effortlessly able to apply forgiveness exercises to everybody in the world at once. And it felt delicious.

Shortly after putting away the groceries, I was still on a gentleness high when the phone rang. Kathy's energy/breath/chakra class was short one person for the afternoon session, and they needed a willing body to fill in. Would I like to attend? I quickly checked in with Spirit:

"It would be fun to go, yet I know energy, breath and chakras are all part of the world of illusion. Will this afternoon class be counterproductive to my practice of the *Course*?"

Not if you don't want it to be. Go to the class if you want to. Just remember it's all illusory and use it as an opportunity for forgiveness.

Kathy picked me up a few minutes later. The class was split into two groups; my group consisted of Kathy and a few guys. I quickly saw why they needed that extra body. The exercises were designed as concentric wheels, people on the outside matched up one-on-one with people on the inside, the inner wheel rotating after each exercise so that everyone had a chance to work individually with everyone else.

The very first exercise: Sit cross-legged on the floor facing your partner, knees touching knees, and stare deeply into each other's eyes for a very, *very* long time. It was designed to be uncomfortable, of course, and meant to break down barriers. The cute boy with whom I was bumping knees, having spent the whole morning doing this kind of intimacy work, was all warmed up and relatively used to it. For me, on the other hand, it was pretty much like the Worst. Elevator. Experience. *Ever.*

Yet it all got better as the afternoon progressed. By the time that same exercise rolled around again an hour or so later, I was ready for it. As I sat opposite my partners one by one with oodles of quiet time between us, I sent long, luxurious forgiveness affirmations deeply into each person's mind, picturing the divine light of the Grill Guy as I did so:

You are holy and innocent, pure and pristine and perfect; you are wholly safe and strong and free; you are limitlessly abundant and infinitely valuable, you are eternally gentle and unconditionally loved and loving. You are radiant light. You are immortal spirit.

As I concluded each forgiveness exercise, I could swear I *saw* the acknowledgment of the message as it registered in the eyes of each of my partners. Not consciously, of course, but somewhere way in the back of the mind. In Kathy and one of the guys, the response was…wonderment. Like it rang a very faint and distant bell, and the news—if it really could be believed—was awesome.

In the other two guys, the eyes grew troubled and uncertain, the brow furrowed slightly; this information could not possibly be true. Not about *them*, anyway. I smiled tenderly at each of them.

I hear ya, I empathized gently. *Been there.* ❖

AND NOW FOR SOMETHING COMPLETELY DIFFERENT

April 15, 2007

Yesterday's forgiveness exercises at the energy/breath/chakra class touched me more deeply than I could have imagined. I would've liked to spend this morning in meditation and contemplation of all I learned there…but no.

Today was our neighborhood's first-ever progressive brunch: Four houses and eight solid hours of eating, drinking and partying. Totally fun. But kind of hard to stick with lessons of eternal oneness while the champagne corks are poppin'! ❖

CAREER COUNSELING

On May 1, 2007 at 3:53pm Carrie wrote:
To: Fran
Subject: Career counseling

You know how you're always telling me I'm supposed to come up with a whole new language for talking about the *Course*? One that's faithful to the concepts yet modern and different from every previous approach? Every time you mention it I roll my eyes and brush it off as having nothing to do with me. I just figure, Oh well, whatever, that's your opinion.

It never even dawned on me to wonder if you were doing your InnerVision thing, reporting on info flowing to you from my higher self. I just assumed you were giving me your random personal feelings about my career path. You'd think I'd know better by now.

This morning I was puzzling over how to structure the book; I couldn't figure out what, if anything, I'm supposed to say about the *Course*, where those parts would fit in to the story or why anyone would care what I have to say about it in the first place.

And then Spirit said: ***Your career lies as a translator.***

And in that split-second timefreeze moment I finally realized it was true, and that this is what you've been trying to tell me all along.

So I still have no idea what form that "translation" is going to take or what my actual part in it will be. I guess I'll find out. Thanks for being persistent with the message—I'm a little slow on the uptake sometimes.

Fran wrote:
Aren't we all. ❖

CHAPTER TWENTY-THREE

TUCSON

May 6, 2007

I'm here in Tucson for five lovely days to visit Lisa for her birthday. So far it's been a nonstop eating and shopping jamboree, punctuated now and then by gorgeous little epiphanies every time I get the chance to do my Course *homework.*

Saturday's lesson in particular was a real beauty. To paraphrase in plain English, it taught that the infinite gifts Heaven has already given us belong to us forever; that we can't lose them or throw them away no matter how hard we try. And everything else we believe to be "outside" those gifts (i.e. the whole 3-D world of form) isn't even real, so who cares what happens with all that? We're completely covered, no matter what.

It suddenly seemed so simple, so safe, and all worldly worry temporarily melted away. I spent most of that day and the evening's birthday party surrounded by an ocean of joy sparkles, feeling more gentleness than I've ever known. Nice.

On May 8, 2007 at 6:33pm, Carrie wrote:
To: Fran
Subject: Strange days

Just got back from Tucson. While the visit was great, the trip home was very dreamlike, extremely strange and out-of-body. On the one hand I was feeling totally connected, able to blissfully "forgive" a whole airport full of strangers… yet on the other hand pulling lots of weirdness out of people, lots of peculiar stares from passersby plus old karmic stuff I have with flight attendants. They just don't like me and they never have. I don't know why.

The stares I was getting were really unsettling. They weren't Death Stares—I haven't experienced one of those since I forgave that guy way back in the brewpub. I didn't know what these stares meant, yet naturally I interpreted all of the weird reactions by going to my same old body-self-hatred place, because that's what I do. Like, *They hate me because I'm ugly and I don't deserve to be here*.

And the whole time I was in it, I was also outside of it, just sort of peacefully observing my own reactions. Unable to stop myself from cycling into the old patterns, yet at least I was feeling no real anger or pain; it seemed to just be crusty old habit without any true foundation.

Got off the plane at Burbank and floated, trance-like, down the hall; I glanced to my left and noticed Flavor Flav, of all people. His arms were draped around two be-hotpantsed lady friends, all three of them a vision in shiny lamé and oversized sunglasses. They were posing for a photo being snapped by a Buddhist monk in flowing red and yellow robes. Only in L.A.

I left them and drifted down to baggage claim, and here's where it gets really peculiar. A suitcase with markings just like mine came down the conveyor right away. I have it marked with tape in four places so I'll know it from every angle, yet I had no sense it belonged to me. Weird. I never experienced anything like that before. I recognized the bag and all the markings but it just didn't feel like it was mine. I let it go around three times before I pulled it off the carousel just to make sure it didn't belong to me. I looked inside the luggage tag that was taped shut just like mine, and my business card was in there but strangely enough I still wasn't convinced. Unzipping an outer compartment, I was more or less satisfied by the sight of one of my pairs of sky-blue underwear peeking out. What were the chances that somebody else would have underwear that exact color? So I zipped it back up and started to pull out the handle, and that's when I noticed a computer-printed sticker on the handgrip.

It had a barcode, flight number and passenger name on it: Smith, Joseph. I had a little confusion-vertigo moment, like, Oh no! I KNEW this wasn't really my suitcase, and then I went: Wait a minute. Smith, Joseph. Smith, Joseph? Isn't that the Mormon guy? The one who talked to angels?

It made me laugh out loud. Spirit's funny little joke, maybe? I can't figure out what it all might mean. Baggage that no longer belongs to me? Founding a church is not my bag? Who knows.

Any two cents you want to weigh in with? It's not a burning mystery, just curious if you have any thoughts...

Fran wrote:
Are you kidding? My two cents is more like a dollar fifty...

To begin with, Flavor Flav and the Buddhist monk: I'm not sure why, I'm guided to tell you that these images represent two extremes of the costumes you've worn to mask your pain. Does that make sense to you? Have you ever gone through a phase where you hid behind an outrageous "look"?

Carrie wrote:
Oh God yes. Several, back in the very angry 80s.

Fran wrote:
Yeah. You hid behind those costumes back then, and later you hid behind the (symbolic) Buddhist monk costume as a different way of distancing yourself from the world. Two extremes of the same coping mechanism. Now

on to the baggage, this is where it really gets interesting.

Carrie wrote:
Yeah, the part I can't get out of my mind is that the bag goes around the carousel three times before I reluctantly pull it down to see whether it's mine…and it feels like somehow that freeze-frame moment is connected to the trinity of birds missing from the wedge that flew over the Death Beach last month. Like it's the identical event playing out in two different scenarios, and it's somehow the "three" that's important in both.

And now that we're talking about this, I'm starting to think I've been looking at the message of the baggage upside down from what it's supposed to be, just like I was misinterpreting the birds. It's not, Here's baggage that isn't mine. It's that this bag clearly IS mine, in fact I packed it myself and I recognize all its markings; it's time to claim it as my own. Same message as the missing birds from the wedge.

Fran wrote:
Yes! That's it! It's time to take your place and do what you came here to do.

Carrie wrote:
Yeah, ok. Thanks. And what about the Joseph Smith thing?

Fran wrote:
What? Who's Joseph Smith?

Carrie wrote:
Ha! Never mind. ❖

The unsettling stares of all those strangers in the Phoenix airport stayed very much on my mind for several days afterward. I could feel that something about this lifelong body image issue seemed to be shifting at last and was grateful for the movement; little did I suspect what sort of awareness was about to reveal itself reluctantly to the light.

ONE RING TO RULE THEM ALL AND IN THE DARKNESS BIND THEM

On May 14, 2007 at 3:21pm, Carrie wrote:
To: Fran
Subject: Hey

You might enjoy this weird glimpse into the twisted workings of the ego mind: Today I woke up a little depressed yet was able to hold it off as I went about my day. Then this afternoon as I was folding laundry, I suddenly heard that crazy ego voice talking, the one that usually keeps itself so carefully hidden away, deep in the unconscious mind.

It was crooning: "Go ahead, let yourself get really depressed. *You deserve it.*" Like it's being my best friend and offering me a special treat. How sick is that?

Fran wrote:
I'm guided to suggest that you take the time to explore what that's about. What makes depression a special treat, and why do you suppose you "deserve" it?

Exploring it sounded like an irritating waste of time, yet I decided to meditate on that just in case she was right. On the off chance there really was something in it to be discovered. I closed my eyes and was immediately flooded with postcards from the unconscious:

Depression is a special treat because most of the time I have to pretend I'm not the poisonous monster I know myself to be. I crawl out naked into the sunlight and force myself to stand upright and interact with regular people, never letting on that there's something terribly wrong with me.

Yet keeping up that fantasy of normalness is both exhausting and futile, since I know I'm not really fooling anyone with my masquerade. How wonderful to drop the act every once in awhile, to slither into bed where it's safe and dark and no one can see me. Surely I've been a good little mutant and deserve a day off now and then?

And the image of Gollum filled my mind.

God. I'd had no idea I felt that way.

My *Lord of the Rings* was a little rusty, so I turned to some quick online research for a refresher on Gollum: Originally a normal child, he was present when his cousin found a hauntingly beautiful gold ring. Falling immediately under its spell, our boy demanded the ring as a birthday present and murdered his cousin for refusing to hand it over. Paranoid that others would try to steal his "Precious," he took the ring and traveled far from the village of his birth, eventually making his home in a darkened cave deep beneath the Misty Mountains. Over time the ring's evil influence twisted his body and distorted his mind beyond recognition, changing him gradually from ordinary boy to unrecognizable beast.

Suddenly it all made sense. In the murky recesses of my ego mind, I had indeed identified with Gollum. That was why I could never seem to rise above my petty obsession with the world's ever-changing response to my looks. It wasn't just that I was abnormal on the outside—it was my fixed belief that the poisonous evil within had twisted my outer appearance to reflect that interior ugliness. Unconsciously I was convinced everybody recognized the hidden repulsiveness each time they looked at me, seeing straight through to my diseased essence, so toxic and deadly it could kill anyone foolish enough to get near me.

In this day and age, physical "shortcomings" like mine are easily remedied. I'd considered plastic surgery plenty of times over the years yet had never followed through, intuitively realizing cosmetic work wouldn't help at all. Now I understood why. Fixing anything about my surface appearance or my self-esteem would be a complete waste of time, as long as my belief in the existence of that festering internal rot went unattended.

Logic—and *A Course in Miracles*—would say none of that monstrous inner ugliness could possibly be real. Well it sure *felt* real. So real and so deep that I would have sworn it was encoded into my DNA itself, making me literally my own worst enemy. Or I suppose, worst enemy status would have to go to the ego mind, designer of that DNA.

We hates that tricksy ego mind and its nasty lies, we does. ❖

CHAPTER TWENTY-FOUR

URBAN COWGIRL

May 18, 2007

*J*eez, what a night. I got back very late from a client dinner in
L.A., so drowsy I could barely keep my eyes open long enough to
climb into bed. And then instead of pleasant dreams, I found
myself wide awake and vision-y, with Spirit leading me on a
tour through the smelly caverns of my own unconscious mind.
I got to observe how I routinely puke up bits of corrosive, guilty
rage and splatter them onto everything and everybody I see. And
I understood that it's impossible for me to perceive any of those
people or things clearly because I've got them covered from head
to toe in my own unholy ick. So all I ever see is the ick reflecting
back at me.

*I did my best to let go of all that acid rage. I decided that I
really want to know my Self—other people, other things—as I
really am. Without the guilt, rage and fear getting in the way.*

Be undefended, *said Spirit.*

*I tried for a while and just couldn't; the very thought of
putting aside all defense (and therefore all attack) was too
frightening to contemplate.*

After a few hours of unsuccessful effort I stopped the lessons and began to drift without conscious thought. And I went…well I'm not entirely sure where I went. It was unlike anything I've ever experienced before. It definitely wasn't sleep or meditation, and if it was vision, it was a more super turbo-charged kind of vision than I'd realized was possible.

It was vertigo with a capital 'V'—and not just any run-of-the-mill room spinning sort of vertigo—rather, the bedroom bucked and leapt and twirled unpredictably, as if the house were riding a giant mechanical bull. And in the vision (although thankfully not in real life) I fell out of bed. Twice.

When the alarm sounded seemingly moments later, I was not what you'd call a happy 'lil buckaroo. Skipping today's workbook lesson, I nabbed an extra hour of sleep instead. I haven't gotten any work done today, although it's been a surprisingly nice day anyway; a "thanks for your business" gift arrived unexpectedly from one of our vendors, a box of awesome, chewy choco-chip/peanut butter/oatmeal raisin cookies. That's not an assortment; all those ingredients are thrown together in the same crazy over-the-top recipe. So today's been pretty much a lost day work-wise, but these kitchen sink cookies are absolutely killer. ❧

And the visions continued. None quite as thrilling a Sensurround experience as the vertigo vision a few nights earlier, thank goodness, yet all were powerful nevertheless.

TERRORBALL

May 20, 2007

I woke up today with an imaginary charley horse in my illusory neck. We've got a swanky outdoor wedding to attend this afternoon; if this thing doesn't let up by then I'll be in my own tiny slice of garden party hell.

Anyway. It's been two very interesting days. Yesterday morning in meditation, I tried once again to grab that all-access pass and go beyond the limits of the ego mind, because I decided it's time to see everyone as they really are. I'm tired of being fooled by those nasty egoic guilt-transfer tricks I use to hide their true identities from my awareness.

Right away in response, I was gently pulled far out into… somewhere. Vast, velvety blackness. And way down there in the corner, I saw a marble-sized sphere of angry roiling turmoil, fireball explosions rupturing all over its writhing surface. It wasn't scary—in fact, its whole existence seemed a little pointless and silly, an exercise in wasted energy. On closer inspection I saw it wasn't even a solid ball, it seemed to be made of a glowing red grid with nothing at its center. I understood it to be a symbol for the 3-D dreamworld of the ego's domain.

"Ok," I asked, "in light of this vision, what should my spiritual practice be today?" Somehow, the usual forgiveness exercises didn't seem quite meaty enough after viewing the empty ferocity of that ridiculous hollow terrorball.

Forgive others, not with words this time. Just remember the serenity of being here with Me in stillness, watching the false terrorball that you made up. You can remember this symbol of the truth on their behalf, and

it will spark a memory deep within the mind of each person you meet.

That sounded like an easy enough exercise. I'd like to report that I was able to keep that memory of stillness and terrorball going in my mind all day, yet it came and went and I used it for forgiveness purposes only sporadically. I'm not exactly a genius at this mind mastery business; I tend to forget about forgiveness a lot more often than I remember. I guess that's why these things take lifetimes of practice.

The next morning's workbook subject wasn't an easy one: Forgiveness carries within it the understanding that minds are joined. It was a little puzzling for me, as workbook lessons often were. I didn't really know what to make of it, so I just opened my mind and waited for inspiration.

After a moment, I asked: "Although I know I'm not ready to experience the true joining of minds for myself, can you show me a metaphor or symbol that would give me some idea of what it's like so I can understand more clearly?" and once again I waited.

And the vision that appeared in answer to my request was…

Sex? Are you kidding me?

I assumed the ego mind had somehow sneaked into this meditation and was messing with me. Time to disregard that last exchange and start the meditation over.

Hold on, said Spirit. *Think about it. Sex is a kind of joining; indeed it's the only kind of joining that you can experience within the 3-D world of form. Sexual union between bodies isn't real, you know, yet it serves a useful purpose as a symbol to help you understand this concept of joining and oneness. Sexual joining is nothing, yet true joining is more wonderful than you can imagine.*

True joining (which can only be accomplished by the mind) is eternal love and ecstasy; contained within that ecstasy is a perfect memory of Self, a certainty of home, of freedom, of limitless innocence and complete joyous fulfillment. Words can't describe how magnificent is the joined state of oneness.

Sex, the illusory union of bodies, is the small and impoverished echo of joining that you allowed the ego mind to devise as a substitute for the real thing. Although you find it difficult to believe this right now, it's impossible to describe just how worthless is the "joy" of sex. Once you truly understand what real joining is, you'll never remember what you thought you saw in it. ❖

These days I was feeling closer to Spirit than ever before, yet not so close that I didn't still feel those moments of profound doubt about our relationship.

NOT ALONE

May 24, 2007

Last night was long and strange, and full of weird mind games. I was lying in bed, minding my own business, when this sudden thought popped into my head:

What if Fran was wrong? What if this isn't my last lifetime? And if she was wrong about that, could she have been wrong about everything all the way back to the Dinner Table Awakening? Maybe none of that wounded healer business is real. Maybe I just made the whole thing up.

And then every signpost, every milestone I've tried to latch onto in this invisible journey of faith melted away, and I was left hanging out there all alone in the blackness.

"Spirit?" I called. "Help."

And Spirit replied: **Don't you know that you could not possibly ever be alone? I am you, forever and inseparably. We are one and the same. You can block out the memory of Me all you want, and yet you can never lose Me, even for an instant. Nor would I ever choose to leave you, dear one, even if I could.**

You need no external signposts to mark your progress. Take My hand now and let Me lead you safely to the certainty and the limitless joy of oneness. For, of the two of us, I'm the only one who remembers the way home. ❖

THE FOUNTAIN

On May 26, 2007 at 4:18pm, Carrie wrote:
To: Fran
Subject: The Fountain

Kurt is in Japan right now, so Kathy and I finally got around to watching *The Fountain* last night. I know you loved that movie, yet I can't honestly say I liked it very much.

After watching it we were confused and annoyed enough that we went to my computer to look up more about the story, and ended up sitting through a whole hour of extras while searching for answers about that guy in his tree-space-bubble. Which we never got. You said he was a space traveler from five hundred years in the future. How did you know that? Does it say it on the back of the DVD box or something?

Despite its questionable storytelling skills, I knew I'd been meant to see that movie. Somewhere within that film there had been a message for me, and something about that mysterious message had scared me in a big way. I didn't want to address it. After Kathy went home I watched a few hours of late-night TV instead of sitting down to meditate. I knew the fear stemmed from that moment toward the end of the movie when Mister Spaceman pulled out of the dead tree's space bubble and took off in his own little one to finish the rest of the immortality/enlightenment journey alone.

After avoiding the fear as long as possible I reluctantly turned off the TV and settled into meditation mode, letting the cause of the disturbance rise into my awareness: Something about that symbolic space-bubble voyage had rung a distant bell. And then I realized it had rung a distant bell of *memory*. Memory, as in remembering having already made the final part of the enlightenment journey myself. This was just a single blip of out-of-time future experience. Yet it was powerful. And deeply unnerving.

Then I heard Spirit say: *No resistance.*

And I knew I was being asked to allow linear time to melt its artificial boundaries and let all experience happen at once. Sort of like what happened on Bear Mountain the previous December, except back then it had scared the hell out of me when time and space began flowing without solid walls between them. This time I didn't resist. Much.

The next morning I awoke to the gardeners performing their high-decibel mow and blow at seven-fifteen. I picked up my *Course* homework, a lovely refresher page called *What are Miracles?* and tried to meditate on it through all that racket.

No resistance, said Spirit once again.

So I gave it no resistance, offering the gardeners beautiful forgiveness affirmations instead.*

The sound of the mowers faded and suddenly I was knee deep in vision, transported to a magnificent, shimmering waterfall of such immaculate sinlessness, purity and innocence that I knew it must be fed by an infinite Source. I find myself groping once again for the words to tell you just how pristine, refreshing and healing these waters were—but there's just no describing the indescribable.

I can only say this: I really *felt* that waterfall's sinlessness. And yes, it specifically felt like sinlessness. It's not a word I use often, yet that water embodied the perfect absence of sin. The complete inability to be guilty of anything.

The quality of the water itself somehow reminded me of my own true identity and true purpose, and this tiny glimmer of memory felt completely good and right. Being in the presence of that water

---

* I've observed that when I offer someone silent forgiveness, they are often inspired to be extra nice to me or else they quickly get out of my way. Very useful.

seemed to heal me, offering release from all pain.

I knew I was only being shown this vision by Spirit; that I wasn't yet capable of letting those symbolic waters heal me for real. Yet it felt so wonderful that I decided I really wanted to know that fountain (I kept accidentally calling it a "fountain," even though I saw it as a waterfall). I wanted its healing waters as my constant reality, and faintly understood that I *am* the waterfall/fountain.

Do you want this waterfall instead of all fear? asked Spirit.

No hesitation. "Yes."

Do you want this waterfall instead of all sin?

Ooh... *all* sin? Pause. Consider. "Maybe...Oh, wait—you mean all sin including my own?"

Yep.

Hmmm. Loooong hesitation. "Yes. I guess."

But you know I didn't mean it. Not really. ❖

DREAMING OF INDIA

June 1, 2007

The next few days after the fountain/waterfall vision were glorious. Everything around me carried a soft, radiant afterglow of sinlessness, and I felt more joyously safe, anxiety-free and genuinely hopeful than I ever have before.

But what goes up must come down, eh? Last night I felt a scratchy sort of ego crash coming on and its dark doubts kept me awake until just before dawn. And then when I finally dozed off I had one of those awful headache-y dreams that leave a body useless all the next day. The dream's symbolism was obvious:

I was walking around lost somewhere in India, trying unsuccessfully to find my way to the airport so I could fly home. Then somehow I got my hands on a rickety little car—a faster vehicle, get it?—yet I still didn't know how to find the airport. The car was just helping me go nowhere more efficiently.

I found myself driving in circles around a crowded, chaotic industrial area. In this crush of humanity two figures caught my eye: A mother sat huddled on the ground with her young son, their faces terrible masks of pain and grief. I briefly considered giving them a ride then quickly decided against it, fearing they might get my car dirty.

So I nosed the car right past them without even slowing down, and drove instead into a big warehouse with lots of people milling around inside. I could have asked someone for directions in there yet decided not to, since I was sure I knew more than they did anyway.

I drove a little farther until my car was blocked by a giant ladder reaching almost to the ceiling; I looked up at the top rungs and saw little incense burners and dime store treasures the locals had carefully placed up there. Well the thing was in my way so I insisted they move it, which they probably didn't appreciate much.

And then the alarm clock went off. Depressing. ❧

CONTROL ISSUES

The next day's workbook lesson suggested it was time to step back and let Christ's vision take over my perception of the world; that I should try judging nothing myself and instead hand out only miracles of forgiveness to all who crossed my path. That sounded really good in an *I have no idea how to do that* sort of way.

I did want to surrender control and try my hand at non-judgment if possible, switching places with Spirit as the *Course*'s workbook said I should. Becoming the neutral bystander with Spirit "judging" the world on my behalf, together we could offer joyous reminders of unguilty innocence to everybody who crossed my path.

Well, it was a nice thought, anyway. And certainly worth a try.

"How do we switch places? How do I surrender control?" I asked. "Please show me."

You surrender control by surrendering control. No one can tell you how; your power of choice alone is the catalyst. And the moment you choose it, you'll remember how to do it.

So far you've chosen to let your ego mind remain in command. You interpret the world through egoic perception, which means you automatically judge and condemn everything. Everyone who believes in the reality of bodies here in the 3-D world does the same. Remember you don't have to keep allowing your ego mind to interpret the world for you. You could choose now to give all perception to Me instead, and let Me do the judging for you.

If you step back and relinquish control, I can show you how to judge things as they really are. For the world is truly not guilty, and the sooner you realize this for yourself, the sooner you'll experience true peace and happiness.

"I'd like to. I guess I haven't honestly chosen your view of the world yet."

No, you haven't. You will when you're ready. And you'll see for yourself how much easier your path becomes after surrendering it to Me.

By the way, how do you suppose that India dream the other night would've turned out if I'd been in control of the car instead of you?

"Well, there would've been no anxiety about being lost, or fear of being among strangers, and I guess we would've stopped to pick up that suffering mother and son…"

And the ladder?

"I don't know the significance of the ladder."

You looked up and saw the top of that ladder, with all the little trinkets and devotional items placed on its uppermost rungs; you saw it didn't reach as high into the sky as the locals assumed it did. And so you judged this erroneous ladder to be blocking your way. You insisted that the people move it, even at the risk of causing them offense.

In other words, you thought you perceived the limitations of their spiritual belief system, judged it an unnecessary hindrance to you, and demanded that it be pushed aside so you could pass.

Had I been in the driver's seat, the car would have traveled right through that ladder as we swiftly made our way home. Nothing is ever truly in your way, dear one. That's the gift non-judgment brings you.

June 2, 2007

Later the same day. The house has been unusually hectic this morning with grownups and kids running to and fro; a prime opportunity to try practicing non-judgment as sticky little hands try to pet the pond fish, or reach up to play with Kurt's vintage toy car collection.

While I haven't been judgmental in the usual sense, I also haven't been able to stop myself from the kind of perceptual judgment that is automatic to the ego mind. How can anybody choose to stop doing something that's automatic? That's like choosing not to sweat when it's hot outside.

"*How do I do this non-judgment thing?*" *I asked.*

Try remembering why you want to.

"*I can't remember why I want to. Something about offering freedom to all I see so I can have it for myself too, but I'm not making that connection right now. I know you've been showing me meaningful lessons about non-judgment all day, and I'm just not getting it. It's frustrating. I see all the pieces yet I can't seem to put them together so they make sense.*"

You can. You will.

And I had to smile in spite of myself, because that's an oft-repeated line of encouragement lifted straight from The Fountain. ❖

Long Time No See

CHAPTER TWENTY-FIVE

NO RESISTANCE TO EGO

There were only fifteen more workbook lessons to go. Funny, the closer I got to the end, the harder those lessons were to remember; apparently the ego mind was reaching deep into its bag of tricks and finding all sorts of ways to hinder my progress.

Speak of the devil, in my morning meditations I had begun to notice one recurring theme: How much longer did I want to waste my time building a case against the big bad ego? I thought of it as my enemy, the ferocious adversary that must be overcome before I could reach my goal. All this resentment and fear was just plain silly; the ego mind was only doing the job I asked it to do. And I knew that the very moment I stopped asking for it, the ego would quietly melt away forever. It was time to forget this imaginary grudge match and move on to more important issues.

Easy to say; a little tougher to put into practice. In those few remaining workbook lessons I was still doing my best to get out of the way and let Spirit take over. Each lesson would begin promisingly enough, yet as soon as I lost focus for even a moment I'd end up knee deep in ego fantasy instead. Restarting the exercises over and over again, I would be clear and present for a few seconds, then the ego would pull me someplace else altogether, long minutes passing before I'd even realize I'd been hijacked.

It was frustrating as hell. Forget choosing this present moment to let Spirit show me answers—I couldn't even stick around long enough to remember to ask the questions. After a week or more of wasted effort, I was starting to feel ashamed of my incompetence.

Try looking at it the other way, dear one, said Spirit. *Each time a fantasy is interrupted by a moment of presence, consider it cause for rejoicing. The ego mind resists your attempts to be present because ego only operates in the imaginary future and the illusory past. Its judgments and perceptions appear to have meaning only when viewed through these two false lenses; its condemnations make no sense in the limitless reality of the present.*

Keep practicing your lessons and go on trying to embrace the "now." Every present moment contains healing within it; as you become increasingly willing to accept the world's true innocence, which can only be fully recognized in the "now," these seemingly separate moments of presence will someday join together into one perfectly healed reality.

"Thank you, I'll do that."

And do try to release your resistance to the ego mind. Although it doesn't exist, you believe the ego is a very real part of yourself. Your frustration with that seemingly real part of yourself means that you find it guilty. And what part of you is fortified every time you assign guilt?

"The ego mind."

Bingo. By attacking the ego mind you strengthen the ego mind. Right now you think that's unfair, yet I will remind you that you're the one who designed it that way. The ego only possesses the power and the ingenuity you give to it. On its own, it is nothing.

"Ok, I'll do my best to put the grudge aside. But it's hard to perceive something so diabolically clever as a neutral nothing. "

Try. ❖

IN OTHER WORDS

Having finally finished writing the initial draft of *The Crash Course*, I'd been wondering how to bring it to a close with appropriate reverence. And then I came across a beautiful *Course* workbook page called *What am I?* On that page, a few paragraphs apart, I found a couple of sentences shining with such gorgeous purity that they summed it all up perfectly.

So I decided to quote the *Course* directly as a fitting way to end my synopsis. Not the whole page—too full of *He*, and *His*, and that sort of thing. I just wanted those two sentences. Although it was vitally important to me to transmit the essence of the *Course's* meaning as purely and correctly as I could, I wanted to keep all my pronouns gender-neutral. Speaking as a person of the *she* and *hers* persuasion, I'd always found it a little bit distracting to persistently see myself referred to as a "Son" within the *Course's* pages, and I suspected this might be a stumbling block for more than a few women. So I figured it wouldn't really hurt anything to omit the masculine references, since according to the *Course* there are no separate genders anyway in truth.

Then I felt uneasy and wasn't sure if quoting the *Course* itself was the right thing to do. So I thought I'd better ask.

No, it's better if you don't quote the Course *directly. And not for the reason you think. You worry that the publishers of* A Course in Miracles *won't permit you to use their source material within your profane and unworthy book, but that's not it.*

You were careful to cherry-pick the lines you wanted to quote, to avoid the many gender-specific references to He *and* Him. *You also shied away from the passages containing terms you felt were too Christian or biblical in nature.*

"Yes, that's true."

You're using faulty egoic perception and judgment to decide which parts of the Course *are suitable and which are not. What you're actually doing is judging the* Course *to be guilty.*

"Oh!"

Don't be distressed by this, dear one. Right now you have no other method for absorbing the meaning of the Course. *And by the time you're able to perceive the* Course *without judgment, you'll no longer need it as a guide.*

For the purpose of your synopsis, rather than deciding which parts of the Course *to leave out, you're better off putting the essence of its message and meaning into your own words instead. That's where your worldly vocation lies, you know.*

"And you'll help me go over it word for word to clean up my misperceptions and misstatements so I can present as correct a synopsis as possible?"

Yes.

"And you'll tell me where I've gone too far over the top into blasphemy in my writing style?"

That's for you alone to decide, dear one. Blasphemy doesn't really exist, of course. To find your writing blasphemous, you're asking Me to find you guilty. And that I could never do.

Your question is based in fear; you're worried about how your explanation of the Course *will be perceived. This is how it will go: Many will be drawn to your plainspoken and irreverent style of expression. Others will be annoyed or offended by it. Neither response is your concern. Your job, dear messenger, is to transmit the meaning of the* Course *in the language best suited to you— and to tell your own stories of the path you walk on your journey home to God.* ❖

ON ABUNDANCE AND LACK

June 5, 2007

I've been paying bills this morning, and noticing—really paying attention—to just how uneasy it makes me. There's a respectable cushion in the checking account and more in rainy day savings to back it up, yet whether we're experiencing lean times or plenty, the unconscious discomfort never lightens up, and the anxiety stomach never goes away. Why can't I ever relax just a little bit? Maybe if we get lucky and choose great investments this year, that'll help take care of the problem.

Spirit commented: *You possess more wealth right now than your parents ever dreamed of, yet you feel no safer in the world than they did. Do you imagine that any amount of money in the bank would really offer you the sense of security you seek?*

Don't be deceived, dear one. The "problem," as you put it, is not your bank balance. It's your belief in lack. In truth, there is no such thing as lack, although by believing that it exists, you've made lack a very real-seeming phenomenon for yourself. Try putting all your trust in Me instead of in your ego mind (which can only teach you of fear and lack) and I will carry you beyond all fearful dreams of poverty to the perfect safety that is your heart's true desire.

That sounded like a great idea, yet I still had no idea how to put all my trust in Spirit. Or even half my trust. And chronic fear of lack seemed to be a deep and very permanent part of me, no matter how hard I tried to alleviate it or think positive thoughts about it or look beyond it.

True, the situation had been improving lately. As other aspects of my life had begun to heal themselves I could sense the unholy issue of lack starting to dissolve at last; the knotted, swollen strands untangling themselves, letting me feel safety and abundance at times. Still it nipped at my heels, this constant fear that my good fortune might dry up at any moment.

You fear lack, yet you also fear prosperity. In your egoic perception, lack and prosperity are equally intolerable states, for both are quite painful to you.

The subject of money holds great anxiety and unconscious discomfort for you. Money is not inherently dangerous, and its purpose is not to lull you into a false sense of security before yanking the rug out from under your feet. Money is only a neutral symbol of Heaven's limitless abundance, and its sole purpose is to flow effortlessly and without restriction.

Abundance is not something you need to go out and get, My dear, nor is it something that happens to you. Abundance is what you are. It takes a lot of extra effort for you to block the natural flow of abundance in your life, because you must deny your very essence to do so. Yet you do this willingly.

I ask you once again to put your trust in Me instead of the ego mind, for this is the one choice you can make that will restore true abundance to your memory forever. ❖

ABUNDANCE, PART II

It was a few weeks later. I'd worked intermittently all that month, and now another non-billable day, the fifth in a row, was staring me in the face and no jobs loomed on the horizon. I'd have loved to spend this time in meditation yet I hesitated, not wanting to provoke Kurt's disapproval. These days he seemed ok with my occasional bouts of unemployment as long as I filled the time with necessary office or household chores, yet became visibly anxious if he didn't perceive me as being "productive."

I felt like I ought to take some sort of spiritual action to end the dry spell, yet wasn't sure what it should be. I used to rely on chanting to break this kind of logjam, but those days were over. And Law of Attraction affirmations like those described by Gregg Braden (or more recently detailed in *The Secret* and elsewhere), didn't feel like the right thing either, yet I didn't know what else to try.

Eventually I stopped wandering in circles; it was time to give in and ask Spirit what to do instead of stubbornly trying to figure it out on my own.

"How should I deal with Kurt's disapproval whenever I'm not pulling my weight? And what's the right action to take, if any, to cause more work to flow? Or should I just try to accept the unemployment situation because it isn't real, and trust in You to lead me wherever You think is best (even if that means willingly embracing financial hardship along the way)?"

Kurt is not separate from you, so the disapproval you feel is your own. Rather than trying to fix the mirror, concentrate on healing your own lack of faith in your spiritual "productivity" and Kurt's behavior will take care of itself.

As for the rest of your questions: Remember that abundance is your true state. Open your forgiveness exercises to the possibility of Heaven's limitless abundance. Let this be your spiritual practice today, and see what happens.

I took the advice. As I practiced on Kurt at the breakfast table...

You are holy and innocent; you are limitless and free; you are infinitely peaceful and joyous. You are perfect love; you are immortal spirit… the exercise suddenly took a new and unexpected direction as this statement was added: *You give all and receive all, eternally.*

I was startled by this statement, yet sensed the freedom inherent in it; the total confidence and safety that were the necessary prerequisites for this wide-open state of being.

You give all. There could be no hoarding, no possibility of fear or lack.

You receive all. It made sense that endless abundance would be the natural result of such limitless giving. Nobody could believe in lack while in this state, therefore only completely joyous fulfillment would be possible. Just picturing it felt wonderful.

I wanted to hang onto the memory of that feeling for as long as I could, so I practiced it again at the gas station, the car wash and the grocery store, silently telling everybody I met that they give and receive limitlessly and forever. It felt incredibly right and good to be able to deliver that message, as if this job of giving and receiving was programmed into our genes and had been lying dormant all along, just waiting for somebody to come along and activate it.

Damn, I thought to myself longingly, *it would feel so great to be able to activate that giving-and-receiving process for real, and not just in forgiveness exercises.*

A nice side effect of all that concentration on giving and receiving: Even for just a few minutes at a time, the anxiety stomach melted away and I was able to relax and trust in Spirit, whatever the financial situation might be. Which came in very handy, because Kurt called me from the road a few hours later to say a rock had hit his windshield and cracked it.   Although grateful to hear that he was unharmed, I shuddered to think what it would cost to replace the windshield on a German import. Yet surprisingly my stomach remained calm.

The timing of this incident couldn't have been coincidental; I supposed it was all part of letting Spirit be in charge of the journey.

I decided then that I'd willingly go along for that ride, and would do my best to just look out the window at the scenery as it zipped by, instead of getting too worked up about the out-of-pocket cost of the trip.

June 22, 2007

It's the next day, and I just spent an hour meditating in the garden. Giving and receiving is great, yet I still can't help being nervous about cash flow. Although I'm tempted to fall back on my usual methods for attracting more work, it seems really important to keep trusting Spirit to guide me instead. At least for now.

During that meditation I put the immediate money question to the side; I sensed I was being asked to examine what was really behind Kurt's discomfort (or rather my own) with allowing me to be "unproductive" by choosing to meditate in the middle of the workday.

As I began to open to this question, a statement was placed into my mind: *I allow myself to be supported.*

And I felt a big spontaneous shift, a sort of "whoosh" of healing, as I recognized that this statement could now be true—if I wanted it to be—for the very first time. I decided I did indeed want to start letting myself be supported, whether by friends and family, or by the world at large. I'd spent a lifetime convincing myself I wasn't acceptable and didn't deserve to thrive. Now it was dawning on me that I was a natural, integral part of an abundant universe, and support was as much my birthright as anybody's.

Then another thought was placed into my mind: *I allow myself to be loved.*

And I let that one "whoosh" too, bringing healing and recognition behind it. Letting myself be loved was something I'd never fully permitted since those long-ago days as an unborn felon, but what the hey—apparently it was never too late to start.

Carrie Triffet **281**

All this spiritual healing was wonderful, I decided, and I was certainly thankful for it. Yet I couldn't help wondering whether it would actually change things enough to affect my employment situation. Would this healing make it any easier to manifest 3-D symbols of abundance?

Post Script

9 days later

It's been a crazy whirlwind week. The dry spell ended first thing Monday morning with a big rush job for a grateful client, and the work has been pouring in steadily ever since. I even have half a dozen jobs (and one new customer) lined up for next week. Feels so incredibly nice to heal things from the inside out, and then see the immediate effects in my 3-D environment. Gotta love those symbols of abundance. ❖

CHAPTER TWENTY-SIX

ON THE FLUIDITY OF TIME

I'd been continuing the abundance work, letting it sink in ever deeper that I was worthy of being supported and loved. And in the meantime the jobs had been flowing in beautifully, effortlessly.

Then the client who'd given me that rush job called late one evening and left an urgent message: The original project had been expanded, he wanted me to call him back immediately to go over the new additions. It was eight o'clock on a Sunday night; there was no way I was going to call him back right then. I added the return call to my next day's "to do" list and thought no more about it.

The next morning upon waking, I felt a small stab of resentment at this guy's presumptuousness. *I pulled rabbits out of hats for that last-minute rush job; did he expect me to drop what I was doing to make myself available every time?*

Then I caught myself. That was an old pattern of mine from way back: First I'd be desperate to bring in the work, because life without a paying job was unbearable. Then the work would come in and I'd be terribly relieved. Then something about the circumstances of the employment would make me fearful or resistant or resentful, or otherwise reluctant to do the work once I had it. So now, *having* the work was unbearable. I would finish the job, immensely relieved that it was safely over with, but then of course I had no work, and soon the whole tiresome chain of events would start up all over again. A couple of decades of Buddhist practice had slowed this self-destructive spin cycle to a trickle, yet still I occasionally felt that old familiar pull.

"I'm so sick of this pattern," I said to Spirit. "I know enough to realize it's never really about the work or the job circumstance itself; no matter how I earn my living or which client I happen to be working for, this is my same old stuff. I just want to be grateful and happy for the employment, because I really do consider it a privilege. How do I stop being at cross-purposes about my work?"

No matter what question you ask Me, dear one, I have only one answer for you. As long as you choose to believe in the existence of the ego mind, this pattern of cross-purposes is what you'll encounter in one form or another. Cross-purposes (being of two minds) is the ego's specialty, its hallmark.

Your ego would prefer that you didn't experience abundance at all. It would like you to remain convinced of your inherent worthlessness, which, in turn, would prevent you from allowing symbols of abundance to flow into your 3-D dream life. Because abundance is flowing, ego will do the next best thing. It will try to drain whatever fleeting joy or satisfaction you might have derived from that abundance.

"Ok so what can You do to help me get rid of the ego as quickly as possible?"

Spirit doesn't "do" anything; the truth merely is, and it waits eternally in loving patience for you to embrace it of your own accord. I would never, could never, attack falsehood or take any action to remove the ego mind before you were ready to discard it yourself.

What I can do to help you is what I am already doing: I teach you about oneness, so you can learn to choose correctly between Everything and nothing. I speak to you in language that makes it sound as if there's really a separate "Me" and a separate "you," yet that's just an expedient device. At your current level of spiritual understanding you'd be unable to accept our communication any other way. Rest assured there is no separate "Me" or "you." We are one. We are exactly the same.

When you're ready, you'll choose oneness. When you've truly made up your mind, choosing to turn your back on the ego once and for all will be the easiest, most natural and most logical step you can possibly take. Yet until you're completely ready for it, there's no chance you'll be taking that step. Wanting it with your conscious mind alone isn't enough.

Readiness is possible for you (and for everyone) at all times, in every present moment; you just have to choose oneness with every part of your mind united. Then, with a mind that's sure of what it wants, leaving the ego behind forever is a breeze. The moment you stop believing in it, your ego simply ceases to exist.

"Sounds so easy, the way You describe it. I just hate not knowing if it'll take decades or lifetimes, or what."

Yes, I know. Don't be discouraged, My love. Remember, there's no such thing as linear time. The entire dream of separation happened all at once, and then it was instantly healed and forgotten. You're experiencing that dream now, yet in truth your fantasy of separation already ended long ago. It only remains for you to take the steps within your dream that have already been taken, to experience the dream's end for yourself.

The time and the circumstances that will result in your enlightenment are fixed, because they've already happened. Don't misunderstand this point; this doesn't mean you should live your life as if the end goal has already been achieved so nothing matters, or as if you're a helpless cog in the celestial machine, unable to affect that which has been preordained. That's not how it works. The choices you make in this 3-D world at every moment are extremely powerful. Your moment-to-moment choices are what determine the nature and length of your journey back to the full memory of Heaven.

All the work of choosing to relearn the truth must always be done in the here and now, while you're having the dream experience of living in a body. If Heaven is your desire, what you think and what you choose to believe in every moment of your dream existence are of paramount importance, for these are the steps that lead directly to—or away from—that state of enlightenment. To decide it's unimportant or futile to work toward your salvation in this life is merely to put off the end result.

Time is "fixed yet not fixed." It's fixed in the sense that it's already happened, but the outcome is determined by your choices from moment to moment. So the outcome (even though it's already happened), is endlessly fluid based on the choices you make right now. Got it?

"Wow, yes, thank you so much for clearing that up. I always wondered how that worked."

My pleasure. Back to your original question about your clients and the work they offer you: Be loving. And when you catch yourself being unloving, offer them forgiveness just as you did this morning. Each moment in which you choose forgiveness instead of attack will hasten your experience of Heaven. ❖

PRACTICE MAKES PERFECT

July 14, 2007

Yesterday was one of those mildly depressed, ultra-sandpapery days; the kind where everything is irritating and nothing feels right. I was so out of sorts I even told Spirit to shut up when it suggested I apply forgiveness to something or other around midday. That was a first, and I wasn't proud of my bratty behavior.

This July heat wave isn't helping things, either. If only it would cool down a little at night, maybe I could get some sleep.

Late that same night, throwing off the sheets and fidgeting from side to side, I could hardly stand one more minute inside my mopey mind and sticky body.

Try joining with Me, suggested Spirit.

Sure, why not, I thought listlessly. *It can't be any worse than where I am now.* Abruptly I peeled mind and body away from myself, and attempted to join with Spirit. I wouldn't say the effort was successful by any means, yet because I was at least a marginally willing participant this time, I came closer to it than ever before.

Joining wasn't comfortable mentally or physically; each attempt made me want to jerk my body away involuntarily. Still it seemed like a worthwhile exercise, so I practiced it until I fell asleep at last in the early pre-dawn hours.

The next morning, when I asked what that day's practice should be, Spirit surprised me:

Practice joining. You're planning to go downtown shortly; join with the sales clerks and your waitress. Join with your friends and with strangers on the street.

"Really? Didn't you tell me joining is like sex?" That seemed like a weirdly intimate exercise to try with a bunch of strangers.

Joining is only "like sex" if you're joining for real. And if you're joining for real, this question of intimacy and strangers is meaningless, for joining is another word for oneness. There can be no violation of privacy in the act of joining.

To join truly is to voluntarily abandon the illusion of keeping private thoughts in a separated mind. Joining is the joyous embrace of pure oneness, and in oneness there's no need or desire for secrets or privacy. In any case, you needn't worry since you're not yet ready to feel the pure ecstatic communion of real joining. Right now by practicing joining, we're just wearing down your mind's egoic resistance to the idea.

To practice joining is a nonverbal form of forgiveness affirmation. It involves a temporary rejection of the ego's interpretation of the world—a refusal to see others as guilty and separate from you.

Try it on as many people as you appropriately can, today. Recognize oneness and innocence everywhere you go. Then see what kind of day it turns out to be. ❖

Not surprisingly, Spirit's advice was the surefire cure for what ailed me. By day's end I had begun to feel like my old self again, and after repeating the joining exercises for a few more days I was starting to feel so much better than usual that I barely recognized myself.

REMEMBERING INNOCENCE

"Good morning! How are You?"

Always great. And you?

"Really good, actually. Feeling uncharacteristically light and sunny today. Listen, I've been meaning to ask: Lately I find myself cringing a little when I discuss my beautiful "forgiveness" experiences with friends, because the word itself sounds so judgmental. I feel like I want to find a different word to describe it. Is that ok, or does changing the language stray too far from the intention of the *Course*?"

The word "forgiveness" (as defined by the Course*) sounds judgmental because it is judgmental. Each time you choose to forgive truly, it means you are judging the ego's dark fantasies to be untrue. This "right judgment" helps heal your fragmented mind by replacing clouded illusion with the light of truth instead. This is the one form of judgment—indeed the only form of judgment—that is of value to you.*

"Yes. Ok. I just wasn't sure if I should try to find another word to describe it or not."

Of course you should, if you feel a need. You hesitate because you're still afraid of overstepping; you still think you have no right to alter the "sacred" language of the Course.

Language is never sacred, My dear. Language is at best a helpful symbol that points toward the truth. When the time comes, you will abandon language altogether, for the communication between joined minds is far finer and more expressive than anything mere language can offer.

As for the wisdom or safety of substituting a different word for "forgiveness"—your desire is to hold the purity of the Course's *message carefully within your heart, is it not? Your intention is not to change its language in order to dumb down or sugarcoat, but merely to facilitate understanding. As long as that remains the case, the appropriately updated language will always present itself to you.*

"Excellent, thank you. So, instead of "forgiveness" I was thinking of calling them "remembering" exercises instead. What do You think?"

"Remembering" is as accurate a word as "forgiveness," in the sense that these exercises are designed to cause you to remember your brother's innocence, as well as your own. You have forgotten what you are and what God Is, so practicing "remembering" affirmations seems logical.

However, the ego mind is a master of subtle distortion, and a generalized word like "remembering" could easily be misunderstood and adapted to focus solely upon the idea of remembering God, while conveniently leaving out the part about your brother's sinlessness. The last thing the ego wants you to do is drop your grudge against the world. That grudge is what keeps the ego mind alive, so it's highly motivated to make sure you go on believing in sin and guilt. Present it with an opportunity to sow cloudiness or confusion through the use of an ambiguous term like "remembering," and it will surely take that ball and run with it.

Separated minds embrace their separation, just as they embrace condemnation of "others." You have sometimes wished you could attain enlightenment all by yourself, without having to include any recognition of shared divinity, or forgiveness of anyone else's "misdeeds," isn't that so?

"Oh, totally. I'd love not to have to include anyone else in my enlightenment, if I could possibly get away with it."

You can't. The memory of your own innocence—which is, of course, what one becomes enlightened to—hinges directly upon your choice to first remember your brother's innocence.

It's impossible to have one without the other, for both are the same.

And there's no putting the cart before the horse; memory of your own innocence will remain shrouded by the ego mind until you voluntarily choose to fully remember the sinlessness of the "other guy." Only then does the shroud disappear, allowing your mind to remember itself as it remembers everyone else, joined in perfect oneness and holiness.

"So...no "remembering" exercises, then."

How about "innocence" exercises, instead? It really means the same thing as "forgiveness" exercises. And "innocence," like "forgiveness," is a specific enough concept that the true point of the exercises should be easy for shrouded minds to remember.

"Thank you. 'Innocence' it is. Although now, frankly, I'm having second thoughts and might just go back to calling it forgiveness. At least for now. That seems safest, since I'm still so prone to making mistakes."

Whatever you choose to call them, My dear, just keep doing those exercises. They're your certain path home to the unshrouded memory of perfect oneness and joy. ❖

CHAPTER TWENTY-SEVEN

TO BOSTON

August 4, 2007

*W*e're killing time as we wait for a plane at LAX; all flights are delayed. That's ok, I'm glad for the chance to sit still for an hour or two. Funny (or maybe not so funny) that I experienced what felt like a major turning point in my spiritual practice a couple of weeks ago, then immediately got so busy I never found time to think about it for even a second.*

One morning in meditation I got clear enough to realize that the ultimate truth of Heaven—the only truth there is—is wonderful through and through; that there's nothing in it to be afraid of; that I really do deserve it, need it and want it wholeheartedly to the exclusion of everything else.

That was brand new, and it felt great not to be scared of Heaven anymore. And from this vantage point I could suddenly identify the mad insinuations the ego had been making all along (way down deep in my unconscious mind), in its attempt to keep me frightened and immobilized: The fear that, if I were to choose ultimate truth, I'd be so blissed out I would no longer care about earning a living, preferring instead to sit homeless and drooling on a park bench; the fear that once I decided to love everyone equally without limit, Kurt wouldn't want to stay married to an enlightened freak; the fear that no one would ever invite me to another cocktail party because nothing kills the party mood quicker than a Christ hanging around.

I think it's much harder to consciously hear the ego's voice than the voice of Spirit. Mainly, I think, because Spirit wants to be heard, yet the ego would prefer to operate beneath the radar, way down in the murky depths where its crazy talk can't be scrutinized in the logical light of day. Only when I stayed consistently focused on choosing truth, could I easily identify the ego arguments that popped up to defend the stinky status quo. Yet here was the good part: No matter how stubborn or fearful the thought, the simple action of choosing to look past it to the truth was enough, in every case, to dissolve the obstruction.

Well, nothing is ever that simple, at least for me. After a very clear and beautiful week of consistently choosing truth, (along with deeper, less conflicted forgiveness exercises than ever before), I started to notice that old familiar "what goes up must come down" feeling, that egoic crash-and-burn coming up over the horizon to get me. When one of those ego crashes arrives, it typically hits like an eight car pile-up and lasts for a couple of weeks.

So this time when I felt one coming on, I paid it close attention. It carried all the same hallmarks as the others, the same twisted ego logic: This was punishment for having flown too high for too long. Or no—not punishment. It was a necessary correction to the flight path made on my behalf, for my own safety and wellbeing. Yeah, that was it. Ego was tearing the wings off my plane to protect me.

I made the conscious decision not to allow it. No crashing, no burning. No depression, no stagnation, no two weeks of spiritual amnesia.

Ego said: You deserve the down time; you shouldn't deprive yourself of it.

"No."

The down time includes hiding in bed under the covers. You love that. You find it healing.

"No thanks. My intention is to forever give up the desire to hide in darkness. I choose instead to reveal myself to the light."

And with that, the ego crash hesitated, lost momentum and then quietly dissolved.

Yet it was a little too soon to pop the champagne corks. Right away on a more subtle level, someplace just beyond my conscious ability to spot it, came a different form of egoic sabotage. Life immediately got busy and never slowed down for even a moment. At the same time, insomnia became rampant. When I finally did fall asleep each morning just before dawn, I had the same recurring dream: In a crowded outdoor plaza under a blinding midday sun, I discovered I had no pants on, and was horrified to realize I'd intentionally exposed myself to the light.

So one way or the other, ego managed to have the last word. And the net effect: Two weeks of stalled forward momentum, exactly the same as if I had allowed the crash.

Pretty sneaky. ❖

LIGHTNING

I'd forgotten what a drag air travel could be. It was late the same night and we'd been flying for hours by this time, legs achy and craving a good stretch. The plane had been hard-bumping along for quite awhile, our flight punctuated occasionally by the sound of rumbling thunder, when random flashes of bright white light suddenly began popping all around us. Paparazzi of the gods. I was startled and didn't like how near we seemed to be to the source of the lightning; it crossed my mind to wonder if perhaps I ought to "do" something to ensure passenger safety.

Should I try to enclose the plane in a protective bubble of light? No, that couldn't be right. It implied there was something fearful "out there" to be protected *from*. Like the bears at Sequoia.

Yes, bravo, dear one, said Spirit. *The bears and the ice and the cactus and coyotes. This is the same thing.*

"So…You're saying lightning is a part of my one Self, and instead of trying to protect myself from it, I need to embrace it and offer it forgiveness?" Ok, then. *The plane, the lightning, the rain and thunderheads are all one. All are holy and innocent, radiant and peaceful and safe…*

I went on to finish the forgiveness exercise and afterward my mind drifted off someplace else. It took a minute or three to realize all signs of the storm had disappeared. ❖

LIGHTNING, PART II

It had been a too-short visit with friends by the seaside, and now we were on our way back home from Boston, flying once again very late at night. Someplace between Milwaukee and L.A., the captain let us know we'd be in for a bumpy ride. He took the plane high above the clouds and a few minutes later the reason for the warning appeared: A light storm, actually two light storms up ahead, unlike anything I'd ever seen before. They were violent beyond description, and monstrous in scope.

And strange, too, beyond their sheer size and power. They brought no accompanying rain, no turbulence, no bolts of lightning or thunderclaps; we encountered only silent smooth blackness, shattered over and over by gargantuan bursts of blinding light that x-rayed the multilayered cloud formations for a hundred miles in every direction.

Even more peculiar: Nobody panicked. The plane was jammed full of passengers wedged knee-to-butt and elbow-to-elbow, and small kids aplenty on board. You'd have expected a few tears or at least some frightened whispers. Yet nobody said a word, and not one of the children even seemed to notice the terrifying light show.

The plane glided quietly along. I felt a little out-of-body as Kurt and I gazed out the window at the silent mayhem. From our viewpoint high above the clouds, it was kind of like watching Armageddon on television, with the sound turned off.

"Wow," I remarked to Spirit, "my one Self is pissed."

Your one Self is eternally serene, infinite and joyous.

"What do you mean?"

When I say lightning or ice is one with your holy Self, I use these examples from your 3-D dream world to teach you what you really are and what you have forgotten about yourself. You have forgotten you are limitless, that you are eternal, immortal spirit. Because you believe instead that you are a small and disconnected body, powerless and subject to the laws of the world you made, you find it impossible to accept the truth: That you are in fact infinitely powerful and one with God.

Everything you see in the dream world around you—whether animate or inanimate, great or small, near or far—is part of the ego dream you made for yourself, and you made all of it from the raw material of yourself. And so in that sense, every part of your world is one with your holy Self, having been fashioned from a deluded fantasy aspect of the self.

The lightning is not separate from you. Along with everything else in your 3-D dream world, the lightning is a part of you. To realize that your world of dreams is all one thing, and that this one thing is all a part of yourself, is the beginning of awakening from that dream. Understand?

"Kind of. Yes. Pretty much."

The light show grew still more intense. I wasn't afraid, exactly, yet couldn't help feeling uneasy as I watched the escalating storm out the window. It reminded me of the Grill Guy vision, in which I stood high above the fray and observed the effects of what appeared to be bombs exploding on the ground, illuminating the cloud cover from underneath. This was like the live action big screen version of that vision, with the unseen "explosions" here a hundred times more violent.

The main storm was taking place to the left of the plane. Directly up ahead and plainly visible from my window seat, storm number two lit the sky in much the same way except now, in addition, it started randomly throwing ferocious bolts of lightning *upward.* And into our flight path. It dawned on me then to wonder: *Is this a life-threatening event?* I knew airplanes were built to take lightning strikes, but could a plane that wandered head-on into a rogue electrical discharge of such ferociously super-sized mega wattage possibly survive?

As I watched out the window I thought again of the Grill Guy vision, and felt a short-circuit moment of dreamworld-interruptus: *This storm is not real. I'm making the whole thing up.* It wasn't a forgiveness exercise; I wasn't saying this to myself in the hope of someday believing it. Instead it was as if some unseen hand had changed the channel for a split second, making me snap out of it just long enough to realize I was not actually living my own seemingly real-life experience. I was only watching it on TV.

More crazy upward lightning. *Is that even physically possible,* I wondered, *for lightning to travel up?* I knew we were perfectly safe as long as we didn't encounter one of those monster lightning bolts. But what if we did?

"I don't really want to die up here, and besides I'm supposed to write books—You said so Yourself. I'm supposed to *live.* Aren't I? Or maybe life and death aren't that big a deal since it's all just one crazy-ass dream state anyway. Oh, Jesus Christ. I don't know anything anymore."

Our chances of survival looked about fifty-fifty to me, yet I didn't know how to pray or what to ask for. It had become painfully obvious I had no idea what was really going on, let alone what the best outcome was supposed to be.

"Ok, Ok. *You win.* I will trust in You completely. My illusory "life" or "death" is in Your hands (even though we both know perfectly well You have no hands), because You alone know God's Will for me."

Excellent, My dear. Your one Self rejoices.

I felt a vague sort of peace come over me, and all signs of the light storm instantly melted away into darkness.

Yeah, whatever. ❖

JUGGLER'S TREASURE

August 22, 2007

I always wish my spiritual progress could be more tidy and linear—get a big realization one day and start building on it the next—yet that doesn't seem to be how it goes. Instead it feels more like I've got a whole troupe of street jugglers leaping around with fifteen or twenty pins in the air simultaneously; every so often, somebody lets out a whoop and they all trade pins without missing a beat.

For instance: After that life-changing realization (The ultimate truth of God is a thoroughly good thing, and I want it instead of everything else), came...nothing. Zip. I guess somebody whooped, and all the pins changed hands. All of a sudden the ultimate truth of God was back-burnered, and now it was all about the light storms and the true nature of reality. And then that wasn't important anymore; now it was about learning to put life-or-death trust into the hands of Spirit. All worthy subjects, yet kind of hard to keep track of while they're all in the air simultaneously.

Now the pins have seemingly come back around to where they started, and I find myself wanting the truth of God again. The other day I had a sudden realization on that subject, an insight of such perfect clarity and simplicity that it seems stupid to admit I never understood it before: The ultimate truth of God IS each one of those people and things around me that I'm having such a hard time forgiving. They themselves are the truth of God, the treasure I've been yearning for all along.

It's as if I've been charging around in circles, stubbing my toe repeatedly on my treasure and bellowing at it, "Get the hell out of my way! Can't you see I'm looking for my treasure?"

Finally I understand that the only thing standing between any of us and our eternal happiness is the bad acid trip we're collectively on, because its illusions distort our ability to recognize the treasure that's right in front of us and everywhere around us and, ultimately, within us.

I know, I know, this is not news; spiritual teachers have been saying it for thousands of years. But this was the first time it made absolute clear-headed sense to me.

What can I say; I'm a slow and juggly learner. ❖

CHAPTER TWENTY-EIGHT

JOINING

The previous year's August 12 trip to Sedona had been on my mind all week, especially the part at the Shaman's Cave, *If you let me, I'll show you what you are.*

I'd been getting ready to perform a backlog of forgiveness exercises for people and situations that had set me off over the course of that very hectic week (pre-tradeshow rush job deadline madness), when the idea suddenly occurred to ask Spirit to come in before I began the exercises so we could do them together.

The Disappearance of the Universe specifically says to always make the Holy Spirit a part of forgiveness exercises, that we should never try to do them on our own. But you know how that goes; no matter how clearly something is stated, there's always a way to misinterpret it or disregard it if we want to. And I wanted to.

Early on, I'd decided not to include the Holy Spirit; I felt I worked better flying solo. I'd give a little nod to Spirit somewhere during the forgiveness exercise, acknowledging that all healing resulting from these exercises was being accomplished by Spirit on our behalf—but I wanted to do the exercise my way, without interference.

This time I finally asked Spirit to take over before the exercise started, and what a difference it made. The exercise itself held greater warmth than I had yet experienced; the forgiveness followed whatever unexpectedly creative directions Spirit chose to take it for maximum understanding and release; and it ended by inviting me to feel a tiny connection between the holy radiance of the object of my forgiveness, and my own holy radiance.

I repeated this new form of forgiveness exercise several times that day and evening, and throughout the following morning. And each time, I was invited to see a bit more of the connection between the innocence of my subject and my own innocence. It felt wonderful.

Soon, predictably, my ego mind was up in arms about the whole thing. This innocence stuff was hitting way too close to home and it wasn't the slightest bit happy about it.

Gone was the sensation of gentleness and safety I'd been enjoying so much. Instead I began to feel vulnerable and fragile, like I wanted to cry, yet at the same time downright bloodthirsty in my vicious internal complaints about the imagined crimes of others.

The desire for attack wasn't even aimed at anything recent or relevant: Two months earlier, some genius* at the Apple store gave me wrong advice on how to program my new phone. One of my tech-savvy friends remedied the situation the very next day, so, truly, no harm was done. Yet two months later I let the Apple guy have it anyway, with both barrels.

The Buddhist term for this kind of backbiting is *onshitsu*. The warning against engaging in onshitsu couldn't be clearer. They say by indulging in this form of attack against others, we actually destroy our own castle from within. The concept always made logical sense to me back in the day, yet now I felt like I fully understood the corrosive effects of onshitsu for the first time.

It took hours of concentrated effort before I could even start to try to *want* to offer forgiveness to the Apple genius and others. And yet somehow, that eventual action of choosing to ignore the ego's urging, and then letting the Holy Spirit take over instead, made the resulting forgiveness lessons sweeter than all previous ones to date.

* No, really, that's what they call their techs. It says so right on the tee shirt.

September 3, 2007

The next day. This morning in meditation I started to invite Spirit in, and then the thought was given me: Ask to join.

And so I happily asked Spirit to join with me together as one, at least for forgiveness purposes. And then I realized why I'd been thinking all week about last August 12—how hateful the idea of joining had seemed back then, as my solo ball of light sped around the other one, trying so hard to avoid the inevitable link up.

Hallelujah, for the difference a year can make. ❖

MEET THE BEATLES

September 19, 2007

We're freshly back from this year's Vegas tradeshow. It's really been a pleasure to watch the show's evolution from two years ago when we started. This year's event was lively, upbeat, packed with people.

Two interesting things happened on this trip. I hadn't been sleeping much, and at around three o'clock one morning I suddenly snapped awake in one of those "standing-outside-oneself-and-observing" states, and was just looking around my hotel room and feeling very lucid and calm.

And then Spirit said: **You know, there's no reason you have to allow yourself two weeks of stagnant ego-reaction time after every forward leap in faith and understanding. It only happens that way because you've decided it should. In fact, your whole journey could move much more quickly and efficiently if you chose it to be so.**

So I chose it to be so.

A couple of nights later, the second thing happened. We had stayed an extra day in Vegas to catch a performance of the Beatles' LOVE. * The whole audience was on its feet for the final number—I think it was All You Need is Love—*when footage of the Beatles themselves appeared for the first time, projected on giant scrims. Four huge heads, one per screen. Talking, laughing, listening, looking around.*

I glanced up at John to my right, then over at George on my left. George gazed around the room slowly, caught my eye for a long moment and smiled what seemed to be a gentle little smile of recognition. And in that smile came one of those unmistakable electroshock moments of communication that I've come to know so well.

* Best. Show. EVER.

George's smile had said: I sent you my message of awakening and you received it. I knew you would.

I jumped back, startled. Surely I'd imagined it. Who gets secret messages from a dead Beatle? Charles Manson, maybe, but not me. God knows I'm willing to entertain some pretty weird possibilities, but really, this was too much.

It must have been a trick of the light, *I told myself.* It only happened because George's gaze had seemed to catch my eye. *As if in answer, George's image faded away and was replaced by Ringo, who laughed gently as he stared me right in the eye…and nothing. No electrical impulses, no messages sent or received. So much for that theory.*

Well, ok then, *I thought, reconsidering the evidence.* Time, space, bodies and the whole entire 3-D world are just an illusion—oh, hey wait! That was the same message George had been sending all along, come to think of it, so I guess I really did receive it—anyway, if everything we perceive is equally illusory, what difference does it make which vehicles are chosen for transmitting spiritual experience? And why should I get to decide which of those vehicles are appropriate or legitimate?

I thought back to the careful construction of that sparkly beaded Om shirt, accompanied by all those Harrison songs played over and over on the stereo; uncomprehending and incurious about the meaning of the lyrics, I had listened devotedly anyway, never once removing the records from my turntable. Then I thought of the Parisian shopping epiphany with Australian Jesus and Within You Without You *playing on the store's sound system; and lastly the terrifying Jell-O-time experience last December in Sedona, accompanied by, what else—the* LOVE *soundtrack on the CD player.*

And then I realized in a rush of warmth and gratitude, that Spirit, working through these unsuspecting pop icons, had been transmitting its message of universal truth in one way or another throughout my entire life. Ingeniously it chose the only open channel I would allow at the time for receiving its message of oneness, patiently waiting decades until I'd be willing at last to develop the ears to hear it. ❖

WILLINGNESS, TRUST, AND SAFETY

One morning in meditation I started to join with Spirit, as was now my habit.

Join with Kurt, Spirit said.

"Really?" I eyed the tousled form sleeping next to me. Joining with a Mind I already knew as perfect and trustworthy was one thing. And the "practice joining" I had tried downtown had been an interesting experiment at best, nothing more. Yet a serious attempt at joining with a regular person, even someone I loved, struck me as foolhardy and a little unsafe.

The idea had seemed abhorrent when Spirit first proposed it in the snowy wonderland of the Sequoias. Yet a lot had changed since then, and I had to admit that Spirit has never steered me wrong. So I gave it a shot. Kurt and I joined (at least superficially) as one, and to my surprise, the joining filled me with an indescribably delicious gentleness and peace.

For weeks I'd been joining regularly with Spirit in my meditations, and could really feel the difference it had made; now, after seeing how great it felt to join with Kurt I was finally ready to sincerely try my hand at joining with other people too. This willingness brought in its wake a brand-new sense of trust, along with a refreshing comfort and safety I'd never known before.

Which was a very good thing, because the old work-and-abundance issue had returned yet again. All my jobs had dried up simultaneously a couple of days before the tradeshow and now, nearly three weeks later, I still had no work at all in the pipeline. In the past I would've been chewing off my own leg to escape the steel unemployment trap by this time.

Having always been one of those people who confused what I am with what I do, throughout my twenties if you'd asked me, "Who are you?" I'd have answered confidently, "I'm an art director." Or, later, "I'm a fashion designer." Whatever career phase I happened to be passing through became my only identity. Naturally that caused a wee bit of existential inconvenience every time I quit or got fired (which used to happen a lot in those pre-Buddhist days). "No job" meant I'd simply ceased to exist; I was a worthless shell devoid of meaning. At least until the next hiring.

Yet in this current prolonged period of joblessness, it seemed like I was being held safe and almost timeless, perfectly supported within a dream state of unemployment. I knew I could take matters into my own hands to manifest full employment if I wished, but strongly suspected that wasn't the response that was required this time.

This time it was about standing still to consciously identify that deep-down awful ego voice each time it sidled up to whisper its ugly nothings in my ear: *You're a fraud—your clients figured that out and they're never coming back. Your husband will leave you and go find somebody else who makes a better business partner. Because you don't deserve to be alive if you're not earning your keep.*

This time it was about letting go and giving complete trust to Spirit; it was about recognizing that maybe I never really knew what was best for me, so leaping once again to the conclusion that *I am lacking employment, which means I am worthless*, and then taking action to quickly slap a band-aid on that gaping wound might just be a way of repeating the same fundamental error over and over again. It was time to try to heal this thing once and for all.

So I did my best to carefully isolate the ego's lies every time it crept in to do its thing, and to steadfastly refuse to allow those lies to stand. And I wasted no time mourning my lack of employment. For the time being, at least, I was sticking with the Holy Spirit's interpretation of events: That I was safe, I was loved dearly, and everything was perfect exactly as it was.

October 3, 2007
A couple of days ago I allowed myself one wistful moment of wishing for employment: It sure would be nice if I could

bring in a thousand dollars by Wednesday, *I thought longingly as I wrote a check to pay the phone company. Then I instantly dismissed the idea as impossible, since there were still no jobs lined up.*

Today, Wednesday, I got an email out of the blue from an old client who'd run into financial trouble two years ago and had been unable to pay me the money he owed; I'd long since written off the loss as uncollectible. Now he's back on his feet, he's sending out a check today for the sixteen hundred dollars he owes me, and he's ready to hire me for a new round of projects.

Curiously, I didn't experience the overwhelming relief, the massive weight off my shoulders that I would normally have felt in this situation. This promise of money and gainful employment was nice, yet I didn't need it to rescue me from the abyss. Instead I felt only warmth and pleasure that my trust in Spirit had not been misplaced.

You see? chided Spirit gently. *Letting go and placing your trust in Me brings only effortless flow, increased joy and peace. Giving control to Me never brings heightened pain or fear, as you had assumed it would.*

"Yes, you're right. All this time I thought handing over control to You would automatically bring on the biblical suffering."

That's a common misperception. Until now, you've made the mistake of believing that "letting go" and "sacrifice" are the same thing. That's because you've always believed maintaining control is both desirable and necessary to your survival, and to let go of that control would be a terrible loss of power—an enormous sacrifice. There is no such thing as sacrifice, dear child. The Course *makes this point over and over again.*

To believe in the existence of sacrifice is to believe in the existence of poverty and lack. You can't possibly lack anything, My dear, because in truth you are Everything.

This is why no one can ever, or will ever, be asked to sacrifice anything along the way to enlightenment. Whenever you try to "give up" something you still find valuable, that's a gift Heaven can't accept, since it's based entirely on the illusion of lack, self-denial and pain. These concepts simply don't exist in truth, which means all sacrifice is illusory.

Lay aside something because you realize you don't want it anymore, however, (as you did when you willingly let go all control and trusted in Me instead of following the ego's plan during your period of unemployment), and Heaven rejoices at the gift. Trust in Me always, dear child, and you'll discover My love will never let you down.

As I contemplated these words I felt cradled, hugged, supported by all of Creation. I understood for the first time that I was intrinsically valuable and completely loved whether I was employed or not, and accepted the gift of that understanding gratefully.

And in response, it felt as if the entire universe giggled and clapped its hands in delight; it was as if it had offered me a glorious birthday cake and was overjoyed to see that I had finally taken a bite and discovered it was good. ❖

CHAPTER TWENTY-NINE

NAKED

October 10, 2007

*K*urt and I are back in Sedona, this time staying for six days
at Fran's place.

*We left home early Thursday morning while the stars were
still out, decaf soy lattes nestled in the cup holders of my sprightly
little spudmobile—baby's first road trip—and arrived at Fran's
house by early afternoon. Not quite as comfy a ride as the Audi,
yet really not bad for a tiny car packed with stuff in the back
and two long-legged people in the front.*

*It's great to be back here, and doubly great to be able to
take some time at last to enjoy Sedona purely as a vacation spot.
After settling in at Fran's for a few hours, we grabbed a bottle of
wine and headed out to visit one of the canyons so Kurt could
photograph the sunset; for him, this trip is all about the photo
ops. For me, it'll just be nice to spend some quality time with red
rocks and good friends.*

The next morning, Lisa and her boyfriend, Scott (the aforementioned
good friends) arrived from Tucson. Back when I'd visited in May
for Lisa's birthday, the three of us had enjoyed a very long and

unexpectedly deep early morning conversation around the kitchen table about all things metaphysical. Lisa and I have been friends since we were thirteen years old, and metaphysics usually isn't one of our top five subjects of discussion.* And Scott, whom I know much less well than Lisa, hadn't struck me as being interested in spirituality at all. Yet as we talked, I kept getting the hit that they really ought to meet Fran. After about fifteen such hits, I said it out loud and made a mental note to arrange a meeting. This trip was that meeting.

In the late afternoon, the five of us piled into Fran's SUV and made our bumpy way up Schnebly Hill Road so Kurt could have his prime photographic moment, the glorious October sun doing its best to cooperate as it bathed the red rock cliffs in its brilliant glow. Kurt had never been to the top of Schnebly Hill; I was happy as always to go back. We were all standing atop my favorite overlook, admiring the view, when Fran tugged at my arm rather urgently.

"C'mon, there's something I need to show you."

We peeled away from the others, trotting briskly a few hundred yards toward a tree Fran has nicknamed the "crucifixion tree." I'd seen it before; it was an ancient juniper, strange and starkly beautiful, its smooth old body twisted in countless striations of gray. One of its two main trunks had been wrapped in barbwire ages ago for use as a fencepost terminus at cliff's edge. Over the years the trunks had grown together over the wound, encasing the rusted barbwire in living flesh.

As we stood facing the tree, Fran pointed silently at its feet: It was surrounded by pristine, dewy mounds of delicate spring wildflowers—in October—a quiet riot of purples and whites, tender greens and pale yellows. I gasped as I felt their message tumble toward me all at once.

---

* Although as kids we did love to light incense and "meditate" to the drum solo from Inna Gadda Da Vida as we sat cross-legged on the bed beneath a huge poster of Jim Morrison's face. But I don't think that counts.

This gray and wounded tree is a symbol for how you've chosen to perceive yourself throughout the ages. This is what you thought you were; you were completely mistaken.

Now you are learning to put your trust in Me, and as a result you're beginning to see you are not what you thought you were. Look down, My love, and see the symbol of yourself as you really are.

I looked down at the wildflowers as they nodded and shimmered in the breeze. I had never seen anything so beautiful. So innocent.

Your healing can progress in one of two ways: You can slowly, carefully unwind the barbwire, strand by strand, painstakingly digging it out of your atrophied limbs, pausing each time to examine the flesh closely for evidence of scarring.

Or you can simply choose to shift your focus away from what you are not—the gnarled old tree in the background—and behold what you are: The luminous spring growth in the foreground, for this is the "you" that awaits your perception any time you're willing to accept it.

That second option sounded awfully good, and as I chose it I felt wrapped in holiness, safe in the glowing promise of a fresh beginning. The Heavenly gladness, the joy and pure delight all around me were overwhelming.

"This is another one of those divine giggles like I felt the other day," I whispered to Fran (thinking as I said it that it was a silly description for such a glorious phenomenon, yet I really didn't care). "Like all of Creation is clapping its hands with glee."

I could have basked there for hours, but was interrupted by the sight of our three companions trooping down to meet us. Together we all walked back to the overlook to view the sunset, which was now in full swing. Standing side by side we watched as the molten orange sun hung full and round just beneath a thin horizontal bank of quicksilver clouds. It shone brilliantly, sending wide sheets of radiant light cascading down onto the canyon floor, with luminous upward rays, equally lovely, reaching high into the sky at the same time.

Still bathed in joy, I felt compelled to stare directly into the sun. My eyes were completely comfortable in doing so; I felt no need to squint against its brilliance, experiencing not even so much as a retinal afterimage when I blinked. Fran moved next to me and said quietly in my ear, "It's shining for *you*."

I nodded agreement. That may have seemed a strange thing to say, yet I knew what she meant. The sun—yet another symbol chosen by Spirit—was demonstrating to me that it was harmless and beautiful (translation: Innocent and holy), just like those pristine wildflowers. And possibly just like me.

The next morning, after breakfast at the inn we all climbed into Fran's vehicle and took off to spend the day out in the land. First stops: The Palatki and Honanki Ruins, both crowded with tourists on that lovely autumn day. We traveled through those sites as quickly as we could, alternately listening to the Forest Service employees and the Pink Jeep tour guides as each told their own versions of the Native American history of these areas.

After that we made our way to the Heartwell. I hadn't been back since my uncomfortable experience there the previous August. Interestingly, it didn't look anything at all like I'd remembered it. True, it held lush vegetation this time, and instead of the prehistoric slugs and bugs it now teemed with small fish and normal dragonflies. Yet the geography itself seemed completely unfamiliar, as if I'd never been there before. I recognized the place from scenic photos yet not at all from personal experience.

I sat down on a rock while the others poked around the site. Ever since we first arrived in town I'd been having the feeling that something big would be waiting for me on this Sedona visit, and I couldn't put my finger on what that something might be. Some kind of important lesson seemed to be clogging up the pipeline, yet the feeling, if it could be put into words at all, was this: *Agree to dissolve the narrow walls of the pipeline itself, and feel what it is to be unconstrained by boundaries.*

Which seemed confusing and a little too airy-fairy and non-specific for my taste. And each time I tried to dissolve those boundaries, I hit a thin wall of fear mixed with joyous anticipation of the future freedom I'd surely be enjoying, just as soon as I got past that nameless blockage. This had been going on for days, and the impasse was really starting to bug me.

I felt the clog persistently now at the Heartwell. *What is this blockage?* I asked myself impatiently. *Please spit it out, I need to get past this thing.* No answer came. We hung around there a bit longer while Kurt took his rocks-reflected-in-water photos, then we piled back in the car and headed for the Shaman's Cave.

For the previous few weeks I'd been feeling strongly pulled to revisit the Shaman's Cave, and Lisa had been looking forward to seeing it as well. Yet the more I described the place to her in anticipation of the trip, the more scared of it I became. It was those shallow toe indents on the short expanse of exposed slick-rock just before the cave mouth. I'd been lucky once, getting in and out of there safely. But my body was just so damned unreliable when it came to agility; surely I would be tempting fate to try it a second time?

Just as she had on that previous August visit, Fran cut straight across the middle of the canyon on little-used Forest Service trails, rather than taking the long way around on moderately well-maintained dirt roads. She raised the SUV's off-road pneumatics and away we trundled over boulder and washed-out creek bed. A few minutes into the trip, we all heard it: A long, drawn out *pssssshhhhhht*.

All five of us got out to look. Was it a flat tire? No, all four tires were fine, yet the left front suspension sagged comically low. The other three sides thankfully seemed to be holding firm, so off we hobbled over the unforgiving terrain in hopes of making it home without having to call for a tow from the middle of nowhere. Getting out to move tall rocks whenever possible, and with Fran skillfully maneuvering the limping vehicle onto the smoothest parts of the trail the rest of the time, we inched drunkenly over the canyon floor.

Whew, I thought to myself, greatly relieved, *Clearly we weren't supposed to get to the Shaman's Cave today after all.*

"Well, we're practically passing right by the Shaman's Cave on our way out of the canyon," Fran remarked an hour or so later. "I feel like we're meant to go there anyway."

Hiking down that familiar slope and up the other side toward the cave, I felt sick with anticipation. But when we finally reached that small patch of slick-rock, I was surprised at how easy and harmless it looked—and wondered why I'd ever been daunted by it. Could it be that *all* fears and phobias of physical incompetence had melted away on that cold December morning when I'd had fun driving the jeep? At the time I'd assumed I had only lost my fear of operating machinery, yet maybe it had been more than that. Maybe my body had altogether stopped being unable to cope, and there was honestly nothing left to be afraid of.

I leapt effortlessly over the slick-rock and into the cave.

Your body hasn't changed, said Spirit. *Yet your perceptions about your body have changed quite a bit. Notice how your interpretation of the dream world around you changes as your perceptions of your own limitations change. The slick-rock, once so forbidding, has become harmless, forming no barrier at all between you and the cave.*

Consider the freedom you might experience if you were to let go of all erroneous ideas about yourself.

The next morning, we savored one final breakfast together before Scott and Lisa put their too-short visit behind them and headed back to Tucson.

Scott, who is very much in tune with nature and very knowledgeable about Southwestern archaeological sites (hence our visits to the ruins the day before), had seemingly not responded at all to the kind of experience of the land that Fran provides. Which was perfectly ok with me. Although our get-together with Fran had been "suggested" during that metaphysical conversation back in

May, this visit had never been expected to accomplish anything of a spiritual nature.

So I was surprised at breakfast, when Scott volunteered a story about a dream he'd had a dozen years earlier: He'd been a passenger in an off-road vehicle, traveling an unknown Western landscape, and in the dream he'd been told by an unseen voice what he was supposed to be doing with his life. He didn't want to do the thing the voice suggested, so the dream consisted mainly of *Yes, you should,* and, *No, I don't wanna,* arguments. He didn't know why that dream had always stuck with him so powerfully all these years, he said, because he felt that it was stupid and clearly not about anything significant.

Except here's the thing: Midway between the Heartwell and the Shaman's Cave, he suddenly realized *we were traveling through the landscape of that dream.*

Fran looked up from her breakfast.

"I know exactly where it happened. We were on a ridge, and you said, '*This is it,*'" she told him. "And even though I was completely preoccupied with trying to steer the car at that moment, time stopped and I went out-of-body when you said those words."

"It was just a silly dream," Scott replied. "It didn't mean anything."

Fran smiled and went back to eating her omelette.

We said our reluctant goodbyes after breakfast. With Fran's car out of commission, it was up to my little low-bellied Mini to carry the remaining three of us around, so the rest of our hikes were chosen based on their proximity to paved blacktop.

We decided on Cathedral Rock, even though I'd declined the invitation to climb its towering spires more than once in the past: Too much elevation, too much slick-rock, too much everything. This time, at Fran's insistence I agreed not only to hike it, but to make it all the way to the top instead of quitting halfway as I normally would.

Fran and Kurt led, and I followed. I wasn't fearful at all, observing myself with surprise as I scrambled up the smooth, steeply angled rock faces. My notoriously weak ankles held firm in all kinds of weird climbing positions, lungs and muscles all cooperating nicely in the unfamiliar exercise.

See how the lingering perception of your own weakness no longer hinders your progress, commented Spirit. *Maybe all your self-definitions are outdated and should be discarded.*

"Maybe," I conceded, "but it's a damned good thing we're not hiking in the peak heat of the day. It's a miracle that my newly sure-footed self can suddenly go rock climbing without fear, yet I'll bet I could never manage it in hot weather."

The next day, our last, I woke up not nearly as sore as I thought I'd be. Kurt asked for one final hike, so it was quickly agreed that we'd head over to Brins Mesa.

"Is it a mostly level-ground hike?" I asked hopefully, not wanting to repeat the previous day's acrobatics, much as I'd enjoyed the challenge.

Fran hesitated, and then laughed. "Well, yes and no," she confessed. "It's a mesa, so the *top* is nice and flat..."

It turned out to be a long, steady elevation hike, with just a couple of patches of nearly vertical slick-rock that I found a lot more challenging than anything we'd encountered the day before at Cathedral Rock. Cathedral, although steep, offered pits or outcroppings for use as hand or footholds in almost every area. Brins' steeply angled slick-rock seemed, in some places, as smooth as a botoxed brow.

Once again I marveled at my newfound lack of fear as I clung, splayed on the utterly featureless rock face like a spider, or a monkey, or a spider monkey.

Did I mention we were hiking in the peak heat of the day?

Relaxing with drinks after dinner, we chatted until very late, reluctant to let our last evening together come to an end. Fran was telling me about the Alliance for a New Humanity's annual conference, where rock stars of the spiritual/human rights/eco planet world (along with occasional rock stars from the rock star world) gather to brainstorm positive global change.

"You should come to the next one," said Fran, and I gasped at the unexpectedly powerful electroshock charge of the idea. Someone like me would never dream of crashing a party full of big-time luminaries—why risk the humiliation and rejection?—yet I knew I was going to do exactly that; in fact, in one of those split-second futurepast blips, I realized I had *already* done it.

Immediately I was slammed by that same thin wall of fear and anticipation that had been dogging me ever since I'd first arrived in Sedona, more insistent that night than ever before. By this time I had a pretty good idea of what it was all about: I was supposed to drop the limiting way I viewed myself; to stop being afraid of what other people thought of me and start being real. I was supposed to let go of something or other, and make room for the next big thing, whatever it was. Yet how to do all that?

Do the TMI revelations never end? Here's one more thing to file under *Way more than you ever needed to know about me:* I sleep in the nude.

I'm a freedom lover, what can I say? Pajamas are too constricting and tend to guarantee I'll get no sleep at all. I've never worn them at home or in hotels, yet in recent years have typically made an exception when staying at other peoples' houses, preferring to invite a little extra sleeplessness rather than risk a surprise hallway encounter if I happened to be up in the middle of the night.

It's not the nudity per se that would have made a late night hallway hello so unthinkable. I mean, everybody's got skin under their clothes; getting a glimpse of mine would surely not have been the end of the world as we knew it. I came of age in the pre-AIDS 1970s, for God's sake—"clothing optional" was the way of life. I never would've thought twice about accidental viewings back then. No, this current discomfort went way more than skin deep; it was all tangled up with that damned Gollum thing, the obsessive need to hide my shameful self from the light at all costs.

On the first evening of our visit Kurt and I had said our goodnights and shut the door, preparing to change into our bedclothes. I needed privacy, yet Kurt was loath to keep the shutters closed as a beautiful breeze was coming in the window opposite the door. And I couldn't bring myself to change clothes with those shutters open.

We bickered about it for a few seconds. Kurt, a little exasperated, pointed out that there was only one neighboring house, and he had positioned the shutters to completely block its view of the bedroom. Didn't matter. This wasn't about logic. Finally I solved the problem by closing the shutters completely, changing my clothes and then reopening and adjusting them to their previous position to let the breezes blow in.

For the next four nights I did the same, yet on that final evening I surprised myself by choosing not to wear the pj's. Deciding I'd rather be comfortable for a change, I was willing to take my chances in the late night hallway. Positioning the shutters "Kurt style," I climbed into bed. It was an unusually breezy night, the cooling air very welcome.

I was still reeling from the effects of the Alliance conversation. I closed my eyes and was immediately engulfed in vivid, overlapping visions; fragmented and confusing, they were shot through with joyous anticipation as seen through a terrifying funhouse mirror. This was that big-ass block in all its unglued glory, and try as I might I couldn't figure out the bottom line: What was being asked of me, and what was I supposed to do about it?

I understood by now that the boundary-dropping request meant letting go of my debilitating self-image; it meant leaving behind all the old fears and anxieties. Yet I couldn't seem to bring all the whirling parts of the request together into one actionable whole. It was kind of like being up inside the Wizard of Oz's tornado, with all of these strange ideas and images boiling in circles around me, none of them standing still long enough to make proper sense.

I don't know how long I was suspended in swirl-o-vision; after a while I got up for a hallway sojourn, afterward closing the bedroom door once again behind me and returning to bed to resume my disjointed ramblings. Suddenly the wind heaved and flung itself full force at the bedroom door: Ba-*BANG!* I jolted awake, only then realizing that the door had been creaking and scratching away at its partially latched mooring ever since I'd returned to the bedroom.

In that same moment, Kurt (beautiful baby Buddha that he is) woke up and said in a calm and lucid voice, *"You need to either close the door or open it."*

Time stuttered as I fell out-of-body at the sound of these words.

Slowly maneuvering myself out of bed, I felt all the disjointed whirly-swirly visions collapse down into one single dimension, one focused understanding: *Yes. Ok. It's time to choose. I need to either close the door or open it.*

I moved dreamily around the bed and toward the door. If we were strictly talking 3-D world logic, I would certainly have closed that door, making sure it was securely latched this time. I paused with my hand on the doorknob, knowing this had nothing to do with 3-D world logic, and everything to do with agreeing to take that next step in faith.

It's time to let go of your erroneous and limiting perception of yourself, Spirit said. *You are not weak or sick. You are not ugly or poisonous or shameful. You are perfect. You are pure divine light, radiant in its wholeness.*

Remember the Grill Guy? You are that.

Release yourself from the prison of self-judgment that blocks your memory of Heaven. Choose now to dissolve the narrow walls of that prison, and learn what it is to be unconstrained by boundaries.

I hesitated, still unsure of what action I was supposed to take that would make me stop the self-judgment and start to feel better about myself.

Don't misunderstand the request, My love. This is not an exercise in self-esteem. You are not asked to replace one negative ego interpretation of yourself with another that seems, on its surface, to be more favorable. Instead you are asked to lay aside all judgment of yourself, whether that judgment seems cruel or kind, approving or disapproving.

"Ok. I'll try."

I opened the door wide.

To lay aside all judgment of yourself, you must also lay aside all judgment of "others," for these others are one and the same as you. Because you fear them, you judge and condemn these others every time you assume they harbor cruel and unloving thoughts about you. Because you fear the judgment and condemnation of others, you are ashamed and afraid to tell your story publicly. Yet the scorn you fear from these others is only a mirror of your own scornful self-judgment.

If you truly wish to remember Heaven, it's essential that you gather the courage to look beyond the ego minds of others. Only then will you understand what they—and you—really are. Be unconcerned with the judgments that seem to come from ego minds, whether those judgments appear to be positive or negative. All egoic judgments are equally illusory and meaningless.

The shutters suddenly started to bang in the wind. In a daze I left the door and moved to the window, opening them all the way, and paused for a long moment to gaze at the sky. It felt strange to stand exposed in the moonlight, newly free of the shame and dread that were my usual companions.

Be unafraid. Lay aside all desire to hide yourself in the shadows; step forward confidently into the public arena, and dare to discover who you are after the anxieties have gone.

Ok, I thought as I lifted my eyes to the trembling stars high above. *I guess it's time to open up that door and let my naked self be seen.* ❖

CHAPTER THIRTY

WHO EATS WHAT?

October 20, 2007

*T*his *morning on my way out to the garage with a load of laundry, a great blue heron and I startled the crap out of each other. With ungainly wingspread beating the air, he reluctantly left his spot at pond's edge and moved to a safer vantage point on the roof. At first I was delighted—he's the only giant water bird I've ever seen in our yard, and I thought I'd interrupted a bath or maybe a drink. Then it hit me: No, I'm pretty sure I interrupted breakfast.*

I watched him as he stood on the roof, drawn up to his full height and scanning alternately for signs of me peeking at him through the window, and signs of fish darting beneath the tangle of lush green pond plants below.

What was I supposed to do? Shoo him away to protect the fish? Everybody needs to eat. What was the difference, I asked myself, between this hungry creature and the chattering crowd of neighborhood birds at our all-you-can-eat feeder stationed just a few feet away?

Well, there was one very important difference: Those fish and the neighborhood birds fell under Kurt's benevolent protectorate. It mattered to *him*, who ate what. Which meant whichever choice I made, somebody was going to get hurt. Clearly there could be no earthly solution to the quandary—only an unearthly one.

I watched as the bird searched intently for signs of me one last time, and then dropped to his previous position at pond's edge. He stretched out his long neck and stared into the water with unbroken concentration.

"Help me see this bird correctly, Holy Spirit. Help me know what to do."

See the heron as innocent and see the fish as safe. Together they are one in eternal happiness, and they know no hunger or fear of death. Trust that this is so, and let them be as they really are in truth.

I felt comforted by these words and chose to allow the bird his innocence in peace. At that moment it seemed almost logical, almost easy to let go of my attachment to the victim status of those fish. Seeing them as safe meant nobody was guilty, since no crime was being committed.

I turned away from the pond with a deep sense of tranquility. Not that I was silly enough to believe I had this issue licked. Would I have been so serene, so willing to back away from the drama and acknowledge ultimate truth if it had been a coyote after my precious Bob? A mountain lion after the neighbor's toddler?

Yeah, right. ❖

WHO EATS WHAT? PART II

October 25, 2007

This whole week has been murder. It started with that heron on Sunday. Kurt and I ran to the garden center that same afternoon for black plastic netting to stretch over the pond, yet it seemed we were too late. As we stood at the pond's edge with our roll of netting, it quickly became clear that the water held only our own astonished reflections staring back at us; as far as we could tell, not a single fish remained.

There had been no sign of struggle; not a single droplet of water had splashed outside the pond, and every time we'd peered out the window at the heron he seemed only to be intently looking, never actually trying to catch anything. Yet now... dozens of fish gone, apparently, in a single afternoon.

I had thought he'd get at most one or two. ("Oh, no way," our pond-savvy client Doug assured us when he heard the news. "Once you get a heron in an unprotected fish pond, he'll clean you out.")

"You see?" my ego whispered triumphantly, somewhere down in the unconscious sub-basement. "Those fish weren't safe at all. That's what happens when you listen to the Holy Spirit's lies."

But Monday and Tuesday were hectic, and I couldn't find any meditation time to address my vague, guilty discomfort.

The following day, a Wednesday, Kurt and I were scheduled to attend an all-day meeting in L.A. to discuss the direction for next year's tradeshow with the company's newly hired brand identity coordinator. Or so we thought. I had been genuinely pleased to learn they'd finally hired somebody for this much-needed purpose, and was looking forward to meeting her.

What took place that day was not at all the team-oriented strategy session I had envisioned. Her presentation instead turned out to be a

Carrie Triffet **327**

damning indictment of my skills, taste level and training. Employing a masterful blend of innuendo, mixed messages and outright attack, she delivered this veiled stewpot of covert disparagement in a manner so subtle, so skillfully camouflaged and outwardly pleasant, that it was completely missed by her new boss, our longtime client Doug, who sat beaming comfortably in the corner of the room throughout the entire six-hour debacle.

This meeting was our first after the previous month's astounding tradeshow success;* an achievement due in no small part, I might point out, to the untiring creative effort put forth by team Triffet. I don't need to be thanked, but I sure as hell didn't expect to be spanked, either.

Mostly I sat and listened; I wanted to hear her out, to give her a chance to express her point of view, even though that point of view seemed to be mainly that I sucked and couldn't be trusted to make my own creative decisions. I realized there was no point in getting into a pissing contest with her; each time I explained my reasons for having chosen a particular design decision, or reminded her that, *yes, I not only know what "brand identity" is, I've worked with some of the best brand I.D. professionals in the business…*I saw that I might as well have been talking to a concrete slab. She would stare impassively until I finished, then restate her original accusation as though I hadn't said a word.

I was genuinely flummoxed, unable to believe what was happening. With a résumé and skill set far less solid than my own, this girl had nevertheless managed to position herself as creative director and queen of all media. And Doug seemed perfectly ok with it. Would she now (in addition to the marketing and brand identity duties for which she had originally been hired) become my boss? Would she be art directing the art director?

---

* A whopping 65.5% increase in 30-day advance pre-registration over the previous year's figures. The actual attendance increase was probably half that, but still. It was a phenomenal result by any measure.

From the way she talked it sounded as if she intended not only to set the company's future marketing direction, but to design each ad herself before handing it over to me to execute. Demoting me, in effect, from highly regarded design and marketing consultant to entry-level paste up/layout technician.

It was as if my normal world had been flipped over suddenly to expose the disorienting backside of the tapestry, with its crazy jumble of multicolored threads running in every direction. I couldn't make sense of this new terrain; couldn't put my finger on any of the under-the-radar tricks she was pulling, or figure out a way to make her stop eating my lunch. I didn't know what was going on. I just knew it didn't feel good.

Silently Kurt and I gathered up our things and headed for the parking lot after the meeting ended.

"She could be a big problem," Kurt observed quietly as he pointed the car toward the freeway, and I concurred. And that was the only thing we said about it, preferring to listen to music for the rest of the long, trafficky rush-hour trip up the coast.

It wasn't until hours later, as I climbed into bed for an evening of soothing Food TV, that I stopped to check in with myself: *That meeting was rough, yet it's over now. I'm safe and comfortable in my own home. Why do I still feel so wounded?*

Oh. Right. Because I spent the whole day getting beat up.

It was the first time I'd consciously acknowledged it.

On cue, Kurt entered the bedroom and said, "You know, it really upset me that she ambushed you like that. It was completely unfair that she forced you to defend yourself and your work over and over again."

And those validating words opened the floodgates of righteous rage: "Hey *yeah*! You're right, that whole meeting was bullshit. And Doug *totally* owes me an apology for letting it happen."

Kurt withdrew to go call Doug and give him an earful.

But now that those gates had been opened, the flood wasn't about to stop its mighty flow: *We were given no advance warning of the attack*, I fumed, *no opportunity to present a defense. She just decided she'd score some easy points with the new boss by slamming our work, and "educating" us about brand identity to make herself look like an expert. Expert, my ass.*

My God, Carrie, listen to yourself.

Take a deep breath, girl.

Upset as I was, I still knew without a doubt that this turn of events was pure illusion. I understood clearly that I had devised the whole scenario to give my ego mind permission to go on the rampage; that its sole purpose was to try and make me forget all about forgiveness. And it was working, big time. I couldn't think of anybody alive who was less holy or more guilty than that woman at this moment.

Here's how it went all through that first terrible night: Recognize her innocence, feel a moment of deep peace. Followed by an hour or so of bitterly compulsive, ranting onshitsu, followed by a brief recognition of the oneness of all things along with its moment of deep peace. Drift off to sleep and awaken a few minutes later in a blind stinking rage. Lather, rinse, repeat.

In an early next-morning conference call, Doug apologized and assured us sincerely that the events of the previous day would never happen again. I remained skeptical, since he'd been completely unaware of the attack the first time around, believing (until we told him otherwise) that the meeting had been a complete success.

"I just want to go on the record," I told him. "You've invited a heron into your pond. Don't be surprised when all your fish go missing."

On October 27, 2007 at 10:50am Fran wrote:
To: Carrie
Subject: Talk?

Sorry to hear you've been having a difficult
couple of days. Anything you want to talk
about?

Carrie wrote:
No thanks. To talk about it now would suck
me right back into feeling all that rage,
and I don't want to give it reality by
doing that. I'd rather go all metaphysical
on its ass.
    Tell you about it later after the wounded
feeling has subsided.

Yet the wounded feeling didn't subside. The pain was so dense it almost felt like physical injury. I was so ungrounded, so knocked off my foundation, that there seemed no point in wasting time on forgiveness exercises while in this destructive frame of mind.

Kathy, my guardian angel, picked me up that evening and took me to a lovely, gentle group meditation, which grounded me and cleared my mind somewhat. Cleared it enough to notice that the reason I couldn't lose the wounded feeling was because *I* wasn't willing to let it go; cleared it enough to realize that underneath the illusion of the wound lay the same old savagely deep acid rage that powers the whole engine of unforgiveness—the unconscious fuel that runs my 3-D world of dreams.

I went to bed that night intending to offer forgiveness exercises, yet instead spent the next eight hours immersed in spluttering outrage:

How dare she lecture me! Why, she's not even… and I'm so totally… and on and on, over and over, all night long.

Spluttering outrage is my ego's favorite meal, of course. And spluttering outrage because I've been unjustly accused, unappreciated *and* betrayed? That's like Thanksgiving dinner. Ego can feast on those leftovers for weeks.

By morning I was thoroughly sick of myself, and sicker still of choosing to be suckered by this very obvious ego diversion. I read a short segment of the *Course*, as I do every morning before meditation, and one concept leapt off the page: *There is a holy light that this world can't give. Yet you can give a holy light to the world.*

Hey, maybe that would work. Until now I'd been concentrating on trying to recognize the light and innocence in other people. But I couldn't seem to locate even a glimmer of light or innocence in others at the moment. Maybe I'd do better in my current circumstance if I offered my own light instead.

I moved into meditation and, with Spirit's assistance, began to emanate a beam of gentle light. My ego started to protest, then faded away as I chose the light instead of its grumblings.

Brand I.D. Girl's image swam into my mind, and I directed the beam of light toward her.

Limitless, said Spirit.

Ok, limitless. I dropped the outer boundaries, widening the light as much as I could.

Unconditional.

Oh. Right. Unconditional. Grudgingly I allowed the rest of the constraints to fall away. I found it relatively easy to keep the high beams going as long as I focused only on her, and not on any of the things she had done. Yet each time I let even a faint memory of her behavior creep in, the light would disappear and I had to start the meditation all over again to get it back.

Overlook these crimes you think she has committed. She is completely innocent. Your memory of Heaven depends on your willingness to look past this 3-D world of guilt and condemnation to the shining reality that lies beyond it.

I kept trying and eventually got the hang of seeing only

innocence when I looked at her. The healing light began to pour out in a steady, unbroken stream until light was all there was. That light felt wonderful; I'd been so busy attacking her I hadn't noticed how bad the constant aggression made me feel. After so many days of nonstop pain it was an enormous relief to stop hurting myself.

The heron's image appeared in my mind. Although it twisted my heart a little bit to do it, I let him enter that same limitless and unconditional light.

Include the fish.

"Include the fish? They're long since digested by now, splattered, I'm sure, onto windshields all over the city."

Not. Things are never as they seem, dear one. Include the fish.

So I included the fish.

Brand I.D. Girl, the heron, the fish and I were bathed in gloriously tranquil light, which seemed to know no boundaries. Melting into that wondrous light, our individual identities seemed to recede, replaced by a shared experience of quiet joy.

I sensed dimly that this forgiveness lesson was being received in all corners of the universe, bringing tiny ripples of healing to all.

And I suspected that Heaven was smiling. Or it would be, if it had lips.

Ok, so I'm nowhere near enlightenment yet, I thought as I opened my eyes and gazed peacefully at the ceiling for a few moments. *Still, every little lesson counts.*

I threw aside the covers, got out of bed and began my day. ❖

A week later, the fish came out of hiding.
The heron has never been back.

THE CRASH COURSE

A WORD ABOUT
THE CRASH COURSE

The Crash Course is my own short-form explanation of *A Course in Miracles*, a breakneck gallop through the 580 pages of the *Course's* teachings. Written in common everyday language, the tone of *The Crash Course* is purposely a little bit blunt and irreligious, in obvious contrast to the often biblical language of the *Course* itself.

Stylistic differences aside, students of the *Course* will notice immediately that *The Crash Course* isn't a strictly literal or chronological synopsis of *A Course in Miracles*. Concepts have been arranged here in the manner in which they flowed most naturally and logically for me, which is not necessarily similar to the way the information is structured within the *Course* itself.

Please note: Although I was scrupulously careful to present the *Course's* teachings as accurately as possible, I'm no scholar and can't guarantee that my work is free of mistakes. I can only assure you that I did my best.

It would not have been possible for me to write *The Crash Course* without the help of Gary Renard's books, *The Disappearance of the Universe* and *Your Immortal Reality*. I owe much of my understanding of the *Course's* material to the broader explanations set forth in those two books. The rest of my understanding is owed to the many patient *Course*-related lessons offered me in conversations with Spirit, as chronicled elsewhere in this book.

THE CRASH COURSE

1. Everything you know is wrong.

2. The world we think we know is upside down from the way we suppose it to be: ugliness is beauty, good is evil, joy is sadness, profit is loss.

3. That's because each of us, without exception, is stark raving mad. And in our madness, we believe that love is hate and hate is love; that light is darkness, happiness is pain, lies are truth, death is life, attack is defense and fear is safety.

Perhaps a little explanation is in order.

THE BACK STORY, PART I

1. God is real.
   First, the good news: Like everything else in this world, we have God all wrong. God, of course, is not Big Daddy In The Sky. God has no gender, no body, no long white beard. God is love and nothing else. And not our messed up, *I'll love you as long as you behave and do what I tell you,* kind of love. The infinite and perfect Mind of God is total love whether we think we deserve total love or not; this total love is wholly pure and impartial, unchanging, eternal and unconditional.

2. God is real, and nothing outside of God is real, because only God exists. Period. There's nothing else out there.

3. There's no "out there" out there. God is everywhere and everything at all times, eternally and limitlessly. And even that's not a strictly accurate description; "everywhere" implies space, and "at all times" implies temporality, yet time and

space don't exist because, by definition, they don't meet the conditions of being real. (Only eternal, unchanging love is real.) So it's meaningless to say, "God is everywhere at all times." The closest thing to a true statement is this: God Is.

4. The Mind of God does not—*can*not—judge, condemn, threaten, get angry, be disappointed, punish or take anything away from anybody. Ever.

    The perfect and serene Mind of God does not do battle or choose sides. No country or religion or political group gets the extra special stamp of Heavenly approval; divine love is offered constantly and limitlessly no matter what we do or don't do in this world. And speaking of battle, there are no Satanic forces in opposition to God, because, seriously, what could oppose God? Only in our confused fantasy do we believe anything could exist separately from, or as a threat to, the infinite power of God.

5. The Mind of God did not create this world or any of the bizarre things we think we see in it; in fact, this world has nothing to do with the perfect, infinite Mind of God at all. Nothing truly exists except eternal, limitless love. Anything that doesn't fit that description is just part of the crazy dream we're having.

THE BACK STORY, PART II
The beginning of time

1. God created one Son of God.

2. And we're it.
    The Son of God, of course, is not male, is not a body or even a lot of bodies. Somewhere along the way the Son of God was given this moniker in an attempt to describe

its relationship to God—the Son being the creation of its Creator. The so-called Son of God can best be described as divine Thought, created perfect and held forever safe and eternally unchanged within the loving Mind of God.

3. True Creation, meaning the kind of thing created by a Creator, is powered by the engine of divine love. And the Creator creates more of Itself; that's what real Creation is. It's the reason that only love, and only God, exists. The Mind of God creates more of Itself, out of the raw material of Itself, exactly like Itself in every way. This true Creation, this perfect Thought, is every bit as eternal, sublime and loving as the Mind that created it. Together the Mind and the Thought are one immortal spirit: Holy, pure and unchanging, joyous and peaceful, limitlessly strong, safe and free. This Creation exists forever within God (since there's no such thing as existing outside of God). Once created, no force exists that could alter true Creation in any way, or divide it from the Mind that created it. And there's no place where the Mind of God ends and the created Thought begins. The perfect Mind and the perfect Thought are inextricably one, sharing the divine Will of God. So, for all intents and purposes, the Creation *is* God.

4. With one very important exception: Although this Creation has all the attributes of God, *it did not, could not, create itself.* The Mind creates the Thought. The Thought is capable of creating in the same way that the Mind creates, yet only if it does so in perfect oneness with God, using divine love as its catalyst and its raw material.

5. And now, the other news: We, the one Son of God, the perfect Thought forever joined with the eternal Mind, started to entertain the idea that we didn't want to be one and the same anymore. We wanted to split up so we could each be

special and unique and different. In other words, we wanted to create ourselves over again—just a little differently this time. Yet God's divine Thought has never had the power to change itself in any way, no matter how much it may have wanted to. So we did the next best thing. We started to pretend.

6. In our pretend fantasy of a separate will, we split our one mind, producing an ego mind seemingly separate from our own. And then we became afraid that we'd done something really bad, something completely against the rules. And the ego mind said, *Ooh. You broke the law; you stole something that belongs to God. You tore away a piece of God Itself! And now you want to kill off your own Creator so you can rewrite the laws of Heaven. That's disgusting. If God ever catches you, you're in for eternal damnation.*

   Listen, I'm your friend. I'll help you. I can fix it so God will never find you. We'll make this new place, and it'll have walls so thick that God can never come in. You'll be safe there, and you can split and subdivide as much as you want. You can rule your own kingdom and forget all about Heaven.

7. And poor old Son of God was so upset by now, so consumed by fear—which doesn't even exist, remember, since there can be no fear in perfect love—that it consented wholeheartedly to the ego mind's crazy plan.

   And so, in a massive outpouring of energy, a universe was formed, powered by the engine of, and using the raw material of fear. Yet fear has no foundation in reality, so the things made from fear share none of the attributes of the things created from love. Things made from fear (besides being completely imaginary) are designed to be love's opposite. Stunted and flawed, unloved, unsafe and impermanent, they're designed to block all memory of God.

Things made from fear are "born" for only one purpose: To suffer, wither and die, lifetime after lifetime. And surely that's what they deserve, isn't it? The little ingrates tried to destroy Heaven and murder their Creator, so they—we—deserve eternal misery in exile. So reasons the unreasoning ego mind.

8. Completely taken in by the ego's version of events, our grief and pain over what we thought we'd done to God (and its imagined consequences, should we ever be brought to justice) was too much for us to bear. We forgot we were only pretending. Driven insane by fear, we buried our intolerable guilt so deeply in our collective unconscious mind that to this day we don't even know it's there. And by forgetting that bottomless pit of unconscious guilt and fear, we also forgot it was we who made the ego mind in the first place, and not vice versa. We still think it's our master, our jailer, and we its many helpless slaves.

We think we're billions of separate bodies with separate minds, fragile lumps of mortal flesh moving around in time and space, each living and then inevitably dying. What we call "life" is a brief, cruel mockery of the real thing, which is holy, joyous and eternal. And what we call "death" can't possibly exist in any form, because real life has no opposite. We are not bodies. We are one perfect immortal spirit, given limitless, unchanging life within the wholly loving Mind of God.

Yet willingly ruled by the ego mind, we cling tenaciously to life as we think we know it. Some of this precarious "life" existence seems to be wonderful and beautiful, and some of it terrible and horrifying. Yet all of it, everything we think of as "the real world" is no more than an elaborate 3-D hallucination, complete with imaginary walls that seem to stand between one separated mind and the next.

It's a self-induced trick of light and shadow, smoke and mirrors. No walls exist in truth between our seemingly split-off minds.

We only *believe* they do. And the limitless power of our belief—remember, we share the same attributes, the same unlimited creative power as our Creator—is enough to make it real for us.

A RAY OF LIGHT

1. Therein lies the way back home. The so-called "separation" never happened; we haven't "sinned against" our Creator. (How could sin, or anything else, exist within perfect divine love? And how could we stand apart from our one infinite Self to sin against it?) We therefore can't possibly carry even a speck of real guilt, unconscious or otherwise. We can only *believe* these things are true; yet if we learned to believe in the fantastical and the untrue, that means we can choose to re-learn the truth to take its place. And belief in the truth is all it takes to set us free and carry our awareness back to Heaven.

    Because in truth, we, the one Son of God have been safe in Heaven this whole time. We never left—where could we possibly "go"? In reality we've been sleeping safely, eternally within the Mind of God. We're just having a really epic bad dream.

2. It's the eternal Will of God that Its Creation be safe, strong and joyous, infinitely peaceful and abundant, radiantly pure, holy and limitlessly free, at home and one within the Mind of God forever. And God's Will most certainly be done. We, the Created, are endowed with free will, yet only in terms of what we choose to do and think, what we choose to remember, and when we choose to remember it. What we *are* remains unchanged forever.

3. The choice is ours: We can delay the memory of Heaven as long as we want, yet sooner or later every single one of us without exception will freely choose to remember our own

shared divinity, to remember the Mind of God and return to oneness. Because that's God's Will, and in truth, God's Will and our will are one and the same.

The memory of God, and of what we really are, may be buried beneath an unfathomably deep mountain of mud, but still that memory remains eternally in each of us, pure, unchanging and untouched by any part of this world. To let it come back fully into our awareness, all we need to do is willingly let go of all belief in the fantasy world we made to replace it.

Maybe we won't make the choice to withdraw our belief from this upside down world we made and return to the memory of God in this lifetime; maybe not even in the next hundred or thousand lifetimes. No harm done. Time isn't even the blink of an eye to Eternity Itself; we're free to mess around as long as we want to go on pretending we're stuck in dreams.

And make no mistake, we're only pretending we're stuck. We're the Son of God, the perfect Thought within the infinite Mind. We can wake up any time we feel like it.

THE PERFECT VEHICLE

1. Remember Jesus of Nazareth, who fully realized that He is the Son of God, forever one with his Creator? This realization itself is Christ, making Him, yes, Jesus the Christ. Yet Jesus didn't corner the market—anybody who attains the same full memory of one Mind and Thought united is also Christ; the whole and complete Son of God in its unseparated glory *is* the Christ, the perfect undivided Thought that knows the Mind of God. So any small chunk of us who comes to remember the truth is one and the same.

2. *A Course in Miracles* (a course taught by the Christ Mind) offers each one of us crazy Sons of God the opportunity to

"undo" the ego mind, slowly restoring our sanity and our memory. Our primary goal: That buried toxic waste dump of unconscious guilt needs to be removed. Partly because it's the power source that keeps the ego mind large and in charge; partly because it's the barrier that stops us from being able to accept the holy truth about ourselves and each other; and partly because it's the source of never-ending unconscious pain to us all.

That pain is unbearable, so we constantly try to rid ourselves of it by finding "others" guilty instead of us, compulsively hurling our own unconscious guilt at every target we see. There are two major things wrong with that strategy: One, the guilt stays exactly where it is no matter how hard we try to transfer it to somebody else. Two, there *is* nobody else; there's only one of us in truth, and although we can lose ourselves in fragmented fantasy, we can't rewrite the laws of Heaven. So every time we toss a bucket of toxic guilt at somebody or something "out there," we're really attacking ourselves.

3. We're given the means to unmake our unconscious guilt while we unmake the ego mind: we're taught to practice what the Course calls "forgiveness." Yet this isn't forgiveness in the usual sense. The world's version of forgiveness says: *You've sinned. I will rise above my desire to blame you for that, and instead find compassion in my heart to forgive and forget what you did.*

    The problem with this kind of forgiveness is that it assumes the fantasy of separation is true. It's really saying: *You are different from me; I am innocent and I stand apart from you and judge you to be guilty. The bad thing you did really happened and has real consequences, but I will overlook it and show you my mercy.*

    And so the world the ego made is preserved. And we

can freely continue to splash our buckets of unconscious guilt onto "others," because this form of forgiveness requires that we first find that other person guilty before choosing to absolve them of that guilt.

Forgiveness as practiced by the *Course*, on the other hand, is designed to gently undo the ego's world by reminding the mind that what it thinks it sees can't possibly be real. True forgiveness says: *Although I think I see you as separate from myself, and although I'm tempted to perceive you as guilty, in reality I'm completely mistaken; I'm not seeing you as you really are. In truth, you are holy and innocent, perfect and pure. You can't possibly have sinned, because sin doesn't really exist. You are divine love, immortal spirit, and you remain exactly as God created you. And you and I are one, eternally safe in Heaven.*

4. Each miracle of silent forgiveness that is offered helps to heal our own seemingly split mind at the same time that it helps to heal the mind of its intended recipient. In truth it helps to heal the entire world, as the Son of God is one Self, and healing received by one is received by all.

That's because another of Heaven's immutable laws is this: Giving is receiving.

Which makes perfect sense when we consider that everything is one. The more we give in truth, the more we receive, because there's only one of us doing both the giving and receiving. This is the reason it's impossible to suffer from lack of abundance—we have and are everything, so how could we ever lose anything? When we give we simultaneously receive. Sacrifice or scarcity of any kind is impossible. When we're lost in fantasy, however, we need only *believe* in scarcity to make it real for us.

This immutable law of giving and receiving is also the reason we're only able to attack ourselves when we try to splash the unconscious guilt around; the more we give blame to "others" for our own unconscious guilt, the more we simultaneously receive the blame we send out.

Luckily for us, the flipside is also true: As we attempt to wake up to the truth, every bit of real forgiveness we offer to others is automatically received within our own minds.

5   And that's *A Course in Miracles'* vehicle for getting us back to the memory and the experience of Heaven. The *Course* tells us the only reliable way to heal our own unconscious guilt is to truly forgive "others," thereby automatically forgiving ourselves. It says there's no other path to salvation than letting the world off the hook for its imaginary sins; only by making the choice to see others as they really are—perfect, immortal spirit—are we able to eventually undo the ego mind and remember that perfect, immortal spirit is what we are, too. And to help us along the way, the *Course* offers us an infallible Guide, a perfect partner to keep our vehicle pointed in the right direction.

THE INFALLIBLE GUIDE

1.   We observe this world with its wars and poverty, its depravity, corruption and cruelty, and we find it hard to believe it deserves anything except our bitterest judgment and condemnation; we forgot it isn't real and we made the whole thing up. We'd rather just toss our buckets of toxic guilt at the mirror and call it sinful.

And that's just the way the ego mind likes it. The ego is only capable of lies. That's the function we assigned it when we made it. And because we freely choose to live in this world—the world of lies that the ego made with our full consent—any attempt to disrupt the ego's thought system by introducing the thought system of truth will be met by unconscious resistance on our part. We're used to looking at everything upside down, so the prospect of eternal life seems like annihilation to us; to be faced with the immediate experience of God's perfect, gentle love seems terrifyingly like damnation and suffering beyond all imagining.

2. When we chose to believe in the ego mind, we chose the worst possible friend and guide. The ego would much rather see us dead than delivered from pain; if we were to find peace and happiness, the ego would have no place to call home. We can't be annihilated, but the ego can.

   The *Course* offers us another Friend and Guide instead. Which is a very useful thing, because the road back to the memory of God can get twisty and confusing at times; the ego will do everything in its power to make sure of it. Without this steadfast and loving Help, it could take a very long time to get anywhere at all. The *Course* calls this infallible Guide the Holy Spirit.

   The Holy Spirit, of course, is not some sort of Casper the Heavenly Ghost. The Holy Spirit is that aforementioned spark of pure and radiant memory existing eternally in each of us; it calls out to us ceaselessly from beneath Mud Mountain, asking us to remember what we really are and what God Is. The Holy Spirit is our own highest Self.

3. The *Course* also refers to the Holy Spirit as the Voice for God. That's the Voice *for* God. God Itself doesn't speak to us. God is fully occupied with being perfect, eternal love and nothing else. The Mind of God can't communicate directly with anybody who believes they're living inside a body in a world made of fear. The thought system of fear and the thought system of love are mutually exclusive—we can't believe mostly in one, yet a little bit in the other. One is pure and eternal truth; the other simply doesn't exist. It's literally All or nothing.

The Voice for God, the Holy Spirit, acts as a bridge between Heaven and our shadow world made of fear. The Holy Spirit remembers the Mind of God—it knows with perfect certainty that the separation never happened. It knows we remain exactly as God created us. Yet it also sees our mountain of mud; it knows what we're going through here in Fear World at every moment. It understands the temptations and obstacles we think we face, it knows our hopes and worries and all our seeming weaknesses. Yet it will gently remind us also of our strengths as it guides us lovingly toward our own eternal happiness.

Each time we offer a silent miracle of forgiveness, it's the Holy Spirit's job to undo a bit of the ego and heal unconscious guilt within the seemingly split mind of the one Son of God. These are acts we're not capable of accomplishing on our own, as long as we still believe we're individual bodies with separate minds. When we practice forgiveness as described by the *Course*, we do so in partnership with the Holy Spirit. Not one of us who believes in Fear World knows how to retrace our steps and get back home to the memory of God. The Holy Spirit, our highest Self, remembers the way. The *Course* asks us to step back and let this eternal Friend and Guide lead us; it assures us that the road home will be much shorter—and infinitely smoother—if we do.

THE GUILTLESS MIND

A Course in Miracles tells us that a guiltless mind can't experience suffering of any kind. Consider what that means: For a mind to be entirely guiltless, every last bit of Mud Mountain has to have been swept away, every drop of toxic unconscious guilt has been dissolved and the mind is now fully healed and whole. Which is another way of saying we've chosen to wake up from our Very Bad Dream, fully remembering and accepting the truth: That we are not separate, we are not bodies, there's no such thing as guilt or sin, and we are all one Thought forever cherished within the Mind of God. We are eternal, perfect love and nothing else.

When our mind is healed and awake to the truth, it means our perception of this world has been completely purified, cleansed of all belief in fear. This enables the Mind of God to lift our awareness back to oneness in Heaven where it belongs. This state of limitless peace and infinite joy is the Christ Mind.

The guiltless state of Mind denies all reality of this world—it sees no death, no pain, no imperfection or unhappiness of any kind, because it knows none of it can be real. Only the eternal Mind of God is real. Although terrible or painful or fearful things may still appear to be happening in this dream world, the guiltless mind remains joyous and serene, responding to these seeming events only with divine love, for it knows that is what it is *and nothing else.*

It's hard for us to understand what that state of life would be like. We hear that if we succeed in becoming Christ we'd have to respond to the events of this world with unconditional love, and the idea sounds terrifying. Maybe it even angers us, as if we're being stripped of our defenses and lured to our own slaughter.

The *Course* assures us no such sacrifice is necessary in the attainment of the state of Christ; not only is it unnecessary, it isn't even possible. The events of this world are not real, and the infinitely joyous and serene Christ Mind knows it. Not as theoretical textbook knowledge; the Christ Mind knows it *and lives it* as its own undeniable experience of the truth.

And because the Christ Mind isn't fooled by any part of this dream world (if it was, it couldn't *be* the Christ Mind—All or nothing, remember?), it knows for certain it doesn't live in a body. And so the body that this particular Christ seems to inhabit has been forgiven by its Mind along with all the rest of the bodies in the dream of separation. And with forgiveness, this Christ's "body" is no longer capable of suffering because the Mind that dreamed it up is no longer capable of suffering. So the body is now pain free and perfectly at peace, because that is the state of the Mind that made it up.

Only infinite happiness, freedom, safety, strength and peace await the Mind that returns itself to God. And what becomes of the body walking around that's seemingly still attached to that Mind?

That's entirely up to the Mind Itself.

It might feel called to teach. It could choose to take its message on the road to the world at large—or it might be quietly content to live out its days in joyous obscurity, offering silent healing to the world without ever stepping forward to speak of what it knows. A Christ's true gift to the world is the silent healing it offers to all seemingly fragmented minds; anything else it chooses to "accomplish" here within the dream is cake.

And when the time finally comes to gently lay the body aside (for all bodies are born to die) the Christ does so with joy and tranquility, because it knows it's going home to perfect eternal oneness with God, and the cycle of birth and death is over at last.

ABOUT THE AUTHOR

Carrie Triffet sports a dazzling array of flaws and vices, none of which seem to dampen her single-minded desire for spiritual enlightenment.

When not engaged in this messengering gig, she works as a designer, artist and marketing consultant.

For photos of people, places and things from this book, and for a more complete list of the "homework" books mentioned in this story, visit www.unlikelymessenger.com

It's a connected world we live in;
    follow Carrie on Twitter.com/unlikelymesngr

Read more of her ongoing adventures on her blog,
    www.unlikelymessenger.com

George Noory